# Thuy - A Life

**THUY - A LIFE**
Chu Minh Hạnh - Lâm Hoàng Mạnh

Cover: Uyên Nguyên Trần Triết
Layout: Lâm Hoàng Lân
Nhân Ảnh Publisher 2025

ISBN: 9798295416064

CHU MINH HẠNH
& LÂM HOÀNG MẠNH

# THUY

## A LIFE

Nhân Ảnh
2025

**A Nhân Ảnh book**

*This book was first published by Nhân Ảnh in 2025*


ISBN: 9798295416064

***Dedicated to the Government and People of the United Kingdom, with our deepest gratitude.***

CMH - LHM

*For my children and my grandchildren*
*and to the memory of Ms Gwenda Hill -*
*a sister and family friend.*

CMH

*"Boat people" – when the Hanoi government hears the phrase, it thinks the word 'dollars'.*

Michel Tauriac,

Vietnam Le Dossier Noir Du Communisme.

## CONTENTS

# PREFACE

War! War! Something that no one in the world wants, but for whatever reason they happen and nobody forgets about them.

Every year, on February 17, the press and media in the country and abroad report what a tragedy it was for the Vietnamese of Chinese origin not only in the history of Vietnam but also in the history of humanity. These reports forget or intentionally forget the thousands of Vietnamese women who married Chinese men. Their experience was miserable, if not more so than the Chinese themselves, but they are never mentioned. Thuy, is one of these.

Thuy's life is like a miniature picture of the fate of the innocent, young girls who married Chinese men. Born in the mid-20th century and raised in the uncertain times of Vietnamese society. Thuy experienced many ups and downs during a turbulent Vietnam. Like thousands of other Vietnamese women who married Chinese men, her life would change forever.

When the Sino - Vietnamese war broke out, the women became victims within their husband's family, forced to endure their fate silently. It seems that history has forgotten to mention these innocent women.

Although the feudal system was in decline, the concept and customs of male superiority and female inferiority were still deeply ingrained in the thinking of Vietnamese people. Women had to endure pressures from their families to social expectations. They suffered disadvantages in all aspects, but they endured and had to adapt to survive.

Thuy's experience was not unusual. The course of her life was filled with obstacles that she had to overcome from a young age. Then when the Sino - Vietnamese war broke out, she became a helpless bystander to her husband's persecution. There is a Chinese custom where the relationship between a husband and his wife is just like a piece of cloth; 'From strangers to a wife. From wife to stranger.'

When the war broke out, Thuy was abandoned by her husband and his family. She was pregnant with their second child and left to fend for herself and their three-year-old daughter. She was ostracised by the Vietnamese government because of her relationship to a Chinese man, who had been expelled from the country. She was now also considered a security threat to Vietnam.

As a wife of a Chinese man, Thuy was put under pressure by the local agencies, organizations and government authorities. She was given an ultimatum, either quit her job or divorce her husband and hand their child over to him, where they would live in the designated areas for expelled Chinese people. It was an unbelievably inhumane demand in the 20th century. Thuy was in the middle of two warring sides: her husband's family and the Vietnamese government.

People have often said that women are the weaker sex. However, when they become wives and mothers, with the inherent kindness of women and boundless love they give, they become determined to protect their children and family. This is when women become the stronger sex.

Thuy knew she wouldn't be at peace in her birth country. So, she decided to leave her homeland to protect her children's future and accept her fate as a refugee.

The journey across the sea during the stormy season from Hai Phong, Vietnam on the 30th April 1979, on a wooden boat to Hong Kong arriving on 1st July 1979 was not an easy one.

With her already poor health, plus being in the final stages of pregnancy, Thuy encountered even more hardships during the arduous journey. Only one bowl of porridge a day was given out to the people on the boat. That was the only sustenance she had to keep her going. Drifting at sea, constantly hungry with a new born baby lacking milk. Death seemed so close.

The UK government extended a helping hand and accepted them as legal immigrants. Arriving in a foreign country, with a different language and culture, but encountering kindness and selfless help.

More than forty-five years in England, starting with nothing, not one penny in her pocket, Thuy was able to fulfil her responsibilities as a mother and take on the role of a father. She raised her children by herself, giving them the opportunities that help them graduate from university, find stable jobs and start a family of their own.

*'Where there is good land, there are birds.'* England has become the second home for Thuy and her children and grandchildren. A simple life filled with laughter.

Now in her old age, happy knowing that her children and grandchildren are doing well. Thuy participates in senior club activities, practices yoga, and occasionally travels domestically and internationally with friends. However, during all these years of change, Thuy has never forgotten the past. She remembers her roots, the place where she was born and raised and reminds her children about the country they left, but is constantly thankful for the people and home they have made in this new country.

*Always be grateful,*
*To the place that gave shelter,*
*To a mother and her children,*
*Living as human*
*Fulfilling the duties of a good citizen.*

Through Thuy's story, it helps us remember what happened during a dark period of Vietnamese history, but also at the same time awakens the love of peace in each person. It is human nature to wish for a peaceful world. To live happily together with love and hope the world can exist forever. This life is so beautiful and precious. We have to preserve it.

*When will the war stop?*
*A truly people life is within our grasp!*
*If there is no love in this world?*
*How boring life would be!*

I would like to thank Hoa Luc for all her time and effort in editing this book.

Summer 2025, London
Chu Minh Hạnh

----

**Note*** In Vietnam, Vietnamese people of Chinese origin are often called Hoa people.

## CHAPTER 1

# Step into a new life

*It's no wonder that truth is stranger than fiction*
*Fiction has to make sense!*

**Mark Twain**

"Mum! Mum! Help me... please! I'm not going anywhere, I don't want to go anywhere…"

Sitting on the back of the Thong Nhat old bicycle, Thuy turned her head and cried for help. Her parents and siblings stood in front of their house, waving their hands. Occasionally, her mother wiped her tears with her sleeve, but no one seemed to pay attention to her pitiful cries. The sunlight began to shine brightly in the late summer morning of the central region, Thuy held on to the saddle of the bicycle with one hand and wiped her tears with the other, her eyes were full of tears.

"Stop crying, sit still. The road is bumpy and we could easily fall off the bike." Sinh, her uncle shouted back.

Thuy didn't hear anything. She cried and wiped her tears with her hand, trying to turn her head to look back.

After going quite a distance, Sinh's steering wheel wobbled on the bumpy dirt road and suddenly the bike fell to the side of the road.

Startled, she woke up. Thuy found herself falling to the ground from a single bed made of two planks of wood placed on a pair of stools in a very narrow room of the women's dormitory. It turned out that this morning, Sinh took Thuy by bicycle, Thuy sitting behind struggling to keep the bicycle from falling over. It had become a nightmare.

Thuy lay down on the wooden planks, pulled the old blanket over her body to keep warm, tears streaming down her face, crying without making a sound, her thin shoulders shaking with sobs. The sky was pitch black, occasionally the sound of a bird. "Catch her and tie her to a pole" the words echoed from the forest, making Thuy even more afraid. Just a few days ago, Thuy was still a happy, innocent little girl, playing and laughing with neighbourhood friends and with Hong, her lovely younger sister. Now suddenly tonight Thuy lay alone, curled up on the hard planks, as cold as a cement floor, without parents, without relatives. The room next to her was full of elderly strangers. Oh my God! She thought. Thuy had no idea what would happen in the coming days. Mum! Mum.... Thuy fell asleep with sobs and hopeless pleas for help.

-----

After finishing high school, Thuy applied for admission to the University College of Hanoi but did not receive an admission letter, while her classmates did. Thuy wanted to know why, so she went to the admissions department of the town hall. Entering the office, she saw an old man in a faded army uniform.

"Good morning sir, may I ask who is the permanent staff worker?" Thuy greeted him politely.

"Yes, I am. What do you want, young lady?" Replied the old man.

"Sir, I applied for a place at the University College of Hanoi, but I haven't received an admission letter, yet all of my classmates have."

The man pointed to the chair opposite. "Sit down, please. Can you tell me your name and address so I can check your file?"

"My name is Le Thi Thuy…"

The man opened the filing cabinet, took out a briefcase and put it on the table. He checked through the stack of files and took out a file, examined it very carefully.

"You are Le Thi Thuy, daughter of Mr Le Van Lan, right?"

"Yes, sir."

Looking at Thuy very carefully and with a sympathetic voice. "Unfortunately, your family background was the national bourgeoisie, so you do not meet the criteria for university entrance exam."

"Sorry sir, my father is a tailor for the joint venture company in the town, how can he be part of the national bourgeoisie?" Thuy said anxiously.

"According to the records, before the merger, your family had three sewing machines and two employees, so when the town launched the movement to reform private capitalism, your family belonged to the national bourgeoisie."

"Sir, that has nothing to do with me, it is my father's story. I only know how to go to school, so how can I be part of the national bourgeoisie?" Thuy pleaded.

The old man shook his head. "The documents were clear, that's why the town's admission committee did not consider you. I sympathize with you, but I am just a member of staff, I can't do anything more for you."

Hearing the man's explanation, Thuy was shocked and couldn't really believe what she was hearing. This meant her path to education ended today. Unable to stand up, Thuy had to put her hands on the table, dragging herself step by step out of the committee door, her mind spinning. Thuy almost collapsed, dizzy, eyes blurred and tears rolling down her cheeks. Thuy staggered out of the Town hall. Thuy's father was just a tailor with three sewing machines and two cousins from the countryside who came to help, but that made him the National Bourgeoisie! The bad elements of the proletarian dictatorship needed to be eliminated, but that didn't change the fact that Thuy's future hopes had slammed shut and just before she turned sixteen.

-----

In 1958, Thuy was only eight years old. On that day she came home from school to see three wooden oxcarts and more than a dozen people, chatting in front of her house. Thuy then saw her father's three sewing machines being dumped onto the oxcarts. Everyone gathered around and pushed them away. Thuy was very surprised and wondered whether her father had decided to sell the machines, but was too frightened to ask. During lunch, her father told Thuy what had happened.

"The three sewing machines were confiscated by the government and taken to the town's garment joint venture company." He explained that from now on, he had to go to work at that company.

That year, the whole province and town was bustling with the program of reforming private capitalist industry and commerce, which meant getting rid of all individual businesses. All handicrafts in the town had to merge into companies or joint venture enterprises or cooperatives. Thuy's father had become a worker at the town's garment joint venture company in 1958, but still the government did not remove the accusations against her family. It had been four years since the liberation of North Vietnam and those papers still existed.

In June 1966, Thuy's resume still had the national bourgeoisie entry. She doesn't even really understand what the national bourgeoisie was. Everyday her father would go to work at the joint venture company and her mother would stay at home to take care of Thuy and her siblings. Their days were spent simply, going to the market, cooking, growing vegetables, raising chickens and pigs and keeping to themselves.

At school, Thuy remembered Mr Hoang, the political philosophy teacher, teaching the difference between communism and capitalism. Thuy learned two things; one, that communism does not have people exploiting other people. There are no masters or servants; all workers are equal. Moreover, all means of production belong to the public to the collective, to the state rather than to any individual.

From this Thuy understood that the three sewing machines which the family had bought gradually for many years, before Thuy was born, no longer belonged to her family. They belonged to the collective, to a company that Mr Mai from the town's People's Committee was assigned to be the head of. But he was not a tailor.

In the school curriculum, all high school students had to write about the 'Petty bourgeois students.'

"All students were petty bourgeois because they had knowledge and education. Unlike workers and farmers, who had nothing, not even education, workers and farmers were the true working class." Mr Hoang explained.

Thuy didn't understand why it was like that, it was absurd, but that was the truth for the government.

Walking slowly home from the town hall, tears flowed down her face. Thuy's mind was spinning, not knowing what to say to her parents. If she told them the truth it would hurt her parents. Her younger siblings would probably have to drop out of school, because if they continued to go, it might mean nothing for their future.

Listening to Thuy recount the incident that morning at the Town hall, Thuy's father sighed and pondered for a moment. "I am powerless to help you, but don't be sad anymore, let your mum and I take care of everything for you."

After saying that, he pulled Thuy close, put his hand on her head and pressed it against his chest to comfort her. That afternoon Thuy played with her neighbourhood friends again, innocently like a naïve fifteen years old who would turn sixteen soon.

A few days later, her parents called Thuy into their room. "Uncle Sinh knows someone who works at the university in our province, he can take you to work in the library of this university. The job is not hard, no degree is required. There are many people in our family now. My work is slowing down every day and the money is very poor and will only get worse. We need you to go to work to support the family."

Thuy was surprised and didn't know how to answer. She knew she had to listen to her parents and do what was best for the family. She thought, I'll be like my father. Everyday I'm going to have to go somewhere to work. I'll come home for lunch, then go to work again, then come back home in the evening. Tomorrow will continue like the day before and at the end of the month, I'll get paid and give it all to my father. Thinking about that, Thuy thought it was quite interesting, both father and daughter would go to work and at the end of the month, they would both have money. So far, in her life all she knew was to go to school, play with friends and look after her younger siblings. Her life was about to change.

Yesterday morning, uncle Sinh took Thuy to the University of Viet Bac. They cycled a long way, through many bumpy dirt roads, over hills full of palm trees, to the row of houses with rough mud walls and palm roofs. Parking the bike next to the shutter door, the two of them walked in. After greeting everyone, uncle Sinh spoke to a woman. Thuy couldn't quite hear what was said. Uncle Sinh then turned to Thuy.

"You will stay here and work hard. Do as you are told, and on your birthday, I'll take you home to see your family."

He patted Thuy on the shoulder and said goodbye to everyone. That was all, he just got on his bike and left for home.

Thuy knew she was leaving her old life behind. She wasn't going to see her parents and siblings for a very long time and she already longed for their mud house with the thatched roof. She wasn't going to be playing with her sister and their friends and the memory of the summer days playing under the banyan trees made her want to cry. From today onwards she would be living in a strange place with strangers.

It was all so confusing and scary, but then a woman in her thirties smiled at her brightly, took Thuy's hand and led her inside. Pointing to the chair opposite the desk, she told Thuy to sit down, then opened the file cabinet and took out a briefcase of documents, which she put in front of Thuy. Her gentle face and warm voice reassured Thuy. "Let's get to know each other. I'm Mai, head of the Organization and Administration department. Tell me your name and how old you are?"

Thuy slowly answered each question, observing Mai's facial expression. Looking at her gentle face, Thuy gradually became less tense and more comfortable.

"Starting from today, you are a temporary contract employee of the school. You'll be working as a staff in the library. The work will be guided by your colleagues. The starting salary is twenty-eight dong*[1] a month, but fifteen dong of this had to go towards paying for the meals at the school canteen and you don't have to pay any other fees. After six months, if you do well and meet the standards, you will be officially employed and your salary will increase to thirty-six dong a month. If you have any difficulties, just come to me. Do you have any questions?"

"No, I don't madam." Was all Thuy could say.

Following Mai, Thuy went to a row of rooms with earthen walls and palm thatched roofs that still smelled of leaves. She unlocked the door to one of the small rooms. The space was about ten square meters. The only pieces of furniture were two wooden planks, with bamboo poles in each corner to make legs. This was the bed Thuy was to sleep on. There was also a wooden box with bamboo legs right next to the wooden bed. Thuy entered the room. Mai placed a new mat on the bed and smiled. "This is your private room. Use this key to keep it locked. This area of the school is the school's women's dormitory. If you need anything just come to me. Try not to worry."

"Yes, madam." Thuy said shyly.

After Mai had left the room, Thuy put her bag of clothes on the wooden bed. She looked around in dismay. Thoughts of this room being her home for years made her heart sink. Tears flowed from her eyes. Thuy sat for a long time just in a daze, then stood up. She arranged her clothes in the wooden box, and walked out of the room. She looked around. In front of her were endless palm trees and behind her were endless palm trees. Along the valley were several rows of houses with earthen walls and palm-leaf roofs. A trail connected one block of houses to another. There were many beautiful floral bushes along the road, but Thuy didn't know what any of the flowers were called.

Slowly walking along the trail, Thuy remembered what Mai had said. The school had just been established, but had to be evacuated quickly and divided into many facilities. Everything was new, but messy. The departments had not finished building their homes for the staff, most of them were staying at local people's houses. Students formed groups to level the ground, they went into the forest to find bamboo and palm leaves to build houses and classrooms.

Suddenly a woman from the next row of houses came out and saw Thuy. She smiled at her. "You're new, aren't you?"

Thuy looked at her and smiled back. "Yes, I'm a new employee."

The woman came closer. "Which department will you be working in?"

"In the library."

"Oh, that's the same department as I am! You'll be living in the other row of houses, right"

"Yes. I think so."

"I'm Nga. What's your name?"

"My name is Thuy."

"It's almost lunchtime. Do you know where the cafeteria is?"

"No, I don't."

"Okay, come with me."

Thuy followed Nga to her home. As she walked, Nga asked. "Do you have bowls and chopsticks of your own?"

Thuy smiled awkwardly. "No..."

"Don't worry. I have some spare chopsticks and bowls you can keep."

"I'll just borrow them from. I'll buy some when I go to the market in a few days."

Nga smiled kindly. "The market is very far away, and it only happens once every five days. Consider it a gift from me to you, on your first day here."

Thuy's face lit up. "I will! Thank you!"

"Not at all! You're too polite."

The communal dining room was simple and was about twenty square meters wide. All four walls were made of woven bamboo more than one meter high and the roof was made of palm leaves. There were a few rows of tables and chairs. The table tops were made of roughly planed boards and the long benches looked the same. This was the first communal meal that Thuy would never forget; a small bowl of rice with a boiled flour dumpling; a bowl of green papaya soup cooked with salt; a small plate with some fried dried shrimp and a small bowl of salt placed on the dining table. Thuy had never had boiled flour dumplings before. Her mother used to steam them like the commercial restaurants would sell them, but when people are so hungry, anything tastes good.

The meal was simple but Thuy thought it tasted delicious because she was so hungry. Nga, who Thuy just met, sat beside her. Thuy could tell she was a gentle and caring woman. This made her feel less lonely. While they ate, Nga talked about the work and activities of the group.

"Our group, which includes you now, has three people, with Minh as the team leader. The university was newly established during the period of urgent evacuation. The work was very messy and books and newspapers ended up being piled on top of each other. According to Minh, the priority is to sort through these piles of books and newspapers."

After eating, Nga took Thuy to the book warehouse. Inside were the piles of books that were spoken about over lunch. Piles of books as high as mountains Thuy thought, her head craning up. Thuy looked stunned and bewildered. How were they going to sort through all of this? There were professional books of different faculties, reference books, documents, news-papers, magazines in Vietnamese and foreign languages (mostly Russian and Chinese). Everyone had to help arrange them by subject: natural science, social science, politics, philosophy, psychology. Every single subject you could think of that should be in a library. They had to be entered into the code book and from there, depending on the quantity, they were divided and brought to the libraries of the faculties in the school. The faculties were divided into different places, the nearest one was about ten kilometres away. Including the faculties of Mathematics, Physics, Chemistry, Biology, Literature, History, Geography. These subjects were at the heart of this teaching region. In addition to working in the University's Central Library, once a month Thuy had to go to the district to buy and collect books and magazines. When she got them back to the Central Library, they were then divided up and brought into their departments.

Looking at the pile of books, Thuy worried out loud. "Where do we even begin?" But Minh, who was about thirty years old, was gentle and reassured her that the team would help her all the way. Minh was also in the school's Youth Union executive committee, which made Thuy worry even more that she might not meet his expectations. She had only lived with her family before. She did help her father with his business, by sewing buttons, making button-holes and hemming clothes. She also looked after her younger siblings and helped her mother cook, but still had the freedom to play with friends and siblings. She didn't really have any worries, but now she was an employee of the state, an adult, not a carefree child, playing hide-and-seek anymore.

Thuy wanted to please Minh and Nga, so worked hard and tried not to bother them. Fortunately, she learned quickly and diligently. After a few weeks of enthusiastic guidance, Thuy gradually got used to the job. She still thought of her family and her home, but her homesickness gradually lessened with each day.

oOo

Nga and Thuy had to leave early in the morning to go to the district post office. After they had collected the books, they stopped by the market to find somewhere to eat before starting the long journey home. The district town was deserted, families had been evacuated and houses were locked up. Food stores and stalls were all closed. They wandered around and right at the end of the marketplace Nga saw a stall selling drinks. It was more like a hut than a stall, there were four poles, topped with palm leaves to protect from the sun and rain. Behind the hut was the base of a giant banyan tree. Inside the stall, a bamboo table displayed a few small ceramic bowls, some jars of peanut candy, a jar of powder candy, a small pile of sweet potatoes and boiled cassava roots. There was also a basket containing hot, freshly brewed green tea. Behind the table, a woman in black trousers and a brown shirt, sat chewing betel leaves. Her teeth were blackened by this habit and she must have been over fifty years old, perhaps younger if it wasn't for the colour of her teeth. In front of the bamboo table, there was a long bench.

Seeing Nga and Thuy, the woman warmly invited the guests. "Hello! Two dear young ladies, please come in and have a cup of tea and some snacks. The tea is freshly brewed, very fragrant."

Without needing to be invited for a second time, the two sat down on the bench. They used their conical hats to fan themselves dry, while choosing a couple of sweet potatoes and boiled cassavas. After eating and drinking a bowl of hot fresh tea, Thuy felt less tired. It had been a long walk to get here this morning, perhaps more than ten kilometres and without any food or water, until now.

The stall owner was eager to start a conversation. "Where have you come from? I can tell you're not from around here..."

Nga smiled. "You're right! We came from the evacuation area. Today is the first chance we've had to come to the district and collect books for our library."

Taking a sip of fresh tea, Nga was curious. "Has everyone in this area been evacuated?"

"Recently, American planes had been flying over here more frequently, so the district leaders announced that all the people had to be evacuated."

"Why didn't you go too?" Nga asked.

The woman laughed kindly. "I am too old, if I leave this place, how would I make money to live? This tea stall is only temporary, until I die!"

"But, where are your children?"

"I have two sons who both joined the army. My youngest daughter just got married in the neighbouring district. I am alone in the house, so I have to carry on and take care of myself. There's no one else."

Nga looked at Thuy and smiled. "Absolutely, you are right, to live anywhere we still need to eat! Thank you for being here. We must now start our journey back."

After paying, Thuy lifted up the pool where the books hung onto the end and they both set off. The sun was beginning to heat up. After walking more than one kilometre, Thuy had to put the pole down on the road. She was panting and sweat was streaming down her cheeks.

Nga glanced over at Thuy. "A seventeen-year-old girl can break a buffalo horn, yet my little sister here can't even snap a straw."

Wiping the sweat off her face, Thuy said shyly. "I'm not even sixteen yet, dear sister!"

Nga teased. "I see! You are as thin as a reed, luckily you have long hair to make up for it! When we cross the bridge, hopefully, the wind won't blow you into the stream."

They both walked and talked, forgetting the long distance. When they were almost at the suspension bridge, Nga said. "Be careful Thuy, this bridge is very shaky."

The bridge over the stream was about fifty meters long, the bridge's sides were made of double cables, tied down to more cables under the rusty bridge, onto the ground. The bridge's surface was made of wooden planks also tied together with cables. Some of the planks were worm-eaten and the width of the bridge was only about three meters wide, just enough for four people to walk side-by-side. Every time Thuy took a step, the bridge shook and swayed. It really tested your nerves. This was the first time Thuy had walked this bridge, but it wouldn't be the last. Thuy had to walk the bridge with the pole across her shoulders, being weighed down by all the books. Underneath her was the rapid river, which was about ten meters deep. Thuy was scared and she could feel goose bumps creep all the way over her body. It did cross her mind that if she stepped on a weak plank, she'd fall through and down into the rapids. Thuy stopped herself from thinking anymore.

Glancing over at Nga, who was calmly stepping on each creaking wooden bar, holding the handlebars of her bicycle with two large bags of books tied to the back. Thuy felt embarrassed she was being so timid, so she mustered up all her courage and strength and carried on across the bridge without stopping. The shoulder pole was pressing down on Thuy's right shoulder, making her whole-body sway with each step. Not only that, both ends of the pole had two baskets full of books, so heavy that they almost touched the ground. They were both shaking and swaying, looking both funny and pitiful.

Nga turned around to Thuy. "Thuy, let me carry the pole for you, you take the bicycle. We've still got a long way to go and we need to get home before it gets dark."

Hearing Nga say that Thuy didn't know what to do, she felt embarrassed that Nga could see she was struggling. She carried on walking, but the two heavy baskets of books pressed on shoulders and weighed her down.

Nga stopped and waited, until Thuy was closer. "Put down the shoulder pole, hold the handlebars with both your hands to lead the bike across the bridge, I'll carry the pole of books for you. Your young shoulders are not used to it, but with practice, gradually, you will be strong enough to carry the burden of work and a husband and then eventually children."

Talk about her being skinny and then mentioning a husband and children turned Thuy's face red. She was also exhausted, but didn't know what to say when Nga talked like that. Thuy put the pole down, wiped her sweat with her shirt, looked at Nga with a grateful gaze and held the handlebars of the bicycle pushing it on their way.

Suddenly, after a short distance from the bridge, there was the sound of an American jet roaring overhead, close to the ravine. They did this to avoid the range of the local anti-aircraft guns, which were being shot, tearing apart the quiet sky.

Nga put down the pole and ran to hide in the bushes by the roadside, Thuy still tried to push the bicycle carrying the books, but Nga called out loudly. "Leave the bike and run here quickly, Thuy!"

"But what about the books?" For some reason Thuy was more concerned about the books than herself. "Books, I don't care about, it's our lives that come first! Throw the bike down, the American planes will turn around and shoot missiles! We'll be killed!"

Only then did Thuy put down the bicycle carrying books on the roadside. She hurriedly ran to Nga. Both of them sat still. A moment later they heard a rumbling sound like thunder again. They raised their heads and saw three jet planes printed with the US flag. It looked like they were heading towards Hanoi. Where they hid was only a midland province bordering Hanoi. It wasn't an industrial zone or had any government headquarters, so planes often flew over and rarely dropped bombs here.

After waiting for quite a while and not hearing any more roaring plane engines or gunfire. Nga said to Thuy. "Next time when you see planes, just drop everything and find a place to hide."

Nga lifted the pole with the baskets of books on the ends, but Thuy couldn't stand up the bicycle because it was too heavy with books. She had to ask Nga for help.

When they finally reached the school campus, they put everything down. Nga took off her conical hat to fan herself. "Today we've finished our tasks. Rest and have a bath, tomorrow we will organise these books."

"Yes, sister."

oOo

In the morning Thuy woke up earlier than usual. The neighbour's rooster had crowed loudly, waking her up and shattering the dream she was having, where she was playing with her siblings. Then Thuy suddenly remembered the work she had to do today. Yesterday, Minh had told Nga and Thuy that the three of them had to deal with the pile of books in the warehouse. They had been taking up too much space for too long.

Thuy arrived at the library ten minutes early, but Nga and Minh were already there. The three of them got to work. First of all, the books, documents, magazines, newspapers had to be piled up separately. The books were divided into subjects. There were books on natural sciences, social sciences, political philosophy, policies of the Party and State, literature and art books, as well as children's books. They had to all be stored separately. Thuy found that there weren't that many children's books, which she thought didn't really matter as it was a school for older students. After several days of continuous sorting, the mountain of books was starting to look a lot less. Relief started to settle on the three workers.

Each pile of books was then divided into sub-piles according to each subject. Thuy had to check and record the quantity, the same book titles, and to divide them into libraries for each faculty in the school. Each faculty had a full range of genres to serve the purposes of studying, teaching, research, and reference. There were also magazines, fiction titles and art books. Books and documents with small quantities were kept in the school's Central Library. Thuy was young and small, so Minh and Nga didn't push her to carry or transport the large, thick, hardcover stacks of books. It would be a struggle to carry just two or three of these sized books to any given place. Thuy was assigned the light task of recording magazines, daily and weekly newspapers and delivering them to the departments and divisions in the central area. Minh and Nga were responsible for foreign language books, mainly Russian and Chinese. After a while, the mountain-high pile of books was neatly arranged according to regulations Thuy was responsible for the Vietnamese titles, recording them for the archives in the Central Library.

From then on, Thuy's main job was to take notes, not to go down to the departments. Records of each book had to be broken down into name, author, year of publication, price, date of import and quantity. Thuy took notes carefully to avoid making mistakes. Minh reminded Thuy. "This is a light and easy job, but do it well."

Thuy didn't want to disappoint her family. They trusted her. Uncle Sinh and her father had instructed her to try to do the assigned work well. It was important that she got accepted into the payroll. Becoming an official employee meant you would have a long-term salary, which meant you could help your parents and siblings. Minh continued. "From the available list of quantities, we will propose a plan to purchase and import books that are missing from our collection."

The books that were kept in the warehouse were covered with dust, partly due to being transferred from the Hanoi library and other places, but also having been sat still for such a long time. In addition, the warehouse was small and with the local climate in the mountainous area, they were prone to humidity, mould, termites and rats. Many books were torn, had either missing corners and pages or both. Some had holes, which had to be thrown away. There were no gloves or masks, so they had to use scarves to cover their mouths to avoid inhaling dust and mould. After a day of work, their bodies and hands were itchy and uncomfortable, the air was stuffy and everyone sneezed continuously.

After finishing the pile of books in the warehouse, Thuy started the main work. Although many of the damaged books were destroyed, there were still hundreds of books that had to be recorded and some of those weren't in good condition either. Thuy often sought advice from Minh and Nga. They were both patient with her and always encouraged her. Both of them treated Thuy like a younger sister, which only made Thuy think of her family more.

Thuy had an older brother who was three years older than her. Chinh was loved and pampered by her mother the most. Although Thuy was the second child, she had to do most of the housework, while Chinh spent all day hanging out with his friends. Sometimes Thuy was allowed out with him.

Thuy had a memory of a time Chinh took her out and forgot it was her turn to cook dinner that day. He wasn't scolded by their mother, but was encouraged to beat Thuy for not coming home to cook! Another time, Thuy's arm was pulled by

Chinh through a bamboo fence until it bled. She was in so much pain, but she didn't dare to cry and didn't dare tell her father. Thuy was afraid that her brother would take revenge on her when her father wasn't at home. So, she kept quiet. Thuy always wondered why Chinh was their mother's beloved one. Always defended by her, while she had to suffer injustices.

Her father went to work early in the morning and came home late in the evening. Everyday Thuy brought him his lunch, but didn't say a word about Chinh beating her. Only later did Thuy understand that, the feudal customs of the Vietnamese at that time favoured men over women. Daughters were often compared to wild ducks. When they grew up, they got married, flew away and therefore weren't of anymore use to their parents. The eldest son however, would be expected to support the family, and later on, to worship their ancestors and so he was pampered.

At work, Thuy's mind would return to the happy and sad memories of her childhood. Nga could see this and knew Thuy missed her home. Minh promised if she did a good job, then the next time the university truck went into town to get more books, he would let Thuy go with him and she could visit her family. This gave Thuy security, so she worked happily. She was praised for her beautiful handwriting and took careful and clear notes.

Sometimes Nga gave Thuy some of her boiled cassava and sweet potatoes. There was usually nothing to eat in the morning, so cassava, corn and sweet potatoes were delicious to Thuy, even more delicious than the sticky rice cake bought by her father at home. Thuy daydreamed that Nga was her older sister, instead of having a lazy older brother who was pampered by their mother and who bullied her.

Sitting and writing continuously too long, Thuy's fingers were numb, especially over the winter months. The wind was very cold. Even with a sweater on and the coat her father had made for her, Thuy was still shivering. Her hands were frozen and it was difficult to write well. She was allowed a break by working with Minh dividing books up by their faculties. When the University was evacuated, it was divided and stationed at different sites. Some of the new sites were more than ten kilometres apart. When the Central Library was finished dividing the books up, the faculties were asked to come and pick up their books.

The books and magazines that were damaged, worm-eaten, or torn, were given permission to be destroyed, Minh would bring them out to the yard to burn. The crackling red flames softened the cold air of the mountains and forests. Thuy was able to warm her two very cold hands over the flickering fire and this helped make the cold winter days more bearable and the days passed by like this.

Working six days a week, leaving the small room in the morning and returning in the evening, Thuy gradually adapted to her new life. In the evenings, there were the union and youth meetings and the emulation movement. When it was launched, everyone enthusiastically participated. On the first day of the meeting, Thuy was bewildered by all this talk. She just sat still and listened.

Mr Pao, a local man and the secretary of the Youth Union, introduced Thuy to the group. "This is comrade Thuy, she's a new employee and today is her first day participating in the Youth Union activities with us."

Thuy felt so embarrassed and just bowed her head, not wanting to meet anyone's eye. After the meeting, Mr Pao spoke with Thuy, explaining the rights and obligations of the young people towards the Labour Youth Union. "You are young and as a new employee, you should be participating in all the organizations of the school, including the trade, youth and women's unions." With a serious face, Mr Pao continued. "You are sixteen years old and not yet a target of the Union's sympathy, you have to work hard for the union, because I know your family composition."

Hearing Mr Pao say these words, Thuy felt sad and cold. Could it be that the national bourgeoisie would follow her for the rest of her life? Mr Pao went on talking, but Thuy could not hear anything more. She only felt confused and frustrated, her head nodding and her words always saying "yes, yes" to be polite.

Finally, Pao finished by saying. "Thuy, I don't want you to worry, all the members of the Youth Union are always by your side and we will help you. If you have any questions, feel free to ask me."

Hearing all this, Thuy still worried about her family and herself. Her high school classmates were all admitted to the Youth Union (at that time, Thuy thought she was still too young). Was it because she wasn't a member of the Youth Union, which meant her university application didn't qualify? Thuy felt lonely and isolated and wondered whether this meant many more doors would be closed to her.

-----

Nga noticed that Thuy had been talking and laughing less recently, so she invited Thuy to come over to eat with her family on Sunday. Nga could see Thuy's hesitation but reassured her. "Come and play with my daughter Lan, she'll be really happy to meet you. Come around 10 or 11 o'clock this Sunday."

-----

Seeing Thuy, Lan smiled, revealing a few decayed teeth. She stood with her arms folded. "Hello, Ms Thuy!"

Thuy was surprised. "Hi Lan! You know my name? Just call me sister. My youngest sister is six years old, the same age as you."

Lan smiled and winked. "Mum said I've been good, so today sister Thuy has come to play with me."

Thuy felt happiness hearing Lan calling out. "Sister Thuy, come here. Sister Thuy, hurry up!"

Then Nga wanted to show off the meal they were going to have. "Yesterday, Quang caught a big carp. I saved as a treat for our guests!" She was so proud.

"What could be better than being treated like a member of your family." Thuy beamed said.

It had been a long time since Thuy had been able to play like she did at home, but she also wanted to help Nga in the kitchen. Nga smiled and said. "Well, playing with Lan is also helping me."

Seeing Nga cooking fish soup, Thuy suddenly remembered her days at home. Early in the morning, she often followed her mother to the market in town.

During the war, the market would open very early, from three or four in the morning There were storm-proof lamps, which made the market look like twinkling stars in the middle of the night. People from every-where would pour in. Buyers and sellers noisily jostled each other in the market. The butchers often came early. The sound of their knives chopping meat and bone was loud on their boards. Thuy would walk by and hearing that, it would give her goose bumps.

Most of the people selling vegetables, chickens, ducks and fish were farmers in the area. They were raising and growing crops mainly for their own consumption, but they also needed to sell some of their produce to buy things such as clothes, hoes and shovels. Thuy's favourite part of the market sold ivory combs, horn combs and pretty butterfly-shaped hairpins. There was also a colourful fresh flower section, which was so eye-catching. The market was truly bustling with life. Thuy and her mother liked to go early to buy shrimp and fish. Her father liked to eat seafood, anything from fried fish to braised fish with fragrant galangal, but her father's favourite dish was fish soup cooked with tamarind and a little dill, salad.

Her father had a funny saying. "Today if there's not enough rice for everyone, then don't blame me.

Please, blame the fish!" Thinking about this made Thuy miss her father and family so much.

It was several months of eating in the canteen, before Thuy got used to this routine. She still missed the family meals, but today, eating with Quang, Nga and little Lan, Thuy felt warm and wanted. She ate well and chatted happily with Lan, whose laughter and chattering made Thuy feel like she was back with her parents and siblings.

Thuy asked curiously. "Sister Nga, is Minh a Youth Union cadre?"

"Of course. He also participates in activities in the party target group. That's why he can be a group leader. The leader must be a party member or at least a member of the youth union executive committee. We're not in any party or union. No matter how senior we get, we're still just low-level employees. Working-class to earn a living." Nga replied.

Nga looked at Thuy with kindness. "You're still young and you're not yet married. You should join all the youth organizations, try to strive to have a future. Did you attend the youth union meeting?"

With a sad face, Thuy said softly. "Yes, Mr Pao, the youth union secretary, said it would be difficult for me to join the youth union because of my family's past."

Nga looked at her husband. Quang said evenly. "It's not a big deal, just do your job well, participate in all school activities and make sure you get along with everyone. You don't have to worry too much, in our team there are many people who are not party members or union members but they still live happily. You will understand tomorrow, but let's eat before the fish gets cold and loses its taste."

Hearing Quang say that, Thuy felt reassured. She tried not to think too much about it, but felt that she might have to be careful around the older people in the departments. There was something about their quietness and reserved manner that made it difficult to read them. She reminded herself to be careful and tactful in front of everyone.

*

*		*

Sundays were the only day off work. There was always so much to do, it was a day to catch up on everything else outside of work. Sundays were also the only day the region's market was open. Thuy and some of the women in the housing area would organise to go there, making sure they could get their essentials for the week coming; sticky rice, shiitake mushrooms, soap. This was also the one day of the week, where everyone had to collect firewood to submit to the communal kitchen. The University law quoted that each person had to collect 30 kilograms of wood every month. If this was short, then their meal allowance would be cut short. The difficulty was that firewood wasn't that easy to find. People had to travel long distances and often would have cut down big trees with an axe or a saw. In the time of war people were on food rations, so their bodies were thin and weak, making tasks like this exhausting work. Many women struggled to reach the quota, so had to recruit younger men to help them. Someone urged Thuy to ask the men in other departments, she said people would happily help her, seeing as she was so small.

Thuy was a skinny girl of fifteen, born into a family that was neither rich nor poor. Even before moving to the central library, she was helping her father with his work. Every day after school, Thuy helped her father with some sewing jobs, as well as looking after her younger siblings. When that was all done, she then had the time to play with her friends. She was carefree then, but suddenly she had to leave her family. She left everything behind and had to support herself. She was still a child, but had to quickly adapt to her new independence.

Most of the people in the school were much older than her. They were husbands, wives, aunts and uncles, many of whom had children of their own. During the summer holidays and bank holidays, including the Lunar New Year festival, they would return to their hometowns. Their families were in Ha Giang, Cao Bang, Lang Son, Yen Bai, Tuyen Quang, which was the Viet Bac region and a few people are from Ha Nam, Thai Binh and Nam Dinh. In the town where Thuy's family live, only Tay and Nung local people can be seen at the market, but at the Viet Bac Pedagogical University, there are many people from different ethnic minorities. Some arrive from the mountainous provinces to work and study.

During festivals or the Lunar New Year, people from these regions would wear their traditional costumes. Colours and patterns on their clothing would represent their ethnicity. There were brocade scarves, silver bracelets and necklaces. The head covering Pieu scarves of the Black Thai ethnic women were beautiful and graceful. The Tay and Nung people would play a steady and gentle melody. The tea hills of the midland mountains were the homeland of the H'Mong ethnic boys. They would play and dance to the rhythm of the pan-flute on festival days.

In addition to the activities of trade unions, Thuy also had to participate in militia and self-defence exercises, like soldiers preparing for battle. They were taught to stand to attention, roll, crawl, practice shooting, balancing and many more. Thuy had to carry rifles on her shoulder that were too big and heavy for her. Most of the time the rifle butt was touching the ground. It was intense military training and Thuy did not dare to complain.

After each training session, her clothes were dirty and soaked in sweat. All she could do was roll onto her bed because she was so tired. Sometimes lying there, she would remember the days when she followed her brother and friends to play pretend battling. That made her smile. They would use dry branches and sticks as guns. They ran, crawled, shouted and charged and shot "pang pang..." with their mouths.

Now, every week during the military training, they would shoot real guns and real bullets, Thuy had become a militia of the school.

People could see Thuy was a city girl. When she held an axe or machete to cut and collect firewood, the tree branches were messy and mangled. Tan and Thai were ethnic men, who were used to farming, so the work of cutting trees, chopping and carrying wood was done with easily and quickly. Thuy only picked up small dry branches and stacked them into piles. Tan and Thai used axes to chop the large dry trees into pieces and carry them home. With the help of the two men, the women reached their monthly quota of thirty kilos to submit to the kitchen. In return, the women made rice balls with sesame salt and green tea juice to serve to the whole group. Tan, from the H'Mong ethnic region, was part of the administrative staff. Thuy remembered him having an upturned nose and who liked to joke. When he laughed, his upturned nose then became even more upturned, which made everyone laugh harder.

This wasn't the first time Thuy had collected firewood. She remembered when she was only thirteen years old, her father gave the three siblings the task of collecting wood nearly 10 kilometres away from their home. They borrowed a wooden ox-cart from a neighbour. At that time her brother Chinh was sixteen and her sister Hong was ten. They packed some rice balls with sesame salt and a flask of boiling water. Leaving early in the morning and not getting back until late that evening, they were able to forage a cartful of wood. There was enough for their mother to cook for a month! Although they were exhausted and it was hard work, they were happy too. They were also happy to be praised by their parents.

-----

In time, the Youth Union assigned Thuy to be in charge of the young children's team. Children of staff members aged six to twelve could participate in the team. Thuy loved this part of her life. She got to play with the children freely. Treating them like they were her younger siblings. It was easy to get along with them, easy to understand what they wanted, unlike the adults.

Thuy planned lots of entertaining activities; singing, dancing and sometimes even helped some of the children with their homework. The children loved and listened to Thuy, looking up to her, like she was their older sister.

The Youth Union praised Thuy's achievements with the team. Everyone's working environment became calmer and people were more at ease, knowing their children were being looked after and entertained. As a reward Thuy was allowed to visit her family next month when the van went into town to collect more books. This was the happiest news for Thuy.

Thuy thought of all the things she would buy at the market for her family. She imagined this perfect day seeing her parents and siblings. They would look at her, surprised at how big she had grown. Her father would ask lots of questions about her job, where she was living and was she eating enough! Thuy would then boast that she had joined the local defence militia and the union and was about to be admitted to the youth union. Then she could tell them all how she was entrusted by the school to lead the school's children team. Her father would be happy because Thuy had bought him the best tobacco packets and some of her salary that she had saved for the family. For her mother she would gift fresh betel leaves and areca nuts. For her brother and sister there would be a bag of sweets. All of this would make Thuy proud. She now had a job, with a decent salary and she could help her family.

-----

The main task of the central library was to organise the warehouse, but every month Nga, Minh and Thuy also had to take it in turns to buy and collect new books. Some months Thuy went with Nga and other months she stayed and worked in the library. Minh emphasised that everything must be organised well, so that the library could soon start operating properly. The number of books had to be entered into the accounting ledgers clearly, divided by subject and book content.

When the Central Library officially opened. There were regulations on opening hours on weekdays, regulations on borrowing and returning books for staff and rules for employees working in the central area. Staff, lecturers and students from other departments were only allowed to borrow books and magazines on Wednesdays and Fridays. There were a lot of rules.

With the ongoing war and region wide evacuations, library staff had to find other resources to build wooden bookshelves. The department heads agreed to use bamboo, reed, and rattan from forest materials to create bookshelves. The book lending room was small, holding only six or seven bookshelves on the walls. The bookshelves were made from whatever wood could be harvested from the forests. They were simple, plain and rustic, but somehow, they also looked good and smelled of forest bamboo.

Thuy's job as a librarian was to lend out books. She, of course, had to follow all the rules for lending and collecting books. Lecturers, students, and staff of departments who borrowed books had to have a letter of introduction and an ID card, which allowed them to use the library. They could borrow the books for two weeks and return or renew them before the due-back date. If any books were lost or damaged, the borrower had to pay a fine according to each level of damage. The librarian had to strictly follow these procedures. Some people thought it sounded regimental and didn't understand the need for such rules about borrowing books. However, in the union meetings, everyone was reminded that it was their duty to play a part in protecting public property and that included books, as well as the building they were in.

As Thuy was the youngest person working at the library, she was sometimes teased and looked down upon by teachers and students. Thuy, however, accepted her position and status, so she always tried to behave in a gentle and friendly manner.

There was one day, while she was arranging the returned books back onto the shelves in the warehouse, she heard a loud noise from outside. It startled her, as she was alone.

Minh was away on a business trip and Nga's daughter Lan was not well, so she was not at work either. Being on her own made her nervous and anxious, especially when the library was deserted. Every time a strong wind blew, the palm branches and leaves would hit each other, creating a rustling sound like a waterfall pouring down from above. It made Thuy feel like the roof was going to flood in. Sometimes though, the wind blew gently, almost as though to lull people to sleep. Without any human sounds, it created a strangely quiet scene in the middle of the day amongst the mountains.

There was the sound again, a loud "pop, pop" hitting the table outside the room. Thuy was startled and quickly walked out to see. A man, about thirty years old, was standing in front of Thuy's desk, flipping through the pages of the book lending list.

"Do you work here?" The man with a cold face, looked at Thuy. His voice was loud, as he looked around to see if there was anyone else in the room.

"Yes, I am sir! Do you want to borrow books or do you need to see someone?" Thuy replied as calmly as she could.

"I want to borrow some documents." The man replied with gruff words.

"Yes, sir. Can you please show me your letter of introduction?"

His face was frowning. "Must I have a letter of introduction to borrow a document? I am a lecturer at the Faculty of Mathematics."

Thuy continued calmly. "Please, sir, read carefully the paper posted over there about the regulations on borrowing books. Even if you are a staff member, you still need a letter of introduction to certify that you are a member of the department."

"I want to speak to Minh and Nga? Where are they?"

"Sorry sir, Mr Minh and Mrs Nga have other duties outside of the building."

The man slammed the catalogue down on the table with an annoyed expression. "Then I'll come another day, goodbye!"

"Goodbye sir." Thuy politely said.

He walked quickly to the door, muttering. Thuy was relieved she didn't have to argue with him anymore.

A few days later, Thuy told Nga about it, she didn't say anything, just laughed and laughed. Thuy didn't understand what she was laughing about, but later discovered that the man was using the excuse of borrowing books to chat to Nga.

-----

Life in the time of war was focused on work and taking care of the family. Very few members of staff borrowed books. There wasn't really time to read books, or read anything else. In the evacuation areas, after work, people were always busy taking care of duties at home.

People with wives and children were living in collective housing areas. These houses were often too small, and some families had many children that had to squeeze into these small spaces. It was a struggle. If there was only one person who went to work, the burden was on their shoulders. They had to work a full day and then carry on the rest of the day taking care of their family.

The wives and children living in the countryside had more free time. Sometimes they were able to borrow books and newspapers from the library.

These were rare moments of entertainment. Most of the people who came to the library were students and lecturers from every faculty. Their faces were often cold, disdainful and they never really smiled at Thuy. This didn't really affect Thuy, she was focused on her work and assumed everyone else had their tasks and assignments too. With time the judging eyes did affect her self-esteem, but it only made Thuy more determined to achieve her ambition of sitting in a university lecture hall and become an intellectual like them.

Some of the older students who Thuy was able to help assist in the library, were full of hope and dreams. After four years of studying, they would be teachers at high schools in the Viet Bac autonomous region. It did make Thuy sad, comparing the future of these students and her future, which was altered, just because of her family background. Thuy was forced to lose her dream. She knew she could achieve academically as well as anyone else. She wanted to have the same experiences and hopes as these students and be excited about her career future.

Students often borrowed specialized books, a few borrowed literature and art books. In time Thuy was able to build a more sympathetic relationship with these students. Most of them were working class, poor and children of ethnic minority party members. Some were children of officials, who were 'the basic elements' as the proletarian government called them. A very small number were Viet people but had lived for a long time in the towns and cities. Some were poor students in the provinces of Hai Duong, Hung Yen, Hanoi, who did not have enough points to enter universities in Hanoi. In front of Thuy these students were proud, after all, they were wearing the university student uniform, while Thuy was just a librarian. This only made Thuy more determined that one day she would also wear the student uniform like they did.

Yesterday afternoon, while eating, Ly and Hoi told Thuy. "Tomorrow, the three of us will go find more firewood for cooking and heating, winter is coming soon."

Thuy nodded and was happy to agree to this, as Thuy did not know how to plan ahead like they did. On the way home that day, Minh followed them and said to Ly. "What time do you want to go to get firewood tomorrow? Let me come with you for fun."

"What's fun about collecting firewood?" Hoi laughed.

Pao and Thai interrupted. "What time do you want to leave tomorrow? We'll go with you too!"

When they all got back to their bedrooms, Ly and Hoi were both giggling.

The weather today seemed to please everyone. In the early morning, the thin layer of white fog quickly dissipated, leaving a beautiful sunny day. The three sisters were neatly dressed. They each carried brocade bags on their shoulders with provisions for lunch. The three young men had been waiting at the foot of the hill for a long time. Minh, a Hanoian, was known as a scholar of the capital, but he had arrived early today.

Everyone nodded in greeting to each other and began their brisk walk towards the forest. The girls discussed the need to only find small dry branches for their own cooking. They had already given in their quota of big branches for the kitchen canteen that month. Without Tan, the atmosphere was quiet. There was no joking around like the previous time.

Hoi started singing softly. She was from the Nam Đinh province, where she was a nurse at the central medical station. She had only arrived at this library two months before Thuy. Hoi was a few years older than Thuy. Her skin was brown, maybe because of the sun and wind of the Red River Delta or maybe from living near the sea. She rarely talked or laughed, but had a gentle nature. She sang folk songs beautifully. She told Thuy that in her home town of Chau Van, she had joined the commune's performing arts team. It made Thuy wonder why she still blushed when she sang, if she was part of a performing arts team. Everyone complimented her singing, but otherwise no one would really pay any attention to her. Thuy, however, did prefer Hoi's company. Ly was ten years older than Thuy, which perhaps made it difficult for Thuy to approach her or be open with her. Maybe it was because she was the assistant doctor at the clinic infirmary?

Thuy started to notice that Mr Minh would follow her wherever she went. Thuy didn't understand why he didn't accompany Pao or Ly? It really annoyed Thuy and made it difficult for Thuy to talk to Hoi alone, who was just content singing softly as she walked. By noon, each person had collected a big bundle. Thuy and Hoi were struggling to find vines, so they could tie two bundles of firewood together. When Pao volunteered to help them, Minh waved his hand to shoo them away. "Don't worry, I'll help them, you go over there to help Ly."

Pao didn't seem to mind. "All right, everyone hurry up and go home early. There's still a Youth Union meeting tonight."

At the union meeting, you had to sit and listen to the secretary talk at length about policies, strategies, and plans over and over again. This made Thuy sleepy, but it wasn't just her. She looked to the side, the other members were all dozing off too!

Thuy was lost in thought when someone grabbed her hand. Startled, Thuy quickly withdrew her hand and looked up. It was Minh! She didn't understand what was going on. Minh acted as if he hadn't done anything, but his face had turned red. So many thoughts raced through Thuy's mind. This man is crazy, holding someone's hand in broad daylight?! Tomorrow she could be accused of being indecent, and having a relationship with a married man. Along with the record of her family background, it was not what she needed to happen.

Since that day, Thuy felt uneasy working at the library and even more so when Minh was in the same room as her. She tried to stay away from him as much as she could, but this was really difficult when he was the team leader. She had to concentrate on her work and try not to be criticized. Her mind was tense and she had no one she could confide in. Thuy found it easiest to forget when she was with the teenagers, teaching them to sing and dance. She could laugh happily and freely and not think about the library.

Thuy sometimes thought she wanted to talk to Hoi, hoping that she might have some advice for her. But for some reason since the day she went to collect firewood, Hoi kept on mentioning Minh, praising him for being kind and gentlemanly. Thuy thought that silence was best, so she kept it all to herself. But over time, Thuy became more and more upset. Not being able to confide in anyone about Minh holding her hand, made her more and more stressed.

She had to constantly try to avoid him, but Minh always found a way to get close to her.

"Ms Thuy, please check this document for any mistakes." Minh said in an annoyed voice.

Thuy attentively looked for mistakes. She could feel her back getting hot, and when she turned around Minh was standing right behind. Thuy slowly pulled the chair away, her face hot, she was trembling and she didn't know what to do. All she could hope for was for Nga to come save her. Minh was still standing there, bending down close to Thuy's head.

"I'm sorry sir, please, let me go to the restroom." She quickly said.

Minh stepped back, then went inside the bookstore. Thuy hoped to end work quickly as soon as possible. The next day, as Thuy stepped through the door and even before she could hang up her bag. Minh was there.

"Ms Thuy, today you have the task of rearranging the books on the shelf to their correct places."

"Yes, sir, I'll do it right away now." Thuy said obediently.

Minh tried every way to approach Thuy, not letting her sit still. Sometimes he told Thuy to go with him to buy new books. He was deliberately trying to spend time alone with Thuy. He never touched Nga. Nga just thought Minh was training Thuy up in her job, making sure she was doing a good job. Only Thuy and Minh knew what was truly going on.

A few days later, Minh gave Thuy a new book, telling her to read it so she could introduce it to other readers. That night, when she returned to her room, before going to sleep, Thuy opened the book. A piece of paper fell out of the book. 'Dear Thuy honey...' There was a letter with her name on it. Two pages full of writing. Thuy scanned the papers and quickly looked at the end. It was signed off, 'Minh, waiting for your reply...'

Thuy looked out of the front door as if afraid someone would look in. Thuy slowly read what was written in the letter. This was the second time she had received a letter from a man. The last time, a classmate wrote a letter hinting that he had feelings for Thuy. Thuy's father caught it and scolded her, forbidding Thuy and the boy from going to school together ever again. She remembered how angry her father was. "You're still in school, you have to focus on your studies. You can't have any frivolous relationships".

Now she was working and lived independently from her family, Thuy felt scared, she actually wished her father was here.

That night Thuy's thoughts turned to what would happen tomorrow when she faced Minh. She had to go to the library to work. Eventually, Thuy fell asleep full of worry and fear. When Thuy saw Minh the next morning, she had no idea what he was thinking. "Thuy, tomorrow you'll come with me into town to buy new books. After that, you can visit your family for two hours and in the evening, we'll return to school."

This news was so unexpected and exciting that Thuy forgot about the letter. Nga was glad to see Thuy happy. It had been over half a year since Thuy had last seen her parents and siblings. She was so absorbed in her busy work schedule, and her life was always changing, that she didn't have time to think about when she could see her family next. Thuy gradually got used to her new life and the child-like look she had on her face when she first started was disappearing.

The old Giai Phong truck (Liberation truck made in China) that belonged to the school was driven by

Phuoc and Tuyen, who was the assistant. Thuy was given the privilege of sitting in the cabin next to the driver. Phuoc was from South Vietnam, so his accent was different from Thuy's. He was about forty years old, with over fifteen years in his profession as a driver. He was cheerful, talkative and told funny stories all the way. The fifty kilometres distance did not seem as long as the day uncle Sinh rode his bike to take Thuy to the school.

The road was full of potholes and bumps, the truck was shaking and swaying and the people sitting inside were being thrown up and down. It was torture riding like this. Minh sat in the back of the truck and must have been shaken up because he screamed in pain. The truck passed through two streams. The water was not very deep, but because it was full of gravel and large rocks, Thuy thought to herself it would probably be more comfortable walking across. The road went through many forests with tree branches spreading out on both sides of the road. Sometimes there was an eerie sound when the branches scraped hard against the truck.

Last night, it had rained heavily and many sections of the dirt road had sunk, leaving behind deep holes. The road was muddy and the tires were covered in clay. There were many times Phuoc revved the engine and the wheels just kept on spinning, without the truck moving. When this happened, everyone had to get out to help push the truck. Every time Phuoc revved the engine, everyone shouted in unison. "Try your best, come on ... come on... on..."

Each time the truck got through mud holes, everyone breathed out relieved. Their hands and feet were dirty, but their faces were happy. When they were all back in the truck again. Phuoc smiled. "I hope it will be sunny all day today. The road will dry quickly and it won't be like this on the way home tonight. We're turning onto the national highway now, so the roads will be smoother!"

"Uncle Phuoc, maybe we should leave early to go home tonight. Isn't it dangerous to go out at night when roads are like this?" Thuy suggested.

"Don't worry, kid." Phuoc smiled. Thuy didn't like being called a kid, so after Phuoc called her that, she kept quiet and didn't say anything more.

On the national highway, the journey was easy. The roads were paved and on both sides, the green rice fields were starting to bloom. In the distance, the tea hills stretched out, looking so pretty to the eye. The sun was starting to rise, it looked like it would be a beautiful sunny day. Thuy looked at the undulating rice fields, floating up and down like waves bending in the wind.

The air was so pleasant, cooler than in the town. Thuy thought her father must be at work now, and her siblings at school. She wondered what her mother was doing right at this moment. Thuy was so excited to see her family. Her younger sister, Hong had written a letter to Thuy telling her that the whole family had to evacuate a few months ago. All of the people in the town had to follow the orders of the People's Committee. The evacuation areas were struggling with supplying food and accommodation for everyone that came. Some people had to leave after only being there for a couple of weeks. To solve this issue, the government ordered families to dig shelters for the area. People continued to live and work there, but they were also ready when the air defence sirens sounded. Everyone was adapting to the wartime situation. The company Thuy's father worked for did not evacuate though, they stayed put.

Thuy thought about her friends, what had happened to them. Had any of them moved away, did they go to university in the end? She missed them, but imagined her life was so different to theirs.

The truck entered the town, passed Dau Cau Street, crossed the intersection and passed the familiar row of banyan trees in front of Thuy's family home. It carried on to the bookstore in the centre of the town.

The town was deserted and quiet, with very few people walking around. On both sides of the road, shelters had been cleverly camouflaged, a sure sign that the war was still present in this town. The bookstore was near the market and the truck arrived before 10 am. The market was mostly deserted, with only a few stall sellers in sight. Thuy could see some baskets of vegetables, shrimp and fish and maybe only a couple of stalls selling meat. A sadness passed over Thuy. It wasn't like the market of Thuy's younger life, which was bustling and full of life.

Minh and Thuy got out of the truck and went to the bookstore where they had an appointment booked. Phuoc and Tuyen drove the truck to get the other goods. Minh met the store manager to discuss what was needed. Thuy slowly looked around the entire bookstore and after about fifteen minutes Minh called Thuy into the warehouse. Back at the central library Thuy had made a list of what was needed and what quantities of each title was needed. Everything was checked over twice to avoid mistakes. The road trips for these collections were so long and difficult, that everything had to be justified. The University head would then approve it, as well as issuing a license for the vehicle that was needed for the journey.

At around 2 pm, after all the books were signed for, invoiced, packaged up and loaded onto the truck, Thuy was then allowed to visit her family for two hours. The bookstore was about a kilometre away from Thuy's family home. Thuy eagerly checked all the gifts she had brought along for her parents and siblings. She started feeling nervous about seeing them, but then excitement as she started running faster towards the banyan trees. First stop would be where her father worked.

Watching from the outside of the building, she could see her father measuring out the clothes for customers. Thuy's father was the foreman. He had many years of experience in the tailor industry. His main job at this company was to greet customers, measure out and cut the fabric, ready to pass onto the seamstresses. The company didn't just make clothes though, it also had a personalised service, suggesting outfits and fabrics to customers. It was doing really well, despite the war. There were about a dozen tailors, all busy working, when Thuy walked in the front door.

Everyone looked up in surprise, including her father. He stopped what he was doing and stood there looking up at his daughter, with his eyes wide. "Oh, my dear daughter... come here."

Everyone stood up and rushed to surround her. So many voices were competing to ask questions. There was an air of happiness as they spoke. Many recognised her and praised her for looking more mature than when they last saw her. During war time, so many families were separated, some reunited, but some lost forever. There was joy and happiness all mixed up. People understood the preciousness of being reunited with loved ones. It was a shared happiness. Thuy's father was so moved that he couldn't say anything, he just looked at his daughter and watched everyone else fuss over Thuy. After a while, the uncles and aunts had to return to their work.

Thuy approached her father and gave him the gift of a golden-coloured water-pipe packet of Tien Lang tobacco. Her father was overcome with emotion, his voice started trembling.

"Are you living well up there? Don't you have enough to eat? You've lost so much weight. Next time you come home, don't use your money to buy gifts for me. You must take care of yourself."

His voice was choked and his eyes started to water. Thuy did not know how to reply. She just nodded softly, yes father.

The pendulum clock of the store rang loudly, Bong! bong! The clock hands showed 2.30 pm. There wasn't that much time left before the truck came to pick her up. Thuy said a sad goodbye to her father.

She had to go on to visit her mother and siblings now. She walked quickly out of the door, feeling both happy and sad. Passing along Trung Vuong Street, she had memories of there being more stalls in front of the doors as well as along the street. There were the longan trees where Thuy and her friends used to play, climb and steal the longan fruit when it was in season. At the end of the row of lush, leafy banyan trees, was the family's beloved home. Only ten more steps to reach it. Thuy ran. The door was still open as it always had been. Her mother and siblings were sitting around the dinner table. Thuy burst in. "Mum! Sister! Brothers!"

The two young boys ran out to hug Thuy. Thuy's mother smiled full of happiness. She scolded her two sons lovingly, then urged Thuy to wash her hands and sit down to eat. Only at this point did Thuy feel hungry. She hadn't eaten anything since 6am. It had been such a long time since she was able to sit down with her mother and siblings.

Today was a special day. On the table was a plate of boiled sweet potato leaves with soy sauce, a bowl of sweet potato juice with tomatoes, a plate of stir-fried tomatoes with eggs (the most indulgent dish on the table) and a large plate of flour dumplings without any filling. Since the start of the war, food was in short supply. Even with rice rationing, there wasn't enough to go around, so the government sold flour or corn instead of rice. This happened all across the north and south of the country. People had to be creative with their meals and in this town, there was a facility that processed flour into noodles or bread.

Thuy's mother skilfully made steamed dumplings, which looked more beautiful and were so much nicer to eat than the boiled dumplings in the school kitchen. The school's catering staff refused to improve or change the way they cooked. Thuy could tell there was no enthusiasm about their work, they just wanted to get the job done and go home.

The dumplings her mother made had no meat filling, sugar or honey, but they were delicious. Her family always made the best of anything, even dumplings! The meal they ate was simple, some might say poor, but Thuy's family was still better off than many others. While they ate, Thuy looked at her siblings and saw how they had grown and looked so different from a few months ago. She felt a pang of sorrow for them. They didn't complain or ask for anything.

"Be good and after we finish eating, I have something to give you all." Thuy smiled at her siblings. She then turned to her mother. "I know it's difficult for you, mother. I have a salary now, so from now on I can give you money to help the whole family. I love you all very much."

Her mother looked at her with love, something Thuy had rarely seen before. After the meal, Thuy called her younger siblings over to their mother. She handed her a bag of sesame candy to share with them, two kilos of sticky rice from the district market (the rare type high-quality upland rice that people today would call a specialty) and a few dozen đồng she had saved from her wages to bring home. along with some of her salary she had saved to give to her family.

Her sister and brothers were excited and asked lots of questions. "How many people are at your work? Are there wild animals in the forest? Are you afraid of ghosts when you sleep alone? Are there many books for children in the library you work in? Do you get bullied?!"

While they were still fun, the string suddenly snapped. At that moment, a car horn sounded outside... a sharp whistle... the school's vehicle had arrived to pick her up; visiting hours were over. Thuy didn't want to leave her mother and siblings, but she had to return. They said goodbye reluctantly. From outside, Minh's voice called out. "Hurry up, Ms Thuy!"

The youngest brother cried and wanted to go with her. Her mother wiped her tears and urged Thuy to quickly get into the truck so that everyone wouldn't have to wait. The two hours of visiting her parents and siblings were over. Time passed so quickly like a beautiful dream.

-----

On the way home, Thuy was very quiet. She didn't say anything or ask anything. All she could think of was the short time she had with her family, and the question she would ask herself again and again, when will I see them next? The days following her visit to see her family, Thuy spoke and smiled less. Nga noticed this change in her mood, but Minh dismissed it. "Thuy just misses home."

The time Thuy had to visit her home was too short, but it left her with so many thoughts. The image of her siblings sitting there with such a simple lunch, just made her miss them more and those images kept on haunting her.

Thuy had forgotten about the letter, but she silently thanked Minh for letting her visit home. He still made her uneasy and she was still worried every time they were in the same room together.

When they were in the same room together, Thuy tried to do her best not to upset Minh. He started, though, to order Thuy to do random things. His voice was often grumpy, unhappy or twisted. "Why are you doing this? Why aren't you concentrating on your work? Are you sleepy?"

Minh's attitude brought Thuy back to the horrid memory of the day she received his letter. After work on a Monday, Thuy met Nhien, a girlfriend who worked as a clerk in the History faculty. Nhien was only one year older than Thuy, so they got on really well. Thuy got to know her background and how she was able to get a job here. Nhien's family were poor and couldn't afford for Nhien not to work. Like Thuy, she was introduced to a job at this school, by a family friend. Getting a job for anyone wasn't easy at all, but because Nhien was a Tay ethnic person, she was accepted straight away. There was a policy of prioritizing the employment of ethnic minority people into the workforce. Nhien was cheerful and friendly to everyone.

From the first day they were introduced to each other Thuy and Nhien became close friends. Finally meeting someone she could call a friend, Thuy felt happy. They were like a pair of birds chatting and walking together. Each time they had lunch together, people in the canteen would stop and watch the friends walk in. Thuy had a new friend. A few men would stare at Nhien's fair and rosy complexion, finding it attractive.

The catering lady, Nhan smiled and teased, when she saw the two girls. "A ha! My dear niece has a guest! Next time remember to tell me about it, so I can give priority to the two of you!"

"Yes, thank you very much indeed, if there is not enough rice to share for everyone, we can eat just one portion between us." Thuy quickly replied.

"Sister Nhan, take my portion of rice to share with these two new friends." Someone joined in. Everyone laughed and there was a joyful atmosphere in the dining room. However, Thuy could see Minh sitting at the end of the table, who wasn't laughing.

In the afternoon Nhien was in the library with Thuy. She was collecting books to take back to her department. Minh wasn't in the library, so the two of them were free to talk openly. Nga handed over the documents and books for Nhien to sign and then Nhien went into the warehouse to help Thuy arrange the books.

The two of them whispered to each other. Thuy told her friend about Minh's letter and the time when he held Thuy's hand the day they went to get the firewood. Nhien giggled and this confused Thuy.

"That's strange right?" Thuy asked.

"Thuy, I also received a letter from Minh, last month!" Nhien smiled.

Now Thuy was surprised.

"He also put it in a book and gave it to me. It's especially funny because the words in both letters are exactly the same! I'll show it to you next time we see each other. We can have a good laugh together." Nhien continued. "Oh, and do you remember Tram? That short girl in the Literature department?"

"Yes, Tram has dimples, right?"

"Yes! Tram also received a letter that old Minh sent. He wrote 'I wrote to you while the raindrops were falling on the palm leaves.' In my letter he wrote rain falling on banana leaves and in yours it was raining on the roof."

Thuy burst out laughing. "Is this guy crazy?" "He is definitely short-circuited!"

"So, after you got the letter, how did you feel? Did you reply and were you afraid?" Thuy wondered.

"I wasn't afraid, but I know for you it's different. You're working in the same department as him. He's your boss, he's got authority over you. I imagine that it is much harder for you to see him."

oOo

Standing quietly in the middle of the cool, clear stream. Thuy stood holding the mussel she had just harvested. Thuy watched the leaves slowly drifting along the quiet water, sparkling under the summer sunlight. In the distance, the palm trees stood calmly after many seasons of rain and sun.

It was a beautiful afternoon and everything seemed to be smiling at Thuy. The palm leaves spread out, shiny under the sunlight, swaying in the wind as if beckoning. They then reminded her of the lines Minh wrote in his letter; *'Tonight, the rain outside is falling on the palm leaves.'* Thuy had no feelings for Minh and had no idea how to reply.

At work she was silent and evasive. Seeing him in the same library every day was extremely awkward and frustrating for her. Even more so, since Minh kept on catching Thuy and Nhien whispering together and then falling silent when they saw him. He became suspicious.

Thinking back to two months ago, like so many other days, Thuy was chatting with the caretaker Nhan after the lunch period. The two of them were happily laughing and talking like usual, Minh walked by without saying hello to Nhan, looked straight at Thuy with a sullen face and said. "Ms

Thuy, I have something to talk to you about. Right away, now!"

Thuy quickly said goodbye to Nhan and followed Minh. Just before they got to the library, Minh stopped and faced Thuy. "The department head has decided to transfer you to work in the Literature faculty."

Thuy couldn't believe what she was hearing.

"Why so suddenly Mr Minh? Can I know the reason? Has the decision been made?"

"If you don't believe me, please go to the department head and you can hear for yourself." Thuy was stunned, her heart pounding. She wanted to ask more, but Minh had already hurried towards the library.

Thuy ran quickly up the hill on the left, towards the department head's room. Her head was filled with questions and doubts. It was only an hour ago when she saw them at the cafeteria. They were talking and laughing with Thuy. There was nothing unusual.

Up until today, Thuy has been living and working in the Literature department for two months. Being moved suddenly, without warning meant that Thuy didn't have time to prepare for the move.

All of the ladies in the dormitory were surprised. Ly was sad but silent. Hoi stayed in the same room with Thuy that night. There was no sleep that night. All you could hear were whispers, occasional sniffles and hiccups. Thuy turned to see a gecko on the ceiling. Its clicking tongue seemed to say, "gecko, so sad, gecko". The women in her dormitory were people she loved, they helped her survive in this strange place and time. Thuy was filled with sadness at the thought of how much she would miss them.

Nga was stunned to hear that Thuy was being transferred to the Literature department. She had her suspicions. “Something isn’t right. Why would they do this to you?”

Thuy heard Nga asking questions, but was too distracted to answer. Believing that the transfer to the Literature department was valid, Thuy left without suspecting Minh. The Literature faculty did not have separate rooms for female employees to live.

-----

The department head was also surprised at Thuy’s transfer and hadn’t had time to prepare. However, they were very happy to welcome the new member and arranged for Thuy to stay with a local family.

Khuong had been a widower for seven years now, her mother-in-law was nearly sixty years old and her daughter, Ty was about nine years old. These three women, from three generations, were living together in a Tay ethnic stilt house.

Ty, the little girl, was extremely happy to have Thuy stay with them. Her mother said she had never seen her smile and talk so much! Every time she smiled, you could see the adorable little dimples on her face. She was a pretty child.

In the evening, the four women would sit around the kitchen fire in the middle of the house. The old mother chewed betel leaves silently all day and occasionally Khuong would also chew the betel leaves. Khuong would work from early morning until sunset on the fields. Thuy could see she was very hard working and it was a struggle to support her mother-in-law and daughter. Khuong had brown skin and a serious, quiet face.

On the first day, Thuy was hesitant to say too much to her. Having grown up in a large family herself and being the oldest of four children, Thuy knew how to integrate quickly and in a week she felt like part of the family. Wherever Thuy went, Ty followed her. Thuy would teach her things she remembered from her school days. She also laughed and played with her, which made Khuong feel more at ease when going to work. It also meant that she warmed to Thuy, asking her more questions and smiling at her more.

Khuong was only thirty years old, but she looked so much older than that. Two weeks after her wedding, her husband joined the army and was then away from home for many years. Ty was conceived during one time visit back home. He soon returned to the fight on the battlefields in South Vietnam and that was the last time Khuong saw him.

Sometimes if Thuy finished work early, she would come home and help wash the family's clothes. She would see Ty's clothes sitting in the corner of the room and put them in a pile to wash along with hers.

When Khuong came back from the field, carrying a plow on her shoulder and leading a buffalo behind her. Thuy could see her trousers rolled up one leg other one loose.

"You're home from work? Leave Ty's clothes for me, you don't have to wash them." Khuong smiled, her two rows of black teeth as even as custard apple seeds.

All the chewing of betel leaves turns teeth black, and in some regions that was seen as beautiful. Khuong must have been one of the most beautiful girls in the village, Thuy thought.

"It's okay, I'm happy to wash Ty's clothes with mine. At home I would wash all my siblings' clothes. You can wash your hands and feet. Your mum is done cooking."

Thuy knew that Khuong's mother-in-law had already prepared dinner, waiting for her daughter-in-law to come home from work. Tonight was like many other nights, the whole family sat around the fire ready for their meal. Thuy spotted some bamboo tubes standing upright next to the stove. She wondered what they were doing there. "Sister Khuong! What are these bamboo tubes for?"

The grandmother looked up at her daughter-in-law and before Khuong could answer, Ty jumped in. "Sister Thuy, my grandma and my mother told me to let you try this bamboo-tube-rice dish tonight. Yesterday, my mother had to pound special sticky rice, ready for this dish."

Thuy leaned her head on the old woman's shoulder and looked at Khuong. "I've never eaten this bamboo-tube-rice dish before and I've never heard of it before tonight. Thank you for thinking of me."

Ty stared at the bamboo tubes next to the fire stove, constantly asking, is it done yet? Why is it taking so long? "Give me two pieces and Thuy the same. Is that okay mum?"

Ty said excitedly. When the bamboo rice was ready, Khuong carefully picked up each bamboo tube. Taking it away from the stove, she used a knife to gently split the bamboo tube in two. Inside the tube halves, the rice was wrapped in a thin, soft white foam membrane that easily fell out of the bamboo tube. Khuong used a towel to line her hands and held the cooked sticky rice out, offering it to her mother-in-law first.

"Where is my portion, mum?" Ty said, sitting up straight.

"Don't worry Ty, everyone will have a good portion to eat."

Khuong then took a portion of bamboo rice and gave it to Thuy and Ty. She looked at Thuy and gently urged. "Thuy, please go ahead and try it. Let me know if it is any different from cooked sticky rice?"

This was the first time Thuy had eaten this unusual dish. If Thuy was still living at home, would she have known about this dish? She then thought about her father, mother and siblings who had never eaten it before and maybe would never get the chance to eat it.

"Yes, it is very delicious." Thuy replied to Khuong's question.

As soon as Thuy tasted the rice, she could smell a strange, light fragrance wafting from the round, white rice grains. They had been soaked in the spring water in the area. When cooked, the rice grains expanded into the spongy insides of the bamboo tubes, being coated and sticking together. The fragrance of the combined sticky rice and bamboo floated through the air. It was like the pure scent of the forest.

Thuy enjoyed the special flavour of the rice and silently thanked the mountains and forests and all its people. That night everyone ate and chatted happily. The homely family gathering was full of love and Thuy knew this was a memory Thuy would never forget.

*

*                *

Outside, the cold wind blew fiercely, passing through the gaps in the bamboo blinds, making waves in the air. Occasionally, the gecko clicked its tongue 'gecko, gecko' on the corner of the roof making it even more sad and cold.

"Thuy, remember to warm your clothes over the fire stove to keep them warm. It will kill the chicken bugs and bed bugs that might bite you while you sleep. It's a cold night, so I've put some more dried banana leaves under your mat for you" Khuong gently reminded Thuy.

Thuy replied with a thank you. The old woman and Ty had been asleep for a long time. Another night away from home, the first cold winter night in a stranger's house, but she was feeling the warm love of everyone in the family. Thuy felt attached, close and how could she forget the first time she got sick when she first moved here.

Moving to this area, more than ten kilometres away from the centre, was right on the day the first cold wind of the season blew in. That night, Thuy felt aches and pains all over her body. Shivering and coughing, she still felt cold even under the blanket. The next morning, Khuong didn't see Thuy get up to go to work. She called out but Thuy didn't answer, so she went into her room to wake her up. There she saw Thuy's face was red and when she touched her forehead it was hot.

"Thuy must have the flu, mom, I'll cook cast rice cakes to help break her fever." Khuong said to her mother-in-law.

After a while, Thuy saw a plate of cast rice cakes placed on the altar. There were three lit incense sticks and two cups of water. Khuong clasped her hands together, bowed her head respectfully and muttered a prayer.

*I bow to Mr and Mrs Flu*
*You are from Nghe An province crawling here*
*This tray of offerings is sacred*
*Please eat it then forgive me.*

When the three incense sticks had burned out, Khuong bowed three times in thanks, took the cup of water and poured it on the ground. She then carried the plate of cast rice cakes over to Thuy. "Ms Thuy, please try to eat it all, then take a nap and your illness will be gone."

Khuong advised Thuy to stay in the home that day. She sent Ty to the Literature Faculty to report Thuy's absence. Not knowing for sure whether it was the plate of rice cakes or the magic spell, or if it was just a cold she had had, but after taking a long nap, Thuy's fever was gone. She was able to go to work the following day.

When she was feeling settled in Khuong's family, the department head then transferred Thuy to live with Luu's family, who was a staff member. Once again, Thuy said goodbye with tears. Ty cried and held onto Thuy, not wanting her to move away.

"I promise to visit grandmother, Khương and Ty from time to time." Thuy said, crying.

Putting the bag of clothes on her shoulder, Thuy slowly let go of Ty's small hand. Thuy looked over at the women one last time before moving on.

*

* *

Luu's thatched house was about twenty square meters wide. On the right, four wooden boards were put together on a pair of wooden stools to form a double bed for Luu and her little daughter Nga about five years old. Next to them, two wooden boards were put together to form a single bed for Thuy. In the left corner of the house, where the kitchen was, there was a large jar of water, two enameled iron basins, several large and small cast iron pots. A few bricks were arranged together to form a fire stove for cooking. Outside were bundles of dry firewood neatly stacked. Thuy looked around and thought, whether she would be moving to another new home soon after this one.

From Luu's house to the office it was about twenty minutes to walk over a hill. It was closer than Khuong's house. The sun had just risen behind the distant mountains and Luu was getting ready to go to work. She was probably going to the kitchen storage to receive a new food delivery. Thuy took her cloth bag on her shoulder and walked quickly to the gate. She was thinking about the pile of books that had been lying motionless for a long time in the archives, so she wanted to get there early to start planning her day.

The dense morning mist covered the mountain range in front of her like a white silk strip. Thuy walked quickly along the small path towards the hill, immersed in the mist like clouds, it was damp and cold. The mist enveloped her, so she couldn't see the path clearly. She couldn't touch it, but it felt like something was pressing down on her head. It was suffocating. Her trousers and hem began to get wet because of the layer of dew on the grass on both sides of the path. Thuy shivered and felt cold. She pulled her coat tightly around herself and continued walking. When she finally arrived at the building, the sun rose to welcome her.

The sun shone on her wet cheeks drying them out. Thuy used her hands to wipe the dew off her eyelids, stroked her cheeks to warm them, and walked quickly into the building.

The Faculty of Literature, was one of three faculties in the southern evacuation areas. This village was in a deep forest, which lacked many facilities. The library was shared with the clerical room. There was a shortage of people, so each staff member did several jobs. The rooms and departments were scattered far apart.

There was Tram, a typist and clerical staff member, who was too busy to deal with the pile of books in the faculty. They've known each other since Thuy worked at the central library, so she and Thuy were very happy to work with each other again.

Tram explained the issue and together they found a solution for how to get through the mounting pile of books. Thuy had come into work early to arrange the books, classify and record them. She did everything from scratch, following the same procedure as at the central library. She applied all the guidance she had got from Minh and Nga and slowly got through the books. After two weeks, the books, documents, newspapers and magazines were arranged on three bookshelves. Thuy had created a neat and pretty work-place.

When the entire library was cleaned, it was finally open for service. Faculty leaders, lecturers and students were excited and everyone started to borrow and return books regularly. The central library did not send anyone to check or help, and neither did Minh visit, even though he was the head of the central library group. Thuy no longer thought about returning to her original role back at the central library. Thuy found her work here was meaningful and she enjoyed the opportunity to help everyone. Thuy and Tram sometimes took the opportunity to visit Nhien at the History Faculty.

Yesterday, Luu had said in advance that this Sunday they would go catch mussels at the stream. Thuy was looking forward to that.

-----

Where Thuy was standing, she couldn't tell where the origins of the stream were. She stood watching the stream flow quietly. Surrounding her were tall palm trees with wide, green leaves growing close together, creating some shade over the forest. The sun shone through the leaves, the scene was cool and beautiful. It was so picturesque with a stream winding through the forest floor. The stream was more than one and a half meters wide and the water was so clear that you could see the pebbles and rocks at the bottom. When the water flowed over large rocks, it made gurgling noises. It was musical along with the sound of the wind blowing through the bamboo stems. A few small fish swam along the stream. They were weaving through the light purple flowers in the water.

Thuy spotted the mussels. There were so many just lying quietly at the bottom of the stream. Thuy called Luu to come over. She rolled up her trousers and stepped down, the water was up to her calves.

Luu had done this a few times before, so she knew exactly what to do.

"They are lying all over the stream, don't rush. Don't bend down to pick them up, your back will start to hurt and your sleeves will get wet. Use your toes to grab them and that way you can pick them up much easier." Luu explained.

It sounded strange, but she watched Luu demonstrate by using her feet to catch the mussel between her toes. It looked so easy as though she was playing a game. The mussels raised their heads proudly and were grabbed tightly by Luu's toes. Thuy tried this method and found out happily, it was a great method. There were so many mussels that in less than an hour, the two women had picked up almost two full baskets of mussels.

Luu, was a native of Hai Hau, a seaside town, in the Nam Dinh province. She told stories of old days at home, raking sand from early morning with a bamboo rake and an iron hook. She would collect clams and oysters all day long with this tool. The work was hard and depended on the tide. She never expected that there would be so many mussels living in a freshwater stream in a forest.

"Let's just pick a few more and then go home. The last few times I was here, there weren't as many mussels as today, so this afternoon we'll have a delicious soup." Luu smiled.

Thuy was daydreaming about the experience and how much she enjoyed it, even more so than when she was at home with her friends playing games. She wanted to write home and tell her family all about today and she wanted to ask Tram to come along next time they came to the stream. Luu's voice called out to her, breaking her daydream. She lingered a little longer to soak her feet in the cool stream before reluctantly leaving to follow Luu home.

The next morning at work, Thuy rushed to find Tram, to tell her all about the mussel, but couldn't find her. At lunch she heard some people talk about Tram being sick. So, after finishing work, Thuy didn't go straight to Luu, but went to visit Tram. Tram was staying with Hue, who was part of the teaching department. Hue was away on a business trip.

When Thuy arrived, she saw several women there. One was sitting on a chair and another was sitting next to Tram's bed. There was confusion and worry on everyone's faces. Thuy approached the bed. She could see that Tram had a fever and was shivering under her blanket. Every now and then she would have convulsions. Her teeth chattered and she was sweating profusely.

Two women hugged Tram tightly, but the convulsions didn't stop. About fifteen minutes of convulsions, Tram was exhausted, her face pale on the bed.

"In my opinion, go into the village and find a herbalist to give her some herbal medicine." A woman about forty years old spoke up.

"It's Malaria! Convulsions like this, you have to catch some earthworms, burn it into charcoal, mix it with cold water and drink it and she will be cured!" Another woman said.

Others said to take Western medicine. That someone should call the assistant doctor at the infirmary.

Everyone had their own opinion, but nobody knew who to listen to.

"Has Tram been sick for a long time?" Thuy asked the person sitting next to her.

"Yesterday, Tram said she was tired, didn't want to eat. She was thirsty and slept lethargically. Then she had a fever and chills and her body was hot and sweaty. She had convulsions."

Thuy had never seen someone so sick before. She was confused and didn't know what to say. She looked out the door and saw the head of the administrative department, along with Ly, the school's assistant doctor.

Lý approached Tram's bed, took her temperature, and took out a stethoscope to examine Tram.

"Please be quiet so the patient can rest. I have decided to transfer the patient to the infirmary at the centre for treatment. Everyone, help prepare the poles and hammocks to help us carry the patient."

Thuy asked the head of the department to let her follow Tram, so she could help take care of her.

Everyone quickly found the hammocks and poles. Four strong young men took it in turns carrying the stretcher. The road from the Faculty of Literature to the infirmary was twelve kilometres. It took forever to get there. Tram's groans in the hammock became louder and louder. The men carrying the two ends of the pole walked rhythmically and carefully, sweating profusely. After every few kilometres, the two other men took over carrying Tram. The small road wound through several hills and through the forest with rows of dense trees. Everyone warned everyone to be careful. Thuy wasn't tired. She walked beside her friend, worrying every time she heard her friend's groans.

The hammock would shake when Tram had a seizure, making it twice as hard for the group of people carrying the stretcher. Thuy kept on praying that Tram was going to be ok. She only had two close female friends. All of them were young and all three of them were far from their home and family.

Thuy started to think of the afternoon, where the three of them sat together, holding the letters in their hands. One person read it to the others, then they all burst out laughing.

"I don't know what that man was thinking when he copied three almost identical letters and sent them to us in the same office. He must have a crazy, steamed brain! It's so funny!" Nhien chuckled.

That day the three girls had a good laugh until their stomachs hurt.

Tram has now been in the infirmary for more than a day.

The assistant doctor Ly had examined and prescribed medicine. Tram's fever had gone down and her convulsions had stopped, but she was still very tired. Thuy made congee with minced pork and fed Tram spoon by spoon, encouraging and comforting her that she will recover soon. When Nhien heard the news, she went immediately to the infirmary to see Tram. Thuy and Nhien looked at Tram with concern, trying to hide their worry. In just two days, Tram had already lost a lot of weight. She was thin, her skin was pale. She looked completely different.

Nga had heard people talking about contracting malaria, when they had been evacuated to the forest. She heard that Thuy was currently at the clinic, so asked Minh if he had seen Thuy yet. She wanted them both to go and see her together.

"You go first, I'm afraid of getting infected." Minh stammered and flustered an answer. So, Nga went alone.

When Thuy heard her voice, she ran outside to greet her. "Hello, sister Nga! How did you know I was here?"

Thuy was so happy to see her. Nga was also happy to see the two girls. The three of them went into the room to visit Tram. Although she had only met Tram twice, Nga had already developed a liking for Tram. All three of these girls were so young and innocent, Nga felt a maternal protectiveness for them. Tram had just finished eating the bowl of congee and had taken her medicine. She was leaning against the bed and when she looked up, her face filled with joy at seeing Nga.

"Oh, dear sister Nga, I'm so sad lying here. I miss home and I'm so sick!" Tram's voice was full of emotion.

"I only heard the news today and I came as fast as I could. You'll get better, don't worry. You have good friends and they'll always be by your side. All you have to do is eat well and take your medicine. You'll be able to return to work soon." Nga said soothingly.

"I asked Minh to come visit you too, but he said he was afraid of getting infected!" Thuy and Nhien giggled, even Tram, who was exhausted, laughed along too.

Of course, Nga was surprised, she had no idea. She just looked at the girls confused.

"We think Mr Minh is embarrassed and doesn't dare see us." Nhien whispered.

"What would he be embarrassed about?" Nga said loudly.

"I don't think you know, but Minh wrote all three of us individual letters. The three letters were very similar. His writing was very flirtatious." Nhien replied quickly.

Nga's eyes widened in surprise, then she lowered her voice. "Now I understand why there was a sudden decision made to transfer Thuy to the Literature Faculty. I had a feeling that something was not normal. Oh, so that's it, he was angry that he 'couldn't eat it, so kicked things down. He was trying to find a way to push Thuy away."

The four ladies chatted happily, until Nga had to say goodbye to go back to work. Thuy wanted to visit some families and their children while she was in the area. Nhien stayed with Tram until she had to return to work too. Later that day Ly confirmed that Tram's illness had improved a lot and that she could be discharged tomorrow. Tram's joy was evident on her face. Her fever was gone, she was alert and eating and sleeping well. The next morning Thuy and Tram returned to the Faculty of Literature together.

-----

After talking to the three girls at the clinic, Nga had a clear picture of Minh and his intentions with these young staff members. It was unsettling to hear this of her colleague, especially as he has a wife and child. This violated the ethics of being a youth union member. Nga was trying to think of the best course of action. Should she keep quiet or tell her superiors? But would they believe her? Frustrated for several days, Nga sought out Mai to confide in her. She was a member of the university head's department and being a woman, she would surely understand and know what to do.

"Mrs Mai, there is something I've discovered about a staff member and I need your advice. I just can't keep it to myself any longer."

"Please tell me, I'm sure it will make you feel better." Mai replied gently.

"You know Mr Minh is the head of the library group where I am working."

"Yes, I know of him. Is there something wrong?"

"Mr Minh had recently suggested transferring Thuy to the Faculty of Literature to work. The situation seemed very normal. His reasoning was that the library at the Literature department needed someone with experience to help. However, why did he not go? Why was Thuy sent, when Mr Minh has all the experience and Thuy was only new to our library?" Nga calmly said.

Mai began to listen attentively.

"Thuy has been over there working for more than two months now, yet Mr Minh has not paid her any visits to check on her progress and the progress of the library out there. The head of the library sent a junior employee to build and consolidate the facility, does that sound right to you?" Nga continued to explain.

"Another further issue, which is more sensitive, relates to three young staff members. Mr Minh has a family and child, but he wrote love letters to these three girls, Thuy, Tram and Nhien. Only when I had visited Tram lying in the infirmary, did they tell me what had happened to them."

"How did the girls react to these letters?"

"None of them responded to his letters. They all tried to avoid him. It was most difficult for Thuy, who worked under Minh's guidance. He obviously didn't like that Thuy didn't reciprocate his feelings, so he used his authority to move her away, to hide his shame. Now it is just me and Minh and working in the same room and knowing all this makes me very uncomfortable."

The revelations from Nga's story made Mai think seriously about the best action for this. As a member of the Party Committee and deputy head for the union representing the voice of women and employees, Mai had to bring this matter to the Party Committee.

*

* *

Last night, Thuy slept so well. The sun was high in the sky, its rays penetrated the middle of the house. Thuy was still deep in sleep, her brain knew it was a Sunday. She heard Luu's voice from outside the door. "Thuy! Today is a beautiful sunny day. Let's go out and get some bamboo shoots. Quickly! We'll go into the forest now!"

Thuy woke up with a start. She had been taking care of Tram these last few days at the infirmary. Tired with worry, she hadn't been sleeping well, until she got back to her own bed. Then she fell into a deep sleep.

"I'll get up right away." Thuy said, pulling herself out of bed.

Thuy had been looking forward to this day where she would go with Luu to collect the bamboo shoots. She washed and got dressed as quickly as she could. The two left the house at 7 am. Luu had woken up early that morning to cook rice for her daughter. She asked the neighbour to look after Nga while they were out. Tan and Le also joined them to harvest the bamboo.

They walked and talked happily together.

"Sister, it's fun to go with a lot of people, isn't it?"

"It is fun but we should look out for each other.

There are things in the forest we need to beware of. That's why Tan is the best person to go ahead of everyone else." Luu replied.

Thuy wasn't sure what she meant.

"If you were walking and you suddenly see a snake crawling out from the bushes, would you be scared?"

"Oh yes, I'd probably faint!" Thuy said, eyes wide.

"It rained last night and the trees are wet. There'll be many leeches in the forest, so everyone be careful."

Tan said, speaking to the whole group.

"There's leeches in the forest! Are they big, Tan?"

As soon as Thuy had finished asking, Tan quickly grabbed his earlobe with his hand.

He pulled the creature out and showed it to Thuy. It was a small, dark-coloured creature, the size of toothpick but shorter. Its head was wriggling on Tan's finger. It clung very tightly, he had to pull sharply to prise it free. His ear was bleeding.

Seeing that, Thuy stepped back, frightened. After more than an hour of walking, they arrived at a forest with many different types of bamboo trees growing in clumps. They treaded carefully to see one or two young shoots sprouting about a foot above the ground. After the rain, bamboo shoots grew in large numbers but small and low, you could only see them if you looked carefully enough. Thuy brought along a sharp, large knife. Tan had a small, sturdy army shovel.

Seeing the bamboo shoots sprouting, Tan used the shovel to dig a large area around the bamboo shoots. He then used the shovel to cut it across and break it with his hands. Luu and Le told Thuy to pay attention. Where there are bamboo shoots, you have to remember to look up. Try to avoid the thorny branches and leaves above that may have leeches clinging to them.

Thuy was careful in her search and when she had found the right bamboo shoots, she called everyone over. There were some thick shoots that grew a little taller. Thuy eagerly dug, following the direction of her elders. You had to have strong hands and a shovel like Tan's to be able to uproot some of these shoots. They were thick and big and well rooted into the ground. These shoots had thick flesh, lots of meat and were crunchy and very sweet. They were worth all the effort.

It was around noon, when everyone had filled their backpacks full of bamboo. Tan had the most.

Everyone then took the chance to stop and eat. Luu took out the rice balls and sesame salt from her woven bag. "You two come here to eat with us, there is a delicious Viet Minh*[2] canned meat dish we've brought with us." Le called to Thuy and Luu.

"Sister Le, what is Viet Minh canned meat?" Thuy asked hesitantly.

"Vietnamese people living in the Viet Bac region who do not know about Viet Minh canned meat are so backwards." Tan laughed.

Thuy and Luu had no idea what this dish was, but were curious and wanted to see. Le took out the bamboo tube and opened the lid for Luu and Thuy to see.

"Oh my God! It's salty fried pork belly with chili salt, you both introduced it as a canned specialty."

"It's packed in a box and not a tin, that's the only difference." Le laughed.

"Do you two know why it is called Viet Minh canned meat?" They shook their heads for Tan to help explain.

"During the resistance war against the French, activists who went on long trips, invented a way to make the most of the food they had. As there were food shortages everywhere, when they bought pork belly, they would chop it into minced meat and fry it with salt and chili. Then they would put it into bamboo tubes. At mealtimes, when they were in the forest and they found bamboo shoots or other vegetables, they would take a little meat out and cook it with the vegetables to make a soup. This dish was so delicious that later on, many people invented similar dishes. They gave them strange names such as 'Chicken fried with dog crying' and Viet Minh ribs'."

Tan enjoyed telling this tale. He swallowed his mouthful of rice and laughed. "In the old days, dog owners would give their dogs the leftover bones to eat. But in the time of war, the bones of chickens and pigs were not wasted. They were chopped up as tiny as possible and eaten with salt and chilli, by the people as well. So, the saying goes, 'The chicken is fried while the dog is crying, as now he gets nothing!'"

Thuy and Luu listened wide-eyed. "How do you know so many stories, Tan?"

"Haven't you heard people call him 'the know-it-all man." Laughed Le.

"Stop flattering me, you'll make me carry everything for you later!"

After finishing their lunch, it was time to go. "Let's prepare to go home early, it gets dark in the forest very quickly in the afternoon. We can still find some more on the way back, if we look carefully."

Thuy dug up quite a bundle of bamboo shoots. She was proud of her achievement on her first trip out. It made her sad thinking about Tram who was still recovering. She would have liked to have made this trip too.

-----

Tram had made a good recovery, after spending a few days of treatment at the infirmary.

People would say at the age of 'breaking the buffalo horn', her health would recover quickly.

Tram was able to return to work without any side-effects of malaria. The two girls worked together in the administrative department. They became close friends. Tram didn't feel lonely anymore. The department felt like a family to her. Now that Thuy was there, when she finished all her paperwork and everything was delivered to the right people, she was able to go to the library. She had loved reading books ever since high school, but as she couldn't continue her studies, she missed the opportunity to have books in her life. After secondary school, she had to find a job. It was only her and her mum and she couldn't afford not to work. Tram had applied for the three months typing and clerical class. When she graduated from that, Tram was fortunate to find work at the Faculty of Literature. Although the work involved a lot of odd jobs besides typing, Tram was not discouraged. She had a sense of responsibility and was hard working.

Everyone was fond of Tram, staff and colleagues alike. Having a library on their doorstep was a dream come true for Tram and Thuy, they spent most of their free time there, whenever possible. The two were like real sisters, constantly chatting, and confiding in each other. They shared all their thoughts and secrets with one another. Tram helped Thuy with tasks in the library, anything so they could be together and because Thuy took pride in her work and was devoted to the library, everyone trusted her.

The library was operating smoothly. Everything was going well and Thuy forgot everything that happened in the central library. She had no thoughts about returning to work at the central library.

Mai had decided that the revelations of Minh's actions towards the three girls needed to be discussed with the Party Committee and all the school's heads. The collective concluded that this was an act that violated the ethics of a union representative. Trying to pursue young, single girls, while he was married broke all the rules of the committee and school and using his position at the school to manipulate a subordinate's fate was a complete abuse of his authority.

The Party Committee, the Board of Directors and the Executive Committee of the school's Youth Union decided to expel Minh from the Union. They were setting an example to the whole school, that behaviour like this was not tolerated. The story spread, everyone in the centre knew about the three letters. Wherever Minh went and whoever he met, he encountered contemptuous eyes, whispers and glances. Shamed by this decision, Minh offered to write a letter of resignation rather than be expelled. He would give the reason that his wife was close to giving birth and that he wanted to take care of his family. The school agreed to this and Minh returned to Hanoi.

oOo

"Thuy! What are you doing? Someone wants to borrow a book."

Thuy was cleaning up and arranging books, not noticing who was waiting. Like a whirlwind, Tram rushed in and as she spoke, she almost bumped into the young man about thirty years old.

"I'm sorry." Tram stammered.

"It's okay, you must be in a hurry. I've also come to borrow a book." Said the man.

The two of them walked into the library. Hearing her voice, Thuy immediately recognized her friend Tram. Thuy was in the room, next to all the bookshelves. She quickly walked out just in time to see Tram and the young man enter the room.

Thuy recognised the man.

"Hello teacher... sir. Hello Mr Nam." Thuy greeted.

"Hello Ms Thuy, I'm here to return this book and borrow another one."

Tram opened her book to pretend to read, but her ears were still listening to the conversation between the two.

"If you can't find the book you're looking for, please write down the name and book number. I'll have a look for it later. I'll register that you've returned this book for now."

-----

Sunday was the only day in the week everyone took time to catch up with family and friends. Luu and her daughter went to visit their friends, so Thuy and Tram ventured over to see Nhien at the Faculty of History.

The two girls passed through the palm forest like many other palm forests in the evacuation area. Although, while they were walking and talking, Thuy realized that it was different from the places she had been before. There were many big, old palm trees here, some with fallen branches and some tree trunks lying on the ground all dried out. Thuy pointed this out to Tram. "Tram, look at all this dry bark around the trees. Are you thinking what I'm thinking?"

"What do you mean? I don't see anything different."

Thuy walked to a tree and pointed at the dry bark.

"I think we can use this dry bark for firewood! Then we wouldn't have to go so far anymore."

"Oh, right! Let's collect this dry wood next week then! Look! There are also bunches of those purple-black palm fruits. Do you think they can be eaten?"

Thuy remembered the time when she was staying at Khuong's house. Khuong spoke about these fruits. Palm fruits look like black plums, although they're not that tasty, they can still be eaten. Thuy thought they should definitely pick some along with the dry bark. Once they had passed the palm hill, a field of myrtle-berries appeared, with lots of ripe fruit. This filled the two girls with joy!

This reminded Thuy of the time when she was at secondary school. Her and her friends were so busy picking myrtle-berries they were late for school and it was obvious to the teacher what they had been doing. The myrtle-berry*[3] juices had given all the children purple lips, they couldn't make excuses for their lateness!

As they picked and ate the myrtle-berries, Thuy and Tram made sure they picked enough for Nhien too.

Nhien lived in the History department's female dormitory. Being Sunday, everyone was out visiting their family, so the area was deserted. This gave the three friends the opportunity to freely laugh and gossip without prying eyes. Nhien made her friends a local dish, which she wanted to share, stir-fried bitter bamboo shoots with garlic. They all agreed it was delicious! They were chatting happily away, when Nhien looked very excited. "Thuy, Tram! I have some hot news for you two."

"What news? Is the news so hot that we must blow to listen?" Laughed the two girls.

Nhien pretended to look pensive and silent, but then she smiled mischievously. This only made Thuy and Tram even more impatient. "You two definitely won't believe this news! Two days ago, I had to go to the centre to meet Nga. She told me about Minh.

Thuy and Tram were edging forward, to eagerly hear the rest.

"What? What happened to him?"

"Old man Minh quit his job at the library and moved to Hanoi!"

Thuy and Tram were stunned. Hearing the reason why Minh quit his job, all of them burst out laughing. It was a fun and delicious lunch. The three girls were together again, sharing the best news possible. Food created such fond memories for Thuy. Eating the bitter bamboo shoots with her friends made the dish even more delicious. They were big and plump. When she ate them, they were crunchy and just a little bitter. She liked the little numb feeling they gave you on the tip of the tongue.

She'd never really seen them when she was at the market back at home.

-----

Tram brought a letter over to Thuy. It was from the central library. Thuy was excited thinking it must be a letter from parents and siblings. It wasn't, it was from the Board of Directors, they want Thuy back working at the Central Library again. Once again Thuy had to say goodbye. It was difficult to know whether she was happy or sad at this news, she had moved so often now. Obviously, leaving Tram and Luu and her daughter, Nga, was the saddest part, but she hoped that they would give Tram her role at the Literature faculty library once she was gone. She knew how much Tram loved books and it would make her happy knowing she was there.

The Literature faculty heads had decided to assign Tram to be in charge of the library. They would both miss being able to see each other every day. They had formed a close friendship, it was a shame to part ways now. Thuy diligently handed over work notes to Tram. Her mind was jumbled up with lots of thoughts, but she kept on reminding Tram to be careful with the books and papers. To make sure she completed the assigned work each day. She knew Tram would do a good job, but the words were coming out before she could think properly. Tram thought sadly that the bitter bamboo shoot meal they had, really was a bitter last meal for her friend.

Thuy had one day to say her goodbyes. She wanted to make sure she saw Khuong before she left tomorrow. That afternoon it was very cold. The wind blew across her cheeks and her nose was numb. She wrapped her scarf tightly around her. As she got closer to the Khuong's family home, she heard someone call her name.

"Sister Thuy, is that you?"

Thuy looked up, startled, then recognized it was Ty.

"Oh! Hi! You've grown up so fast! Are you now herding buffaloes too? Has your mom come home yet? I've come to visit you all."

Ty was really happy to see Thuy and ran up to her to hold her hand. "Tonight, you must have dinner with me! Grandma will cook for you!"

"I would really like that but today I can't. I miss you all, but I've come to say my goodbyes because tomorrow I have to move back to the central library." Thuy explained sadly.

When they were near the gate to the house, Ty shouted out. "Grandma, sister Thuy is here to visit, have you cooked a lot of rice?"

The grandma slowly walked out from the kitchen, chewing betel. She looked happy to see Thuy. "There might not be enough for anyone else, but for Thuy, there is always rice for you to eat here. Come inside, it's very cold out."

At that moment, Khuong came back from the field, her feet covered in mud.

"Thuy, come inside! I just had to bail some water out. It hasn't rained for several days and the fields are short of water. Everyone has been taking turns to water." Khuong called out.

It has been a long time since Thuy has had dinner with the Khuong family. Today there were stir-fried bamboo shoots with garlic and addition of Vietnamese coriander. It made it taste different from Nhien's dish.

"Grandma and mother, Thuy has to move to work at the central library. I will miss her so much."

Again saying goodbye to this family, but moving much further away this time, Thuy really didn't know when she would see them all again. The central library was more than ten kilometres away, but she promised if she was back in the area, she would come and see them.

*

* *

Thuy surprised Nga by turning up without warning.

"Thuy! When did you get to the centre?" Nga exclaimed in surprise.

"Sister Nga, what happened? Please tell me everything." Thuy wanted to get straight to the point.

Nga was happy to give Thuy the good news. The library would soon employ more people. At the moment there was only herself and now Thuy.

She explained in more detail about Minh's departure and how he moved to Hanoi. Nga was delighted that Thuy was back.

Thuy walked quickly up the hill towards the women's dormitory. Her mind was unsettled, because this was the first place she had lived. It was her first home away from home. Having moved several times since then, returning here was like the very first day again. It felt like she was starting from the beginning again.

Reaching the collective house, Thuy loudly called out. "Sister Ly, sister Hoi! It's Thuy! I've come back to live with you."

Hearing this familiar voice, Ly and Hoi hurriedly ran out. The three of them hugged each other. There was lots of chatter and questions and laughter. It was a good reunion.

That night Thuy slept well. It felt good to live near Ly and Hoi again.

As she had always done before, Thuy woke up early to prepare for work. Her mood was different though, perhaps knowing Minh wasn't there anymore. She felt lighter and more at ease. She didn't ever have to see Minh again. When it was nearly 7 am, Thuy walked down the slope and turned towards the library. Nga was just opening the doors to the library. The scene inside had not changed, but the silence was strange. Thuy started dusting. Her first job of each day. She would dust down the bookshelves, the books and the desks her and Nga worked at.

"Does it feel different now that it's just you and me?" Thuy asked.

"Well, last week, I was alone in the library. It was a bit lonely and sometimes I did feel a bit scared. So, I understand how you're feeling right now. You'll get used to it and soon there will be more people working here."

"I did get used to the days at the Faculty of Literature. I'd forgotten everything that made me move over there, but it was still a surprise to hear what happened to Minh. I actually thought I would not be working at the central library again. I was happy over at the Literature faculty, but I know I can be happy here again too."

Nga was pleased to hear that. She discussed the current work situation, promising that they would make a good team. The two started the day full of confidence, when a figure walked through the library door. Thuy wondered who would need the library so early in the morning.

The two women looked up at the same time. Recognizing Nam, Thuy smiled and greeted him.

"Good morning, teacher Nam! You're here borrowing books early?"

"Good morning, you two! Yesterday I was at the Faculty of Literature library to return books and that's when I found out that Thuy had transferred back to the central library." Nam blushed for some reason.

Nga looked at Thuy, then at Nam. Then she understood. A smile crept on her face.

"So, from now on, don't go to the Literature department library, just come straight here!" Nga suggested.

"Well, I teach at the Faculty of Chemistry, so it is closer and more convenient to come here. Also, the central library has more books and documents than the Literature department library anyway." Nam answered innocently.

-----

At the youth union meeting that evening, Thuy met everyone in the area again. There was a relaxed atmosphere and Thuy felt calm. During the whole meeting, Thuy was silent and took everything in. She didn't feel guilty or uncomfortable like at the beginning. Perhaps Thuy was starting to understand her situation and her circumstances better.

Nam, the chemistry lecturer was a regular to the library. It was beginning to become clear that he had feelings for Thuy. Each time Nam came in, Nga would leave the room, so that Thuy and Nam could talk to one another. Thuy discovered that Nam was born in Hanoi. He came from a revolutionary family, who were well-off. He achieved a doctorate from Russia. He was the type of person admired by many girls. There were many female students inside the school, but for some reason Nam paid attention to Thuy.

She felt like an ordinary employee compared to the other girls. Returning to the centre's activities, Thuy continued to be in charge of the youth team as before. She regularly participated in activities with the children, singing, dancing and again sometimes helping them with their school homework. Thuy was enthusiastic and passionate about her activities with the youth team. The school's Board of Directors praised and commended Thuy's achievements.

-----

The library was busier than it had ever been. More and more people came to borrow books, so Thuy and Nga were always busy. Still no new staff were appointed to help. Therefore, Nga and Thuy had to arrange and schedule their work carefully to keep on top of all the tasks at the library.

The library was open regularly and new books were always being added. The work plan was discussed and agreed upon each day. Thuy made a lot of progress and had many innovative ideas to apply to her work. Days went by quickly.

Thuy and Nam became increasingly close with each meeting. Nam often went to the library, not to borrow books but to meet Thuy.

Once Nam boldly told Thuy his thoughts. "Thuy, I know you are a studious person and I understand why you had to start working before your time. I have a suggestion."

"What do you advise me to do?"

"In my opinion, you should go to university. Although you have taken many years off from education, you might feel like your knowledge is behind. I think you should review the general education program and apply for the university entrance exams. There is still time. What do you think?"

"Actually, I used to think like you, but I've been out of school for too long. I've forgotten everything and I'm not sure I have the mental strength to take the exams."

"Of course, you do! I'll help you find the right books to practice for the exams. Just think about which major you want to take the exam for, natural sciences or social sciences? I'll suggest the right books for you."

Knowing Nam cared and feeling like he really wanted to help, made her think it was right to try to get into a university. She wanted to study like other students did. She had fallen behind for several years, but she was always thinking about it. Nam's advice gave her the motivation she needed. She was touched by his belief in her and felt like she truly loved him for that. She decided to tell Nam that she was going to try out the exams.

After Mr Duc at the Organisation department had told Thuy last week. "If you complete your work well and we can see you are achieving all your goals. When the school has set the plan to train members, you will be allowed to do extra classes. This is only after working for four years or more here."

Hearing that, Thuy didn't dare to have a far-fetched dream as going to university. In her mind, she was always haunted by her 'family background', and not being a child of an ethnic minority, there felt like no point in hoping.

Thuy met some old high school friends who were studying Physics at the university. They encouraged her and suggested that she apply to the Faculty of Physics at the school. Thuy's father wanted her to study pedagogy.

"Thuy, I don't agree with you applying to the University of Construction or the University of Transport. As a girl, you should think carefully before deciding."

Her father argued. Her father's words still lingered in her mind, but now she has a good friend in Nam, a lecturer in the Chemistry department, who she knows is doing really well. She believes in his vision for her.

Nam knew all the right science books for Thuy, and finds them for her. Having missed school for a long time, Nam suggests Thuy should spend more time reviewing the general education program.

Two days a week. Nam comes to help Thuy at noon. He is enthusiastic and attentive and Thuy, the student, is diligent and tries hard. An invisible thread has connected the two of them together.

Being a teacher, Nam is busy preparing lessons, teaching in class, while also going to the centre to help Thuy study for her exams.

Everyone in the department and the centre notices the relationship between the two of them. A man and a woman, who are not married and forming a close relationship is normal. But life isn't simple like that, there is always extra gossip happening. Some people were happy and completely supported Thuy, thinking they made a good couple and encouraged their relationship. While others gossiped and criticized her.

Thuy focused on working eight hours at the library and then attentively studying after work. The rest of the time she participated in union and youth team activities, trying not to pay attention to the gossip around her. She believed what would happen.

There were comments that were difficult to ignore though. There were whisperings amongst the students and staff of the Chemistry department. Nam also heard these.

The decent university lecturer likes the female employee without a degree. Came the nasty comments:

*Hanoi boy, mountain girl*
*Climbing high falling hard.*

They're too different to be on the same level. He must have bad eyesight or something, as he can't see so many other beautiful and smart female students at school.

It went on and on. At first, Thuy ignored it, thinking, I didn't want this to happen with Nam. He was the one who approached me. He wanted to help me to continue my studies. It was an honest friendship. But over time, all the gossip got to her and made her feel so uncomfortable. Her old inferiority complex resurfaced.

She once witnessed, directly, the attitude and eyes of students who came to borrow books. She could see their jealousy and contempt. Taking it personally, it was as if something was pressing against her chest, making it difficult to breathe. Nga knew about Thuy and Nam's friendship, so was able to talk to her openly.

"Thuy, did Nam come to the centre yesterday afternoon?"

"No, I didn't see him. But according to the schedule, he should have come to help me yesterday afternoon," Thuy replied.

"I heard that Nam was blamed for something." Nga said quietly.

Nam was a party member. He was in the department's committee, so was criticized for having a relationship with a girl from the bourgeois family. Such a relationship was 'non-political, non-class love', which was a deviation from the Party's guidelines and principles. The Party had imposed its rules on Nam's heart, forcing him to obey the Party's regulations. Nam's activities were monitored and the evidence was presented at the committee meeting. Thuy didn't believe what she was hearing at first, but then many people told her the same thing. She felt shunned and looked down upon and it nearly destroyed her self-esteem.

"You must keep on studying hard for the university entrance exam, only then will life be brighter." Nga encouraged Thuy.

For many nights, Thuy thought about all the things people were saying about her. It was depressing to keep on repeating it in her head. She thought about Nam and felt sorry for him and for her. What had they done which was truly wrong? After a few afternoons when Nam hadn't shown up Thuy disappointedly decided that she didn't need Nam any more.

Although every time she thought about him, she felt a lump in her throat, as if he had insulted her directly. But she knew it wasn't Nam's fault for breaking his promise to help her study. She knew as a party member, he had to follow the Party's rules and policies. With this knowledge, Thuy continued to study, more determined than before. She would do the entrance exams without Nam's help. She must try for this change in her life, so she can have a better future.

Soon a new person was employed to help in the library. A girl from the provincial library elementary class. Her family had contributed to the revolution, so she was given this permanent position at the school. The work in the library was progressing well. The three of them worked well as one unit. Nga was the group leader and Thuy was elected as an advanced worker of the year.

The Board of Directors praised Thuy for her achievements in the youth union work and going above the Library's targets. She was also recognised for having good public relations. The nurses at the infirmary also encouraged Thuy to concentrate and study hard.

Many times, when she saw Nam coming to the library, Thuy had to avoid him, and then not long afterwards she didn't see him at all. Hearing all the gossip about Nam, and how he was criticized and reviewed by the Party committee, Thuy knew her decision was right to ignore him. Thuy used her hope and determination to help pass the time and forget about things from the past. She intended to wait for an opportunity to apply to study a Library course. She tells the organization department her wish and Mr Duc, the Deputy head of the school supports this idea. The Youth Union is holding an admission ceremony and Thuy is excited for this event.

The admission to the Union was only normal for young people, but not those from bourgeois or petty bourgeois families. People had to also be members of the Youth Union to be considered for intermediate vocational schools and universities. Thuy had previously not met any of those criterias. Step by step, Thuy matured over the years. She was a small bamboo shoot in the past, but has now grown into a resilient bamboo tree, standing firmly in the dense forest full of thorns and poisonous snakes.

The following year, the school had a target of training and improving the qualifications of civil servants and employees. The Party Committee, the Board of Directors and the School's leaders evaluated Thuy's achievements in all aspects over many years of work and decided to send Thuy to study the specialized course at the Hanoi University of Theory and Profession. Even though she had stopped going to school more than five years ago, Thuy tried her best to complete all the entrance exams. Then she waited for the results.

-----

**Note**:

*[1] dong; The standard monetary unit of Vietnam.

*[2] The Việt Minh is the common and abbreviated name of the League for Independence of Vietnam.

*[3] Myrtle berries; Upright bushy evergreen shrub about 3m in height, with small, aromatic, glossy dark green leaves, and profuse dark blue flowers 2cm in width with central tufts of white stamens going in mid to late summer or autumn, followed by purplish-black berries.

# CHAPTER 2

## The Small Family

*I do not live for what the world thinks of me but for what I think of myself.*
**Jack London**

**Five years later**

"Ms Thuy! Is that you?"

Thuy pressed the brakes on and turned around to see who was calling her name. On the back of her bike, sitting on a rattan chair was Hien, her daughter. She could see a hand waving at the front door of the bright red tiled house, it was Nga.

Thuy slowly led the bicycle across the road towards the woman. "It's so early, where are you two going in such a hurry?" Nga asked, looking at the little girl.

"I'm going to Ha's place first. I have to be quick, so I can get to work on time."

"So why didn't you leave the little girl at home? She looks tired."

"Binh isn't home. He's gone on a business trip for six days this week. He'll be back on Sunday with a pile of dirty clothes that smell of indigo!"

"Is your house newly built?" Thuy said looking at the spacious brick house.

"This is my mother's house. Yesterday, my family came by to visit." Nga smiled. Then remembered something she wanted to give Thuy. She hurried inside the house.

"Wait for me a moment, please?" Nga came out with a package wrapped in dried banana leaves. "Take this sticky rice package for your baby."

"What do you say?" Thuy turned around to her child and asked. Little Hien was sleepy, but hearing her mother's instructions, sat up straight.

"Thank you very much aunty!" Hien said quickly.

Nga looked at Hien and patted her on the head.

"Hien is such a cute girl. Off you go before you're late."

Thuy said her goodbyes to Nga and stepped on the pedals quickly to go.

Looking at Thuy and her daughter's figures fading away, Nga thought of the first time she had met her. Was this the same Thuy, from the evacuation area? It didn't feel that long ago, she was still a shy, timid girl. Nga had teased her and called her a skinny girl. Life forced and made people adapt to their situation, whether they wanted to or not.

When the war ended, it was everyone's hope that the country would have a peaceful reunification, and that food and clothes would be plentiful for all. After liberation day, the plan was to restore the country and build a strong economy. Under the leadership of the Communist party, the government had grand ideas, but in the end were powerless to enact them. The socialist faction, especially the Soviet Union and China, cut aid because the war had ended.

The US government imposed an embargo and economic blockade and Nixon's promise to compensate four billion dollars after the war never materialised. He reasoned that North Vietnam had violated the Paris agreement by invading the South. After the war, the economy of the North was on the verge of collapse. Agriculture and other industries were suffering severely. For several years, there were natural disasters, which contributed to crop failure. Policies of blocking rivers and access to markets made the lives of the North more difficult and miserable. People had to 'tighten their belts' fend for themselves and be self-sufficient. Everyone had ration cards, but there was never enough food to go around. People were going hungry.

While cycling, Thuy thought about the changing country. Time seemed to be passing by so quickly, and it was evident each time she saw Nga, that time was constantly moving faster. Quang, Nga's husband, was a quick and resourceful man. His job, as the school supply staff, gave him opportunities to make a bit more than others, so Nga's family was better off than most people. At that time, people used to say to each other, 'honest people eat porridge, rude people eat rice'. Honest and upright people like Thuy's family relied on the salary of 'three piles - two piaster salary.' There were all these sayings, but everyone was lacking in something.

Before returning from his business trips, Quang would buy some sort of meat to bring home to his family. To avoid the checkpoints from confiscating or taxing the meat, Quang would boil the chicken (or whatever meat he could get), or if he had fish, he would fry that first. As cooked meat couldn't be taxed or taken away, Quang could bring this extra food supply back, this made a big difference to Nga's family life.

Thuy arrived just as Ha was about to leave for work. The two met after Thuy graduated from university in Hanoi, to work at the Department of Culture. They were good friends. Ha worked at the provincial Forestry office, she could get a permit paper for Thuy to buy one cubic metre of wood and three bags sawdust every month for cooking. Because now no one was allowed to go into the forest to collect fire wood like in the past.

"Did you check the workshop schedule for when the firewood arrives? Don't let them run out, before you go to buy them! And have you finished knitting the things I asked you for?" Ha reminded Thuy.

"I'll be knitting the sweater tonight and I'll give it all to you tomorrow, you can add up all the items at the end of the month and please tell the owner to pay me."

After saying goodbye to Ha, Thuy hurriedly got on the bike to take her child home on time for work.

*

* *

Collective housing area one, was where Thuy's family lived. This consisted of two rows of thatched houses, each row containing ten rooms. Row one of the houses were for families with children. Each room was about twenty square meters wide, and behind each house there was a small plot of land about five to six square meters. This was used for growing vegetables, keeping chickens or making a pig pen. Having this space improved everyone's lives. There were three people in Thuy's family, which was a comfortable size compared to other large families.

Row two of houses opposite had smaller rooms for people without children. The first room was a nursery, with three baby sitters responsible for looking after twelve children from birth to three years old.

Arriving at the alley leading to the housing complex, Thuy heard a commotion amongst the people that lived there. There was shouting and cries, everyone sounding their opinion. Later, Thuy found out that the owner of a pig had given food to the animal who then rejected it. Of course, this made the owner extremely worried. Having lived in the housing complex for more than two years, Thuy was the quietest person there. She didn't like to get involved in anyone else's business and she didn't have time. There was a saying "no time to participate in the white or black cow tooth" story.

People crowded around the woman and her pig, and started worrying about their own pigs!

"Have you given your pigs medicine?"

A woman asked. Everyone was in an uproar again.

"Take a cold tablet, mix it with a handful of bran to make it fragrant. The pig will eat right away and get better!" A very large woman shouted out.

"I'm trying to raise it for a few more months until it weighs more than 80 kilos. Then I want to sell it to help cover all my bills. But now it's acting like this, how much can I sell it for?" The woman with the pig complained

"The fastest medicine, light and convenient, no need to worry, just give it a "Zao de Sunphate" pill (slang word: to kill by one stab) and it's done! Anyone who needs pork, they can go to your house, and the whole family will have a delicious meal!" Someone in the back of the crowd suggested, only partly joking.

"Well, big or small, I've worked hard to raise a pig I can sell! I don't dare to kill it. I want to sell all of it, not daring to keep even just a small piece. My children crave a small piece of good meat but I can't give it to them." Cried another man.

Some people were laughing at the suggestions and others just shook their heads at the situation. When your investment becomes sick, that is a worry, because of course, 'Mr Pig is money and extra income' for their family.

The truth of the matter was due to the 'blocking of rivers and banning of markets' period. Professor Van Nhu Cuong's family lived in a collective housing area. His wife raised pigs, and the pig manure clogged the sewer. People reported this to the police, who issued fines. The police came to make a record stating "Mr Van Nhu Cuong's family raises pigs, making the collective housing area unsanitary."

Professor Van Nhu Cuong scratched his head.

"Please, can you write down; the pigs raised Mr Cuong's family." The Professor insisted.

The police officer was stunned, his face blank with confusion as to why he wanted to have this written down.

Professor Van Nhu Cuong slowly explained, "My family's extra income depends on the pigs, so the pigs raise us as well." After a moment the Professor continued. "Actually, I think you should write this down. It might be easier for you and others to understand. 'Pigs and Van Nhu Cuong raised each other.'"

It might seem like a joke, but the blocking of the rivers and the markets being banned were implemented by the Socialist North Vietnamese government in the 1960s to 1980s.

-----

Thuy took her child to the nursery and left her with the nannies. She then went quickly back to her house to check the chicken coop and the pig pen. While cycling, Thuy made a checklist in her head. She stopped by Hue's house to ask for chopped banana trees for the pigs. Tonight, she had to finish knitting that sweater and deliver it to Ha, then she would get this month's wages. Thuy arrived at the office on time, even earlier than her colleagues. A voice came from outside.

"I would like to inform everyone, the food store sent the truck to get rice to the warehouse, so tomorrow there will be rice. Remember to line up early or 'the slow buffalo will drink dirty water.'"

"Do you know if this time it is mixed with corn or flour?" People started asking the announcer questions.

"What kind of stuffing is it that you don't want to buy, ladies? The street next to my house sold horse tooth corn a few days ago." The announcer replied.

"My sister bought it and even after boiling it for hours, it was still hard and she couldn't chew it. My sister's mother-in-law broke her last molar because of horse tooth corn!"

Someone complained. There was a burst of laughter, but everyone's faces showed pain and sympathy.

"Why is Thuy so quiet? Do you have any good ideas?" A woman wondered out loud.

"No, I don't. It depends on what they use to bulk the rice up with. My child is too young to eat horse tooth corn. Last month, I sold mine and bought more rice for her. My husband and I ate ours with coix grain seeds." Thuy replied slightly startled with the direct question.

Horse tooth corn could be boiled in a pot. After a few hours, the kernels would puff up as large as a big toe, which put a lot of people off eating it, as it would take some much chewing to help digest it. Chinese aided coix grain seed (still in the un-hulled husk) was normally used to feed livestock and poultry, but due to the food shortage, the government distributed it to the people to eat instead of rice. Thụy's standard rice allowance was 13kg, her husband's 15kg and baby Hien's 5kg per a month, which was enough to get by on. All day long, the news that the store would be receiving rice for sale tomorrow, was the most important topic for everyone in the office to discuss.

At 5 pm, which is the end of the working day, there is a bustling atmosphere, as everyone prepares to go home. There is a Vietnamese saying, 'In the morning a civil servant goes to work with an umbrella, in the evening, they come home with this umbrella.' Which basically means they were doing nothing at their office. The issue is with the low salary, making it difficult for employees to have any motivation.

Everything from food, such as rice, fish sauce, salt to consumer goods such as clothing, laundry soap, toothpaste, all use monthly coupons. These coupons are divided up depending on rank, position, and salary. There are lots of coupons but no goods, and at the end of the month, the coupons were discarded because they had expired.

One afternoon, when Thuy was passing by a general store in town, she heard a crowd of people. She got off her bike to take a look, out of curiosity. A woman wearing local ethnic clothing, clapped her hands on her thighs and shouted loudly.

"Oh my God! Other people's children were born into the regime, so they can buy sugar and milk, but my children were born as ordinary people and even when they are sick, we can't buy sugar and milk! How is this fair??!!"

Some people in the crowd smiled and some shook their heads. "This woman is bold, stirring up a hornet's nest, poking at buffalo horns, grabbing a tiger by the tail. She'll probably end up in handcuffs, eating government rations and sleeping in public housing before long," someone whispered. There were a lot of whispers, but no one tried to stop her. After much clapping and screaming, the woman was tired and out of breath. The audience thinned out, as they were afraid of being implicated with this drama.

There was the Trade Union, an organization that protects the rights of employees according to the principles and goals set by the government. From the central to provincial cities, all industries' employees had to pay monthly fees of 2% of their salary. What these fees pay for isn't made public.

In 1976, the Hoa Binh Provincial Trade Union Executive Committee held an annual congress chaired by Mr Quach Hy. During the break time, while the delegates were laughing and talking, a security guard around fifty years old, held onto a large bowl filled with tea. He then took out a packet, which contained food stamp coupons, that were cut into small pieces. He put the bowl under a tap to fill it with water. He then held the bowl up to his mouth and before drinking said loudly.

"Can't buy with ration stamps, so cut them into small pieces, mix with water to drink, it's also quite nutritious and very nice!" With the water in his mouth, he chewed the ration stamps, then swallowed it in one big gulp. Looking at the people around him, he just smiled.

"It's really delicious, if you can't buy your monthly ration, just eat them! They taste so good!"

All the delegates were surprised, their mouths were wide open. Only Quach Hy's face turned purple because he didn't expect to see such vicious slander.

oOo

Like everyone else, Thuy quickly cycled home because there was always so much to do. First chopping banana tree trunks to cook bran for the pig. It was only one part of bran with eight parts chopped banana tree trunk. Combined with leftover food collected from households in the slum, it was made into a meal for the pig.

Thuy also had to finish knitting the sweater ready to be delivered tomorrow. When she got to the gate, she heard her daughter crying for her, along with the scolding of the babysitter. She was telling Hien off as she walked with her, carrying little Hien naked from the waist down. With the other hand, Loan was holding baby pants, which were being dragged on the floor.

"Shut up! What are you crying about? I'll take you to the pond to wash next time! Don't poo in your pants, remember to tell me, okay?"

Thuy saw and heard everything. It was heart breaking to witness, but she had the sense to deal with this situation carefully. Quickly stopping the bike at the door, Thuy took little Hien from the babysitter's hands and slowly spoke.

"Oh, I'm so sorry! I apologize to you, next time she won't dare to poo in her pants."

Then turning to her little girl. "Apologise to aunty, my child."

Thuy was also soft with her words to Hien. Hien was sobbing, tears were streaming down her cheeks, still having to try to speak through sobs. "I'm sorry aunty."

Loan, an ex-farmer, from Nam Dinh province. She was the younger sister of the deputy head of the administrative department. She had never been trained to become a baby sister, but has now been babysitting for three months. She was nearly forty years old and unmarried and some say looked like a man.

Seeing Thuy and her child Loan was also apologetic. "Okay, you're a very good girl, I love you so much, but it's cold, I don't want you to be like that. Be good and back to your mum now, so I can go home and rest too."

Loan said, stroking Hien's cheek. Thuy said goodbye to Loan. When they got home, she put Hien on the bed, so she could make dinner. It was going to be stir-fried green papaya, with an egg from their chicken, which Thuy had collected this morning. It was a delicious meal for the two of them. Thuy took boiling water from a Chinese thermos and poured it into an enamel basin to wash her child. As she washed the little girl, she carefully checked to see if there were any hidden bites or scratches.

Thinking about Hien being half naked, being carried off to a pond to get washed in the freezing cold, gave her a sense of despair. What should she do? After dinner with Hien, Thuy took her next door to play with the neighbour's children.

-----

Lan had three children, four, five and six years old. One child born each year. All of them were well-behaved and liked playing with Hien. Thuy was then able to do a lot of work before going to bed. Lan worked in the Finance Department and her husband, Tuan, was a Propaganda officer. Lan was cooking pig feed. Many families with children raised pigs and chickens to earn extra money.

"Your husband hasn't come home yet, sister?" Thuy asked as she entered the kitchen.

"He never comes home on time. Even when there's no meeting, he hangs around chatting. I thought only women gossiped." Lan sighed.

"Let them relax a bit, sister. My husband is on business trips all year round, all week, all month, and we hardly get to see him. I'm used to it now.

How he eats, where he sleeps, I have no idea. At the weekend, when he comes home on Sunday, instead of bringing home a salary, he brings home a pile of dirty clothes that smelled of indigo."

Thuy continued. "Hien is always asking about her father. It's not until the weekend before she sees him. Then he takes her out for the day."

Lan looked at Thuy with sympathy. "You were born with disadvantages and hardships, but in return, you have a cute, obedient and lovely child, who everyone loves. Keep going."

"Yes, I am lucky. I have good neighbours, like you. You and your children help me out so much, and I'm really grateful. Sister, I'll let you get back to your pot and your laundry. I think it might not rain tomorrow."

"I forgot to remind you, the rice store will have rice tomorrow. Buy some before it runs out. If you want I can arrange a place for the two of us tomorrow?"

"Yes, that would be good."

After finishing everything, it was 9pm. Hien was fast asleep. Thuy covered her child with a blanket, then took out a knitting needle. She had to finish knitting tonight. Suddenly she heard a knock on the door.

"Thuy, are you awake? Can I come in?"

Thuy opened the door. "Hi! Thoa! What's up?"

"I just found a new job for you. It's light work and you can fit it around your day."

Thoa took out a bunch of nylon bags and a big bag of roasted peanuts. "Pack the roasted peanuts in a small nylon bag, return it to the owner, and the owner will deliver them to the retail stores and cafes. What do you think?"

"Of course, of course. The extra money is always handy." Thuy happily accepted. "Are you alone tonight?"

"He's in Hanoi for a few days for work. Without him, I can't sleep. It's a bit scary." Thoa said only slightly embarrassed.

"Then sleep here tonight with me and my child. You can show me the best way to pack these peanuts."

That night, the two of them stayed up until almost midnight before going to sleep. Thuy finished knitting the sweater and putting all the peanuts in their little bags with Thoa will deliver to the owner in the tomorrow.

Ring! Ring! the alarm clock went off. Thuy was sleeping soundly, startled, looked at the clock, it was almost 4 am. She suddenly remembered she had to go to make a reservation to buy rice. She asked Thoa if she could keep an eye on Hien, so she could go out and do this. Thoa replied yes with a sleepy voice.

The weather in the midlands was unpredictable. Thuy put on a thick coat to keep warm. At four o'clock in the morning, the sky was still dark. There was light from the lamp posts on both sides of the road. It shone down on the figure of a small woman pedalling her bike quickly on the dirt road and around the fields of lettuce and kohlrabi. At the end of the curved road to the main street of the town, Thuy cycled straight to the rice store.

From afar, Thuy could see there were already many figures waiting. People had arrived earlier than Thuy. The queue was three meters long, with some people standing in the queue itself, but quite often people would place either bricks, baskets or anything that could keep their place in the queue. Sometimes the owners of the objects stood right next to them. If someone accidentally pushed them out of line or moved them to the back, the owner of the bricks would immediately shout loudly "do you think bricks and objects can't talk??!" Many left the markers where they were.

Thuy quickly found two rectangular bricks and placed them in a row. Objects were marked so their owners could claim them. Looking around, there was no one she knew to entrust her bricks to, but

Thuy had brought red tape and stuck them over the two bricks.

Last month, because she was worried about leaving her child at home, she finished arranging her spot and ran home, when she returned ten minutes later the bricks had disappeared. Luckily a man gave up his place, because he didn't like coix seeds, so he went home without buying anything.

Today though, Thoa was home with little Hien, so Thuy could wait patiently for the store to open. The news of the arrival of rice spread faster than lightning, everyone was waiting eagerly. Rice was the main food source, so it was everyone's priority. Hunger gnawed at people's hearts during the rationing period for decades. Everyone kept their family rice book in a safe place, as it was probably the most precious possession each household had. People often said that anyone who was unhappy or sad was often compared to "being as sorrowful as if they lost their rice book."

"I wonder if the grain rice is moldy or not today?" Someone asked casually.

"You would be lucky, if you were able to buy rice. Be patient and pick out the worms and maggots, what else can you do?" Everyone started to chatter.

"I'll sell it and buy more good rice."

"You would have a lot of money! Why do you have to line up then? Why not go to the market to buy the good rice? Poor people like us, we still have to eat stale rice."

The laughter and chatter of the crowd dispelled the coldness of the early morning, helping time pass faster. Thuy was silent, listening to everyone talking, wondering what kind of rice there was today? What food would have been mixed with? And was there enough rice to sell? Last month, Mr Mai Xuan Hai, a researcher at the Han Nom Institute, lined up to buy rice, when it was his turn, the store employee, with a cold face, declared.

"We're out of rice!"

Everyone's face was stunned.

"Tell me, when will the rice arrive?" He pleaded. "Will it be available tomorrow?"

When you were asking the rice seller you had to be gentle and sweet. Everyone was afraid of offending, the rice seller, who had great power.

At that time, the rice, meat, fish sauce sellers had more authority than doctors, engineers, and teachers. Their faces always showed how arrogant they were. Thuy was afraid that the same scene would happen again today and was also anxious because of little Hien at home. The store would not open for another two hours. Thuy couldn't wait here for that long.

Suddenly though, she saw Kieu, who worked in the printing factory.

"Where are you placed? Have you been here long?" Kieu asked.

"I left my child at home and got here about 4 am. The bricks are marking my spot, over there with the red tape."

"Are you going to wait for them to open? Will anyone come to hold your place for you?"

Kieu offered to hold Thuy's place for her. She said she had asked for the morning off to try to buy rice. Last week, her family ate cassava instead of rice. She was sick of eating cassava. Her local authority was making everyone plant ten cassava trees to prevent hunger.

Thuy thanked Kieu, got on her bike and pedalled quickly home. Thoa had fed Hien breakfast. Thuy could see the two of them checking to see if the hen had laid any eggs yet.

In the cage, the pig was raising his long, big snout and screaming for food. This was a lazy pig. After eating, he would lie there like a lazy fat man, but everyone had to take care of him. He needed to be comforted and he couldn't go hungry or get sick. He was a 'money tree!' People would say.

*Money as a fairy, a Buddha*
*As the spring force*
*As the measure of a human's hearts*
*As the laughter of the young*
*As the health of the elderly*
*As the spring of fame*
*As the umbrella that covers the body*
*As the scale of justice*
*Money is everything!*

"My mum is back, Aunty Thoa!" Seeing Thuy, Hien shouted and ran to welcome her mother.

"What are you two doing?" Thuy smiled. Hien ran to hug her mother. Then Thuy went out and took the bran mix to feed the pigs. She glanced at the vegetable bed that was still wet with dew and thought to herself, it would be good to water it in the afternoon.

Hien had a big smile on her face, she called out to her mum. "Mum, do I look good in the dress you made? Aunty Thoa helped me put it on."

"What did I say to you when I finished making the dress? Don't you remember?" Thuy looked at Hien with a serious face.

"I remembered, but Aunty Thoa found it in the suitcase and said she liked me to put it on."

The little girl mischievously blamed Thoa.

"That's right, it's my fault, okay baby? If your mum doesn't like it, I can change your dress right now." Thoa looked at Hien and laughed.

Hearing that, Hien looked at her mother worriedly. Thuy could see her daughter was happy and didn't want to upset Hien, so softened her voice. "I know my daughter is good and listens to her mum. This time it's okay, but there will be no next time, remember? Today, when you go to the nursery, keep clean, if you want to pee or poo, remember to let Loan know. If you get dirty, you won't have a nice dress to show your dad."

Hien smiled, said yes loudly and hugged Thoa happily.

"Thank you very much for your help. If you can give the bag of peanuts to their owner and let them know if there is more work, I can do it tonight." Thuy said.

"Yes of course, if there is more work I'll bring it right over to you. I have some free time right now so I can pick Hien up and give her some food. I'm happy to look after her until you get back from work?"

"That would be good, I might have to work a bit later today. Does that sound okay?"

After feeding the pigs and chickens, she took the washed clothes out to the yard to dry on the line. Thuy picked up little Hien, hurriedly walked towards the nursery and dropped her daughter there for the day. Thuy was given permission by her office to come in later that morning, so she could queue for the rice.

She cycled as fast as she could, in the hope that Kieu was still keeping her place for her. People were sitting, standing, dozing in different positions, looking exhausted and frustrated.

-----

"The store is open!" A loud voice from the doorway called out.

Everyone stood up in a panic. The store employee started opening the windows, the main door. There were no more dozing people, only fully alert faces now. Now the fight began.

"Why is this woman here?"

"Oh my god, who pushed my brick out like this?"

"Who threw my basket away?"

So many accusations being thrown, but with no answers. Faces full of aggression and defensiveness waving arms, pointing fingers, pushing, shoving. Some people falling, some people standing strong with hands on their hips.

Thuy and Lan ran quickly to the position of the two bricks with the red tape. Kieu had wisely placed her brick between Lan and Thuy's bricks, calmly protecting the three places. Thuy nodded to thank Kieu with relief. The three women were silent and did not join in with the quarrelling. Then all of a sudden, the woman standing second in the line shouted loudly, her voice almost crying.

"Oh my God! Everyone! Where is my rice book?" She screamed out while searching her bag which she had been carrying on her shoulder, but she couldn't find it.

"Where is it?? Look around you everyone, it might have fallen on the floor!!"

Then she realised. "Oh no, who cut the bottom of my bag??!!"

"How did they do that? Who could have done this so fast??"

There was confusion and worry in the crowd. People started clutching their bags tightly. As the first person came out of the store, the focus returned to the buying of the rice again.

"What kind of rice is that? Is it mouldy?"

"What filler have they used?"

"Coix seeds, everyone!"

Queuing should be a simple civilized form, but in a country with a large population and a shortage of everything, it's often hard to be civilised. If it's your turn and there's nothing left, then frustration and disappointment take over. There's no room for being civil.

Desperate people sell the food they've just bought or meat stamps. The black-market traders are then able to sell those on for three or four times higher than the state price. At that time, a new class emerged in society, they were called 'the small smuggler gangs.

Hearing about the coix seeds, Thuy patiently waited. She would then take them to Nga's family to ask for help in finding a buyer. With that money she could buy some good rice for Hien.

There was a raffle at work. The prizes were new bicycle tires and Tien Phong*[1] plastic sandals. These were both very valuable to anyone. Thuy had to go to the office to participate in the draw. Last month was an unlucky month for Thuy. Her bike tires were so worn out, she desperately needed those new tyres.

First though, she had to go to the administration office to get a certificate stating that her husband was away on the business trip. She had to bring along her husband's authorization letter, which gave her permission to have the transistor radio in her possession. This had to be shown before she was allowed to purchase batteries to operate it. The paperwork was amazingly mechanical and bureaucratic. Anyone who questioned or complained would get the same answer. Those are the rules and principles that must be strictly followed. People endured all these procedures, because there was no other way.

Last month, at Lan's husband's company, her husband was lucky enough to win to buy. He won a pair of Tien Phong plastic sandals but didn't fit it him so, he sold them on the black market for four times the original price. His family was able to have one day's meal that was better than the others.

Mr Phung Nghi Man, a police lieutenant, who worked in Hue, needed money to buy a train ticket to the North. He sold a pair of Tien Phong plastic sandals and got twenty dongs, which meant he didn't have to take the coach. The goods distributed at that time were rare and truly valuable!

-----

When the store had rice, people talked to each other when they were lining up to buy. If they couldn't take the day off, they asked their family members to help, but most of them hired people to buy it.

The team of people you could hire to buy and arrange food for you was very large. These included unemployed women, who were willing to 'help' single-parent families.

Thuy's situation was difficult, like many others like her. Her husband's family lived far away. Her mother died when she was young, her father had to keep on working and her siblings were busy going to work themselves.

In general, everyone had to fend for themselves and couldn't rely on anyone else. Salaries were low, there wasn't enough to buy food, let alone hire someone to queue up for you.

During these times, people only wanted simple things:

*_Rice that wasn't spoilt, that didn't have additives, or weevils;*

*_To be able to buy soap to wash clothes with;*

*_To own a bicycle for transportation;*

*_To have a pair of Tien Phong plastic sandals to wear and in the summer, to have an electric fan.*

In the old days, there was a folk song that began with

*'One worthy of being a man had been going to Phu Xuan and Dong Nai provinces.'*

At that time, people were more realistic with material things.

*'One worthy of being a man must have Favourite bike and transistor radio.'*

Anyone who had a small electric fan that was made in Vietnam, would be very happy. These fans were easily recognisable, as the base wasn't properly balanced, when the blades rotated, the fan would jump up and down. It was called the 'toad fan' because of this humorous action. Hien loved seeing this happen, she would jump up and down herself, laughing and clapping her hands.

It had been such a long time since she had visited her father. If Binh returns on Sunday, then they could go together to visit her father. It wasn't that long ago, maybe two months, that Binh's parents came to visit. The two of them had to wake up at dawn to catch the coach and arrived at the house that afternoon. Thuy was in the kitchen when she heard someone calling.

"Thuy, someone is looking for you!" The old man called.

Running out, she saw two old people with cloth bags on their shoulders. Their clothes were all dishevelled, their faces pale. They stood outside the gate. Oh my God! Hien's grandparents! This was Thuy's first reaction.

"Good afternoon, parents-in-law! Please come into the house. What time did you leave? You must be hungry and tired." Thuy ushered them in.

"Oh dear! Why do you live so far away? Wǒmen (we, in Chinese) left this morning, now the pain is unbearable." The old woman replied slowly.

"I brought the castrated rooster from my house for your family. My son loves this meat. But the authorities were so cruel, they took it off me, saying that no one is allowed to carry animals from one district to another." The old man was visibly upset as he spoke.

"Someone told me, before you leave, you have to get permission from the Commune Committee State who you were visiting and what you were bringing. Then you got a stamp and signature to approve your travels. I thought that was enough, but I forgot to declare the chicken, so they confiscated the animal. Since that's happened your father has been so upset and absent-minded."

Thuy felt so sorry looking at the two of them, but she didn't know what to say.

"Let me get some hot water for you to wash your face, hands and feet, Binh will be back soon. Tomorrow is Sunday, so you can stay with us tonight."

The two of them looked at each other confused. Thuy took her parents-in-law into the house and explained. "Binh often goes on business trips all week, only coming home on Sundays. You two can rest. I will make us dinner. We can talk more later."

"Where is 'wǒ de zhízǐ zài nǎlǐ?' (my grandchild)" The old woman asked in Chinese.

"She's at day care. I'll pick her up after school."

Thuy was relieved she had enough food to put together a decent dinner for them all. She had bought peanuts the day before and will mix the crushed nuts with salt water to fry in with cooking oil. Then there are eggs from their chicken and with a bunch of spinach, she could make soup.

The old man lay down on the bed to rest, so the mother went into the kitchen and whispered to Thuy. "Thuy, I had made a bag of rice crackers and rice cakes to give to you, so you could gift them to your neighbours, but they confiscated all those too. After much begging and pleading, the young man left a small portion for us to take. My little Hien can have those."

"Mother, times are tough these days, we must grit our teeth and bear it. I'm sorry we've not visited you and that you now had to make that long journey yourselves."

Thuy felt guilty towards her husband's parents, knowing that Binh often went on business trips and had no time and even his small family was constantly absent.

Binh graduated with a History degree from the University College of Hanoi in 1966, worked at the Viet Bac Museum, then transferred to the Museum Conservation Office in the Department of Culture. Due to the special nature of his job, Binh and his colleagues often went to remote provinces and districts to survey and conduct archaeology. Born and raised in the border province, his Chinese parents fled to Vietnam.

Binh was fluent in Chinese and the local indigenous language, so he was suitable for this job. On business trips, he often had to live with the locals for 'the three together' (eat together, live together, work together). Sometimes not returning home for two weeks, because if he went to a remote area, transportation was difficult.

Every year, the standard leave for civil servants was only twelve days, too little, so they often combined their leave with the Tết*2 banks holiday. This gave them the chance to return home to visit their parents.

Binh rarely talked and confided in Thuy about work. It was not known whether it was due to rules or lack of time together, but it gradually became a family habit. She did not complain, confide, or tell anyone, silently enduring because she sympathized with Binh's work. Now seeing her in-laws old and weak, having to travel a long way to visit, Thuy felt very guilty.

"Don't worry, I know that you're very busy with work, but I miss you so much. If we were near I could help a little bit and you look so thin and paler than when we last saw you." The old woman said kindly.

Thuy was touched, looking at her mother-in-law she wanted to cry, she was kind and honest. From the first time Thuy met her, she had liked her. She had been a daughter-in-law since she was sixteen years old. From what Thuy could see, there were no feelings between the two of them. She could see this old woman was afraid of her husband.

He was completely different from Thuy's father, who loved all his children. Thuy helped her to bed to rest. Her mother-in-law's back was more bent than before. Thuy felt sorry for this woman's fate. She had heard about her life story from the neighbours. Her family had borrowed a high-interest loan from her father-in-law's family. The years went by quickly and the interest grew and grew. Without being able to make the payments on time, there was only one solution, their youngest daughter was handed over when she was sixteen years old. This was the only way to clear their debt.

The first several years, when she couldn't get pregnant, her husband's family scolded her harshly.

"Feeding you is a waste of money. At least with pigs, they give birth a few times a year. This is a deaf tree without flowers and fruit!"

Even when she became pregnant and gave birth to their first daughter, there was another round of scolding and nagging. They were hoping for a boy to continue the family line and then when she gave birth to several boys in a row, she was only cursed more. This poor woman. Working hard all day, then every night she lay holding her child with tears streaming down her face.

Thuy remembered when Hien was born, how her father and siblings were so excited and happy for them. Her husband's family, though, were silent. There were no celebratory words or visits from them. Thuy felt sorry for herself and for her daughter. The ideology of male superiority and female inferiority that had existed for generations, was still prevalent in the country.

oOo

Hien's maternal grandfather's house was in the same town, so they didn't need to complete any paperwork to visit. Still, it had been a long time since they last visited. Thuy knew she should visit more, but her life was so restrictive. From outside the gate, Hien sang happily, mentioning her grandfather. Hearing her voice, he hurriedly came out to the gate to greet them.

"Hello, Grandpa!" Hien said happily to the old man.

"Good morning, Dad." Thuy smiled, then led her bike into the yard.

"What are you doing, Dad? I bought 'Phở'*3 for you, it's from uncle Thu's shop. It's delicious and you must eat it while it's still hot."

"Why did you buy it there? It's expensive, a waste of money." The old man turned to his granddaughter. "Does my puppy want to eat 'Phở' with me?"

He then lifted Hien from the back of the bike. "Oh, my puppy is wearing such a beautiful dress today? Can I borrow it?" He teased Hien.

"Grandpa, that's the dress my mother made for me. It's pretty, isn't it?" Hien was happy to show off.

Hearing little Hien talking about the dress, Thuy remembered to ask. "Dad, do you have any extra scraps of fabric in the house that I could have?"

"Knowing you like I do, I've collected a small bag of fabric pieces for you. Remind me before you leave. Also, I have two meters of black silk, which I won in my company's lucky draw. I want you to have it so you can make yourself some nice trousers."

Thuy thanked her father, he was still thinking of her and worrying about her. The two of them ate pho, talking and laughing happily. Thuy took the opportunity to clean the house, occasionally asking how her younger siblings and her eldest brother's family were doing.

"Is Chinh and his wife planning to come back to this town to work and live with you? It will be good for you to have them take care of you."

Mr Lan was silent, sighed and didn't say anything else. Thuy could sense there was something he didn't really want to tell her. He loves his son and wanted him to work with him at the garment factory.

Thuy went out to the garden to look at the jackfruit trees. There were a lot of fruits on the branches this year. Her father had beautiful custard apple trees too, and they were lush and full of buds. There were tea trees planted around the fence. The green was deep and cool to the eyes. Her father loved drinking black tea. He trimmed the bushes and took care of them every morning. Once Thuy even heard him whispering to them. "I love you, I want you to grow up fast! Be green and beautiful!

Do you hear me? You're my good friend, aren't you?"

Thuy was sceptical at first, but this whispering seemed to make a difference. Every tree was green and growing rapidly, with lots of young buds. There was also a huge peach tree in front of the door. It was starting to bud, surely this Lunar New Year it will have beautiful flowers, thought Thuy. With all these flowers, fruits and green trees as friends, Thuy hoped that her father wouldn't feel alone. She knew they made him happy and they kept him busy, which she thought was important to also keep him healthy.

Unable to stay long, Thuy said goodbye to her father and apologised for not seeing him enough. There was a water spinach field near the house, she wanted to go by it and to collect apple snails for dinner. It helped to improve her health. Last week, in just half an hour, Thuy had harvested a big bagful of apple snails, she ate them over two meals, they were delicious.

Then she hurried home with Hien. She had lots to do that evening; there was more packaging of the peanuts and Ha had also given her more wool for a child's hat knitting job.

Thuy's daily life was as regular as clockwork, but Thuy and her husband were like the sun and the moon. They hardly ever saw each other. They both worked six days a week, Binh always away for his work, leaving Thuy at home to take care of Hien by herself. She was like a single mother, quite often forgetting she had a husband. Binh was not present for his wife or daughter. Thuy didn't feel sorry for herself, she didn't actually have that much time to think about it. She was like a machine, doing a job, except she has flesh and bones.

-----

There were only two people working in the office, Thương was in charge of distributing books and documents to the district libraries. Thuy would read and study the content of each book, then classify them. There were always new types of books arriving. All of them had to be read and recorded with comments on their content. Sometimes Thuy would be so engrossed in reading the newly imported books, she would forget the time. She was so curious to find out more about subjects before the country was unified.

All books about movies, pre-war songs that were stigmatized as 'yellow music' sentimental or any literary works that were published under the Republic of Vietnam regime and brought to the North were labelled as reactionary and decadent.

These were not freely distributed, but people passed them around to read in secret.

Once Thuy was caught reading these banned materials. She was so engrossed in reading, she didn't notice someone standing right behind her, until a deep voice spoke loudly.

"Thuy is working so hard, she doesn't even want to go home."

Thuy jumped and looked up to see the deep voice take the book from her hand. At the end of the week, Thuy had to write a self-criticism. She had to state how she violated working hours, that she was reading banned books with bad ideas and reactionary content.

-----

Books that she was caught indulging in were a pre-war title, The Self-reliant Literacy Group (Tự Lực Văn Đoàn)*4 and The New Poetry (Thơ Mới) book. These were both published by the Republic of Vietnam regime. Fortunately, as this was the first violation, Thuy was only criticised and given an internal warning. However, if it happened again, she would be forced to quit her job and then be expelled from the cultural and educational sector.

In July 1954, the government of the Democratic Republic of Vietnam took over the North according to the Genève Agreement on Vietnam. The Party and the State focused on building an educational culture based on extreme communism. The culture and arts of the old regime, including books, newspapers and musical works, were confiscated and banned from circulation. These included the Self-Reliant Literary Group (Tự Lực Văn Đoàn), the New Poetry Movement (Phong Trào Thơ Mới), and the Yellow music (Nhạc vàng). In 1975, after the two regions were unified, the Vietnamese Communist Party and State considered the literature and arts of the Republic of Vietnam to be decadent and reactionary and banned them from use and circulation.

In the late 1980s, when the leaders of the Party and State learned the painful lesson that extreme communist policies had hindered social and economic development, they launched the Innovation (Đổi Mới) and the Untie and Open the Doors movement (Cởi mở và Thông thương). This gradually helped improve people's outlook on life. Many works of the Self-Reliant Literary Group were adapted into films such as Giông Tố (Thunderous), Số Đỏ (Lucky Number), Nửa Chừng Xuân (Halfway Through Lady's life). These were widely released nationwide, forming the new era of cultural and educational awareness.

oOo

Last Sunday, Thuy's husband didn't come home, but this Saturday he was home early. Thuy had gone to pick Hien up from the nursery.

"Thuy! you've got to go home quickly! Hien's father has already picked her up! Go make dinner for him!" Loan laughed.

Thuy smiled, said goodbye to Loan and rode her bike home. From outside she could hear the giggles of father and daughter. Thuy parked her bike outside and went into the house.

"Mum, dad bought me a very pretty doll, it knows how to open and close its eyes." Hien said happily, holding the doll up to Thuy. She hugged the Chinese doll, stroked her cheeks and hair, talking to it all the while. "You can't cry, you have to be good, I love you a lot."

Thuy looked at her husband and spoke softly. "You didn't come home last Sunday. We waited for you all day. I wanted to go and visit my father with you." She continued with a slight frown on her face. "Anyways, we were able to see him a couple of days ago. He's still healthy and going to work regularly. He asked about you..."

"Why did the department head let you go home early today?" Thuy asked, cautiously.

"Honey, on a business trip I met some people from the lowlands. They said they were trading goods in China and they make a decent living from it."

"Are you saying you want to do the same? But you don't know anything about trading goods. If you're honest, you could lose everything and also, we're government officials, we can't violate policies and laws." Thuy said worriedly.

"I'm just telling you what I saw and I only want to keep an eye on this business."

Thuy quietly went into the kitchen to prepare dinner. Her husband has always been honest, but to be good in the trading business you have to be cunning and deceitful. He had some savings, but if he goes into this business, he might not be able to make any money and might even be cheated out of everything he owns. These were thoughts that Thuy did not say out loud to her husband.

She hears all over the place people talking about the trading industry. Sometimes, even Thuy has thoughts about this business, but only if she didn't have a husband or a child. She would have done this to help her father, then he wouldn't have to work so hard himself.

Thuy hears about these people from the men working in the office, who, although they don't trade in organisations or go on long trips, they still have extra income coming in. She heard of a desperate incident, where a whole family was admitted to hospital with acute diarrhoea.

"What did your family eat that caused food poisoning?" The doctor had asked.

"Doctor, it's the same as every day, nothing special. Boiled spinach rice, pickled eggplant. That's all." The husband replied.

"Strange, do try and remember if there's anything different from your other days."

"This morning, I lined up to buy half a liter of fish sauce at the town's food store. It had been such a long time since we last had fish sauce, I was so happy to be able to buy a bottle. We used it that evening. Dipped boiled spinach in it and even mixed it into the rice." The woman whispered.

"Oh, no, you bought fake fish sauce that's been mixed with hand sanitizer! The women at the store do that!" The patient lying in the bed next to the woman interrupted.

"Oh, my god! What did you say? Mixed with hand sanitizer?"

"Yes, lots of people have seen this being done, not just me. They had received a 100-liter barrel of fish sauce, but some workers secretly took a few liters home. Each day, they used a basin of water to wash their hands while working. At the end of the day, they would pour that same basin of water into the fish sauce barrel to make up for the amount they had taken. When customers came to buy, they simply drew the sauce from the barrel and measured it into bottles for sale."

The doctor listened to all this, shaking his head and writing it all down in his medical record. The wife, who was seriously ill, stayed in the hospital, while the others were given drugs to help ease the diarrhoea.

Stealing by store employees is very common. It's like a disease that spreads quickly. A woman who sells rice using faulty scales could easily steal 10 kilograms of rice a day. She will then go on to sell that stolen rice to the black-market dealers. The beverage store seller steals draft beer and syrup to bring home to her husband and children. Just by working as an employee at one of these stores you would be visibly rich, with gold earrings, gold necklaces and wrist watches, after maybe six months of dirty trading. They are the worms of society and no one can do anything to change this, because they are the wives, children and relatives of leaders from the socialist regime.

Since the liberation of the South, the economy had become increasingly depressed. Everyone was looking for ways to earn more to support their families. The fear of losing their jobs and of public opinion though, forced people to live a lie. After work and on days off, people secretly sold and bought goods brought from China. There were transistor radios, clothes, shoes, fabrics, wool, batteries, anything you could possibly want. Nga and her husband had suggested it several times to Thuy, but she was too scared.

She still had those memories of her family being outcast as bourgeois, haunting her. After she graduated from university and now working at the Department of Culture, she had a husband and child to think of. Thuy did not dare to do anything illegal. She just wanted a peaceful life with her family.

Mrs Mo, who worked at the Department of Culture, had in-laws living near the Chinese border. Whenever her husband went back to visit them, he would return with all kinds of Chinese goods; fountain pens, plastic sandals, perfume, face cream and sometimes even opium. This gave their family a higher standard of living than most. 'The forest has its ears and so do the walls.' A self-explanatory saying. There was always someone who was jealous enough to report you to the leaders and the police. Last week, Mr Mo was arrested at the checkpoint and all the smuggled goods were confiscated. He was disciplined and suspended from work.

After work, while picking Hien up from the nursery, Thuy gave Loan two ounces of sugar, which Loan was very happy with.

"Thank you very much, this is so precious. I have been really tired these past few days and today you've given me sugar, just in time to boost my energy!" Loan wittered on.

"Oh, do you know Mrs Thi's husband? He lives in the same row house as you."

"I know them. Why?"

"Thi's husband went to the South to visit his homeland and brought a lot of things back!"

"Well, then congratulations to Mrs Thi." Thuy wanted to leave, but kept on getting caught up with Loan's gossiping.

"He came back with two bicycle frames, a transistor radio, a huge doll and a big backpack."

"Well, they do have three small children and aren't on a very high salary. This is something good for them, hopefully making their lives happier."

Thuy left immediately after saying this. Carrying her child home, she didn't want to stand there anymore listening to Loan drone on.

While bathing her child, she could still hear voices and chatter all over the building. There was no privacy in the housing complex. People cared and paid too much attention to what everyone else was doing. Thuy started imagining that her actions and movements were being watched by Loan.

The pig was squealing for food. It didn't know whether Thuy was at home or at work, but it just kept on squealing until it could see Thuy's shadow approaching.

It was going to rain that night, so Thuy didn't need to water the vegetables. They were growing taller and their leaves were getting bigger. This made Thuy happy and forget about everything else. Tonight, she could go out to the garden to collect snails and slugs. This would make a good bran mix for the pig. Thuy knew that adding snails would make it eat with real enthusiasm. It would truly live up to the saying, "as gluttonous as a pig!"

The number of people from the South who gathered to visit their home towns in the North increased day by day. Most of them brought back goods that were scarce in the north, while in the South they were sold everywhere on the sidewalks and in flea markets. There were also people who didn't have relatives in the South, but made the journey down to buy goods and to sell in the North to make a profit. The desires and greed of people cannot be measured.

The constant comparison meant that if someone has it, then you have to have it too. Thuy had a relative who had some money, they went to the South, came back North with a Honda motorbike, drove it around the town to show off. He also intended to move his whole family to the South.

Thuy's agency had recruited a PhD graduate from the Soviet Union. At that time, studying abroad was the dream of tens of thousands of young people. The dream, however, was only for the children of the Red families.

The goal was to train 'the young successors' for the Red revolution. The idea of studying abroad was to advance the knowledge of the home country, but this opened up the opportunity of legal trading. Just as ex-Prime Minister Pham Van Dong said to the group of students at Ha Noi train station returning home the summer of 1972. "Hello students, our legal traders, you've returned with money and goods!"

-----

After many years of studying abroad, no one knew whether the knowledge was being passed onto the country, but everyone could see the crates of goods being transported home on the trains. The carriages were filled with Simson motorbikes, Mifa bicycles from the German Democratic Republic, Favourit bicycles from Czechoslovakia, Rigonda, electric radios, irons and electric Elephant Ear fans from Russia, but there were no books coming in.

Parents and siblings coming to the station to welcome these student home, had beaming faces as they could see crates of goods filling every corner of the station.

Any society is like a colourful, rich and diverse flower garden. During the war, every family had a husband or child joining the army. When the war ended, millions of soldiers remained lost in the battlefields. Tens of thousands of wounded and sick soldiers returned alive and were reunited with their families. After the war, both governments won, the only losers were the people. There were many stories from the war.

Thuy's neighbour, Huong, whose husband had joined the army before the Lunar New Year (1967). For more than ten years she hadn't received any letters from him or about him. There were rumours that he had died or there was news that he surrendered to the Republic of Vietnam. Then suddenly at the end of 1977, carrying a heavy backpack with a big doll, a bicycle frame on his left shoulder and a transistor radio on his right shoulder, he burst into the house. His parents, wife and children were all moved, crying tears of joy.

A different return story was with Mrs Tinh's husband. He had been in the army for more than twenty years Again, there was no news of him, except rumours that he was missing in action or he had died in battle. Mrs Tinh didn't believe any of that, she kept on waiting and hoping. On the day he returned, he carried with him a soldier's backpack.

His wife and children were of course extremely happy to see him. Neighbours came to share the joy, glad that he had returned alive. He took out from his backpack, only a few packets of candy, enough to share with the children surrounding him. He told everyone that he had been seriously injured and was transferred from one hospital to another. His wounds had healed and after he was discharged and given an invalid certificate, he waited for the war to be resolved. Tinh's family had their father returned, but not another source of income. Day by day, month by month and now in his forties without a degree or a job, he only had many wounds to show for his many, years away. Several friends who had also been discharged from the army suggested he get involved in the smuggling trade. What other options did he have?

One evening, Thuy and her daughter were having dinner.

"Mum, today me and uncle Lan's children went to visit uncle Toan in his house." Hien boasted to her mother.

"Oh, you did? How is uncle Toan's family? Are they all well? Did you play nicely there?!"

"We were very good, so uncle Toan gave us milk to drink."

They said that at school, in the textbooks, there were words like 'milk' and 'cheese'. The teacher had made them practice writing these words, even though they had never drink milk. It was heart-breaking to hear. There wasn't enough food, let alone money to buy milk and butter.

A few days ago, Hang had confided in Thuy.

"You know, yesterday everyone in my family was happy."

"Why? What was the good news?" Thuy smiled, looking at her friend.

"A friend of my younger brother came to my house to tell us the news. Both of them were discharged at the same time. They were close friends, they had joined the army at the same time, so when he received his discharge papers, he went straight."

"What about your younger brother?"

"Oh my God! He said he was staying a few days to say goodbye to everyone. When my parents heard the news, they were so happy, they cried. Soon we're going to see him."

Hang wanted to share the news with everyone she knew. During wartime, soldiers struggled between life and death, unable to avoid injuries, loss and sacrifice. Those at home didn't have an easier time either. They were hard-working and carried on, silently enduring the hope that their children and relatives would return safely. Therefore, any good news was like a tonic and a sedative, like it was for Hang's parents and family.

However, who would have thought that even after the next day, the next week, the next month, he still did not return. It wasn't until much later did Hang's family learn that the very next day, there was an order to send the entire battalion to the Cambodian battlefield to carry out a new mission.

Two years later, when his mother was old and weak from worry, the two sisters got married. One married the friend from the same army as their brother. He was a communist party member and had medals for his bravery in defeating the Americans. He quickly rose to the leadership ranks of the construction company. Even with much needed income from the new son-in-law, everyone in the family still waited for news of their younger brother. Then one hot, humid summer day, Hang's family received a death notice, her younger brother had died on the Cambodian battlefield.

The relationship between Vietnam and China became strained from the end of 1977. China stopped all assistance and aid activities. They prevented goods from being transported by rail from the Soviet Union and Eastern European communist countries to Vietnam. Beijing radio continuously broadcasted propaganda (broadcasting time at 6 pm and 8 pm in Vietnam) with distorted, divisive and inciting arguments against the Hoa people living in Vietnam. In addition, there was a lot of gossip from border traders. They caused confusion, fear, disruption and upheaval in the lives of honest and simple local Hoa people in the border area.

Meanwhile, the Vietnamese government had not yet made an official announcement or decision on policies towards the Hoa people. False rumours still spread faster than fire and fuelled many gullible people to sell their houses and flee to China. However, the majority of local people lived on, in fear, listening and waiting to see how the situation would develop before making any decisions.

The situation on the southwestern border between Cambodia and Vietnam was also unstable. Since 1975, the Pol Pot regime had frequently invaded Tay Ninh province and other areas along the Vietnam - Cambodia border. In Cambodia, Pol Pot had forced his people to do hard labour. After a few years, more than three million innocent Khmer people died tragically at the hands of this dictator.

On 25 December, 1978, Vietnam officially sent troops to Cambodia. Within two weeks, Pol Pot's troops fled and the Democratic Cambodia Government under the auspices of the communist government of Vietnam was established.

During this time, the government for Thuy's province issued a high-alert war warning. People were ordered to dig a personal shelter according to regulated specifications.

Thuy started digging her shelter during her lunch periods. She was six months pregnant with her second child and she was more tired than with Hien. She had a craving for large edible snails and Asian pears! Digging was definitely more tiring when you're pregnant, but Thuy like everyone else in her province carried on as normal.

On the outside everyone was calm and silently obeying the Party's rules, on the inside everyone had their own worries. It was the lunar New Year 1979. Thuy had bought sticky rice and mung dal beans, hoping to take these ingredients to her father's house and make Chưng cakes*[4]. As these were so time consuming to prepare and make, they were only made at this special time of year.

Thuy's mother had passed away a few years ago. Her younger sister Hong, had got married and her youngest brother, Hung, joined the army. Her father had lived alone for a while, but then remarried a woman that lived nearby. She then brought her son to live with them. Thuy didn't know this at the time, but it was to be the last Tết she would celebrate in Vietnam with her father.

Binh had gone back to his hometown to celebrate Tết with his family. They lived near the border of China. When he returned, he looked solemn and down.

"Honey, the situation in the countryside is very tense. After Tết is over, my mother and siblings will run to China to work on a farm."

"Will it be safer there for them?"

"They've heard that the farms are accepting Vietnamese people to work on their land."

"Is your father going with them?"

Binh shook his head. "He refuses to go. He said he'll regret leaving his house and land. He told me not to worry about him."

Listening to her husband talking about his family in Lang Son province, Thuy became more confused and worried.

One day during a meeting at work, someone notified Thuy she was wanted.

"Sister Thuy, there are some people outside asking about you."

Thuy asked for permission to go down to see who it was. She saw two adults and two children wearing Tay ethnic clothing. The man had a cloth bag on his shoulder and a small child in his arms. There was another child, maybe six or seven years old, hiding behind his mother. Everyone looked tired and worried. Thuy didn't recognise them. She walked close to them.

"Hello, Third aunty!" The man spoke.

Thuy was surprised, she didn't know what to say. Why was he calling her aunty?

"We're from the home town of Bā shūshu (Third uncle in Chinese). Your mother-in-law gave us your address. She said you would help us, let us stay with you for one night." The woman continued for her husband.

"Well, okay. Wait a minute, let me ask permission to leave work early, then I'll take you to my house."

The people working in the office looked on curiously. Having been granted time to go home early, Thuy took her bike and led everyone home. Asking lots of questions to the man and woman, Thuy realised the situation in her in-law's hometown was changing rapidly.

"Why didn't you go with them?" Thuy asked.

"Your mother-in-law was going with uncle Thoong and uncle Thong's families to the China. We want to go back to our wife's hometown in Pho Yen."

That night, sitting together on a mat, rice mixed with dried cassava, vegetable soup grown by Thuy cooked with salt, boiled eggs bought by the family, no meat or fish, but everyone ate with relish, as if they hadn't eaten for a long time.

Looking at the two children eating ravenously, licking their lips continuously, Thuy felt sorry for them. They didn't know each other, but she had empathy for their situation. Forced to leave your home was traumatic for any one. Will these innocent children find a safe home and peace in their lives?

"Eat slowly or you might choke." The wife said to her children. She then looked at Thuy with embarrassment.

"I brought a few sweet potatoes and some sticky rice cakes, but the children ate them all yesterday morning. We haven't eaten cooked rice for two days. We were all so hungry."

"What are you planning to do when you get to your parents' house tomorrow? Stay there or go somewhere else?" Thuy asked, concerned.

"Well, we don't know what to do yet. If we get there and we can earn a living then we'll stay, if not then we'll carry on somewhere else."

Looking at the scene of the couple with two small children, Thuy felt sorry but didn't know what to say. It was very different in the homeland. Families without children went to China to work on farms.

Those with children went to many different places, some with money, some without. Houses and belongings were left behind and could not be sold in time, so where did they get money? It was very chaotic, they pulled carts to carry their belongings back to China.

"It's still quiet down here, no signs of anything, rest tonight. Tomorrow morning you can get a coach station to your hometown."

The adults talked until late at night before going to bed. Little Hien and the two children slept early. Children are innocent and don't know anything. Thuy tossed and turned, unable to sleep, little Hien next to her was sleeping and smiling in her sleep. Looking over, the mother and children lying next to her turned constantly. On the floor, the husband's snoring could be heard, probably tired after several days of traveling, now sleeping peacefully.

At four o'clock in the morning, Thuy quietly got up to cook a pot of pig feed and put a pot of porridge for everyone to eat breakfast. At about five o'clock, after finishing the porridge.

Thuy saw them off for a while, waited until they were ready to leave. When they said goodbye, she gave the woman money. "I don't have much, just a few coins for the two children to buy bread for the journey."

Everyone was worried for each other as they said their goodbyes. From that day onwards, a few people from Lang Son came to stay for one night at Thuy's house, before heading onto their final destinations. Sometimes there were just a couple of people and sometimes a family of five stayed.

-----

After Tết (1979), the situation became more tense, Chinese spies disguised themselves as Vietnamese of Chinese origin from the border areas, infiltrated the village through smugglers, causing confusion and chaos. Local officials were subjective and lost their motivation in their roles, the situation became more chaotic.

Some local militiamen and officials took advantage of personal hatred and resentment to illegally arrest and detain the Hoa people who were hunted down, beaten and shot, including Thuy's husband's brothers.

"Find and capture Cat Thong and Cat Thoong, they are Hoa people."

Thuy's father-in-law was not at peace, so scared that he ran away to hid at an acquaintance's house. He sent a telegram to Thuy's husband, *'come to pick me up right away!'*

After receiving the telegram, Binh took a coach to pick up his father. Two days later he took him to live with Thuy's family, then Binh continued his business trip as usual.

Again, life would change for Thuy. On the first day of his arrived, he told to Thuy and his son his demands.

"Every day there must be three meals without additives must be meat for me. Remember I don't eat fish and I have to have hot water to bathe in."

Thuy's neighbours had been watching and paying close attention since Thuy's house opened up to strangers moving down from the borders. It was now more important than ever that Thuy reported her father-in-law's temporary stay with them. Her movements were now being monitored very closely.

Each day when Thuy returns home from work, she has to be cheerful and polite. Her duties as a good daughter-in-law were firstly to take good care of the father-in-law. She has to do this quietly and obediently and without thinking or questioning.

Her daily work routine is the same as before, working eight hours a day. Then there is Hien she cares for after she finishes work and alongside the pig and chickens, she has to make sure the vegetables are thriving. With the addition of the old man, the family's rice allowance is shorter than before. Hien and the old man get the good rice and

Thuy often just eats sweet potatoes and cassava alone.

The baby is growing and Thuy's workload is also growing. The most difficult thing was the water they used every day. Before, her carrying two buckets of water was easy and chopping wood wasn't that hard, but now with no one to help her with these heavy tasks, it was a struggle to do them all by herself. Only on Sunday, when Binh came home and filled the water tank, the day was lighter for her. The old man lay down all day. He didn't lend a hand to help with anything, he didn't even play with his granddaughter.

Thuy still had to send Hien to play with the neighbours' children after work. In the morning, after feeding the pigs, Thuy had to carry a basin of hot water for the old man to wash his face. She would then have to prepare his breakfast, which had to have meat with it. During her lunch break, she had to quickly to cook for his meal and feed Hien, then she would go back to work until the late afternoon. After work, she came home to water the vegetables, cook the dinner and feed the pigs. In addition to all this, every two days, the old man demanded hot water to bathe with. Thuy was still taking on knitting jobs to earn some extra money, so her days never seemed to end.

------

One Sunday, when Thuy's father was visiting, he could see his daughter doing one chore after another, not stopping at all. It broke his heart to see her heavily pregnant and exhausted.

"Oh! No, no! My dear child, if you continue like this, you're going to collapse. After you give birth, you will come stay with me in my house, I will cook and take care of you."

On 17 February, 1979, China opened the front to attack the entire border area of Vietnam. The Sino - Vietnam War officially broke out.

-----

**Note**

*1 Tết; Vietnamese New Year is celebrated on the same date as the Chinese New Year, following the lunar calendar.

*2 Tien Phong plastic sandals were made in Vietnam but the production quantity was very small and were not for sale to people during that period.

*3 Phở is a Vietnamese soup that's made with all the good stuff: broth, rice noodles, beef or chicken, pork and lots of mix-and-match toppings. The best thing about pho is that it's such a restorative food— the comforting soup is savoury and rich, while still feeling clean and refreshing at the same time.

*4 The Tự Lực Văn Đoàn was an influential literary collective founded in 1932-1933 by Nhất Linh and Khái Hưng. They were one of the most significant political and literary movements in twentieth-century Vietnam and published significantly via their two journals, *Phong Hóa* (Mores, 1932–1936) and *Ngày Nay* (Today, 1936–1940, 1945) as well as their own publishing house Đời Nay. The group used these journals and novels to articulate their social and political ideals, as well as experiment with new literary forms such as the ground breaking Thơ mới (New Poetry Movement), new modes of reportage and the modern autobiography. The group promoted Modernization and Westernization rejecting Confucian traditions which they deemed anachronistic. Tự Lực Văn Đoàn's core members included Nhất Linh, Khái Hưng, Hoàng Đạo, Thạch Lam, Xuân Diệu, Thế Lữ, Huy Cận and Tú Mỡ.

*5 Chưng cake; "Bánh Chưng" is a traditional and irreplaceable cake of Vietnamese people in the Tet holidays and King Hung's anniversary (10th March Lunar). For the Vietnamese, making "Bánh Chưng" is the ideal way to express gratitude yo their ancestors and homeland. It is made with glutinous rice, mung beans, pork belly, and green banana leaves then boiled about 4 to 6 hours.

# CHAPTER 3

## Sino – Vietnamese War

*When sorrow come; they come not single spies*
*but in battalions!*
**William Shakespeare, Hamlet**

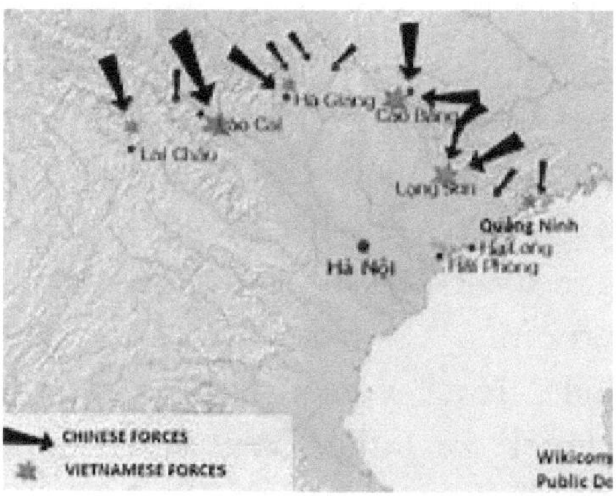


War breaks out on the Sino-Vietnamese border,17-2-1979

At midnight on February 17, 1979, the Chinese army launched a full-scale attack along 600 kilometres of the Vietnam - China border. Caught off guard, with no time to react, the provinces of Quang Ninh, Lang Son, Cao Bang, Ha Giang, Lao Cai and Lai Chau quickly fell into Chinese hands. The

Chinese leader, Deng Xiaoping, declared he would "teach Vietnam a lesson - that ungrateful neighbour who kicked the bowl after eating."

The war raged for twenty-seven days, from February 17 to March 16, 1979, under the command of General Xu Shiyou.

In Thuy's town, life was no longer peaceful. Beneath the surface, tension simmered like a current running under a calm river ready to erupt at any time. The ethnic Chinese residents in big cities like Hanoi, Hai Phong and Nam Dinh seemed to receive the news faster than those in smaller provinces.

That noon, when Thuy came home to prepare lunch, she was surprised to see her husband's younger sister and her father-in-law talking in the living room.

"Hello! Have you just come to visit? I'll make some lunch for father. Will you stay and eat with us?" Thuy asked.

Her sister-in-law stood up. "Sister, I'm taking father to Hanoi. From there, we'll take a boat to China. The situation here is too tense we can't stay any longer."

"Does Binh know about this?" Thuy asked, startled.

"Yes, he knows. Please hurry and make lunch. After we eat, father and I will take the coach to Hanoi."

Thuy hadn't heard a word about this plan. If Binh knew, he hadn't said anything to her. She quietly went down to the kitchen, unsure what to think. The old man and his daughter were fleeing like fugitives. Thuy told herself she had to understand they were frightened, confused, running for their lives.

That afternoon, when Thuy came home from work, the house was empty. Still, she felt as if unseen eyes were watching her. She parked her bicycle on the sidewalk and went to pick up Hien from the nursery. A chill ran down her neck.

Like a machine, she went through her evening routine bathing Hien, feeding her dinner, then tending to the pigs and chickens. She watered the vegetables and mixed pig feed for the next morning. Finally, she washed the family's clothes. Now that her father-in-law was gone, she didn't have to run around after him anymore. For the first time in weeks, Thuy felt a little relief, as if a heavy weight had been lifted. But just as one burden left her shoulders, another far heavier came crashing down.

That night, after many exhausting days, Thuy finally lay down and drifted into a deep sleep.

Suddenly, there was a loud pounding on the front door followed by shouting.

"Open up! Open the door! Quickly!"

Startled, Thuy called out, "Who is it? It's late, what do you want?"

"Open the door right now! We're the local militia here to check your property!"

Thuy jumped up, heart racing. She didn't even have time to put on her slippers. Barefoot, she ran to the door. The moment she lifted the latch, two men with rifles on their shoulders burst in like a gust of poisonous wind.

Everything blurred. She barely saw their faces - only flashes of uniforms, a beam of light, the cold glint of metal. One man shone a flashlight under the bed, into the cupboard, even beneath the chairs. The other used a stick to lift the mat off the bed.

Thuy stood frozen, stiff as a tree trunk, too terrified to move or speak.

Why were they searching her house in the middle of the night without a warrant? She didn't dare to ask. What could they possibly expect to find under a thin sleeping mat?

Behind her, Hien clung to her mother's leg, eyes wide and unblinking, lips pressed tight in fear.

The men moved to the next bed - her father-in-law's and one of them barked a question.

"Who sleeps here?"

"That's my father-in-law's bed," Thuy answered softly.

The man's tone grew harsher. "And where is he now?"

"He went back to Hanoi with his daughter yesterday," she said, her voice trembling.

"Why didn't you report it?"

"This is a collective housing area, I've already reported it to the local authorities. And who exactly are you?"

Ignoring Thuy, the man barked another question.

"Where's your husband? Or don't you have one?"

"My husband's on a work trip, in one of the northern provinces. He'll be back this weekend."

After yelling and turning the house upside down, the two men found nothing. Without another word, they left disappearing into the night like ghosts. The poisonous wind had passed, but its cold breath lingered in every corner of the house.

There was no more sleep for Thuy that night. She held her child close.

"Mum, I'm scared," Hien whispered. "Will they beat us? I'll tell Dad."

Thuy stroked her daughter's hair, trying to calm her and herself. "Go back to sleep, my love. Mum's here. Don't be afraid." But her heart wouldn't rest. Something deep inside told her dark days were coming. Would her husband be safe on his trip? Would her father-in-law make it out by boat? She thought of her own father and siblings they had no idea what she was going through. Her two younger brothers were still in the army. She prayed they'd survive the fighting up north.

When the rooster crowed, the first light crept in through the window.

From that night on, someone came to search the house almost every night. Thuy and Hien could never sleep peacefully again they just had to endure, quietly, without a word of protest.

By Saturday evening, when Binh finally returned home, Thuy told him everything that had happened. He said nothing. He didn't ask, didn't comfort her. His face was drawn, his eyes clouded with worry. He sat there, silent. Thuy looked at him and wondered was this still her husband? She didn't even ask about his father or sister. She just sat quietly, swallowing her tears.

On Monday morning, Binh packed his bag for another work trip. That same day, Thuy received an order to move house.

The authorities had reassigned her family to an apartment in the provincial housing block a four-storey building right in the centre of town, across from the police station.

There was no time to prepare. She was given two days off work to move only the essentials.

She had to do it all on her own. Thuy asked Hue's younger brother to help, borrowing his wooden ox cart to carry her things.

The new apartment was barely eighteen square metres, just one small room with a tiny bathroom. Cooking, eating and sleeping all had to happen in the same cramped space. There was no yard to grow vegetables, no pen for the chickens or pigs. It felt like a box - a cage.

Thuy sold her remaining animals and vegetables to Lan. It broke her heart, but she had no choice. The bed, the cupboards, the pots and basins all were loaded onto two ox carts, with Hue's brother helping her carry them to the new place.

Their new home was on the third floor. The nursery was a kilometre away, which meant Thuy now had to make the trip four times a day carrying her bicycle up and down the stairs each time. It was exhausting.

The new apartment had a kerosene stove. She no longer had to worry about collecting firewood or sawdust, but kerosene was just as hard to find. And when the stove was lit, the entire room filled with thick, choking smoke. Outside, on the wall across from the police station, a slogan read: *"Ensure Public Safety and Hygiene."* The irony wasn't lost on her.

The housing block was full of strangers. They nodded politely in passing, maybe exchanged a few words, then disappeared quickly behind their own doors. Like flocks of birds, they flew out each morning to work, returning each night to their small, silent nests. The whole building felt like a giant birdcage, one the police could watch at any time.

A week passed. When Binh came home that Saturday, he found his wife and daughter already settled into the new place. That evening, while Thuy sat knitting, he quietly took a seat beside her.

"Honey," he began softly, "my younger sister has found a boat. I can go to Hong Kong."

Thuy froze, her knitting needles still in her hands. "What? You're going alone? What about me and little Hien?"

"I have to go," he said flatly. "The department driver, Mr Than - he's Hoa and they sent his whole family to Lam Dong to work."

Thuy stared at him. "Then why can't you go there too?"

"No. I have to go to Hong Kong. If I stay here, they'll kill me," Binh said, his voice calm - too calm.

Thuy felt the blood drain from her face. The bitterness that had been building in her chest for years finally rose to her throat. Tears spilled silently down her cheeks.

"Stop crying," Binh muttered. "You'll wake the baby."

How could she stop? The words she'd swallowed for years now burst out. She had no strength left to hide her pain, no reason left to hold it in. The man sitting before her - her husband - was about to abandon her and their child.

What would happen when the second baby was born? How would the three of them live? Even though Binh was often away, at least Hien still had someone to call "Daddy." Who would she have now?

Thuy's mind was full of questions but Binh had no answers. He sat there, unmoved, as she wept quietly beside him.

Time seemed to slow after Binh announced he was leaving for Hong Kong alone. He didn't seem worried or guilty about what he was about to do. There was no mention of how Thuy and their child would manage after he was gone. Nothing at all.

Thuy's head throbbed with resentment and grief. Her whole body burned like fire. Outside, the night was pitch black, the air heavy and suffocating early summer pressing down on her like a weight. She tossed and turned, glancing at the man lying next to her, a man who suddenly felt like a stranger.

She thought of her father's warnings and felt a deep ache of regret. Her fate, she realized, was just like the girl in the old folk song:

*"Girls are like falling raindrops.*
*Some fall into the palace,*
*Some fall into the ploughed fields."*

oOo

Sunday twenty-four long, silent hours. The house was thick with tension. Little Hien was still innocent, still smiling and playing with her father, unaware of what was coming. Watching them, Thuy's heart filled with love for her child.

Suddenly, a sharp pain shot through her belly - the baby had kicked hard, as if sensing her turmoil. Thuy gently rubbed her stomach and whispered, "Be good, my little one. Stay still and listen to me. It's not safe out there. I'm sorry… I couldn't keep your father here with us."

The next morning, he packed his bag and left for his so-called "work trip," just like every other time. Thuy stood watching, her eyes wet with tears.

"I'm going now," Binh said quietly.

He left without a word to anyone, no farewells, no explanations. Just silence. Thuy stood by the window, watching his figure disappear down the stairs. Unlike all the other times he'd gone away, this time there was a deep, hollow emptiness in her chest.

Out of habit, she still prepared to take Hien to the nursery, then headed to the office to begin another day. She couldn't tell anyone what was happening. The weight of it all sat heavy in her heart, her thoughts spinning endlessly.

The road from the nursery to her office felt longer than ever. The baby pressed down on her belly, making it hard to balance on the bicycle. The hot asphalt shimmered in the sun, releasing a sharp, tarry smell that stung her eyes and nose.

Was it really this hot already - so early in the summer? Or was it her own sorrow and exhaustion making the heat feel unbearable?

Thuy entered the classroom as usual.

"Good morning, students!"

"Good morning, teacher!"

The room echoed with cheerful voices. Her students smiled warmly at her, waiting patiently for the lesson to begin. They were still the same young faces full of faith, hope and unshaken optimism. None of them had any idea what Thuy had been going through.

After several months together, a quiet bond had formed between them. Looking around the room, Thuy remembered the first days of teaching this group; - twelve young staff members - from different districts, sent to attend a three-month elementary course on library work. There was only one week left before the program ended.

Before continuing with the day's lesson, Thuy addressed the class.

"Dear friends, I hope you all had a good weekend and are ready for a new day. As you know, this is our final week of the short-term course. I'd be grateful if you could spend fifteen minutes sharing your honest feedback about the course content, the teaching methods and my own performance as your instructor, so I can learn from this and improve future programs."

The class responded enthusiastically. The atmosphere felt almost like a family gathering open, warm, full of laughter. Thuy listened carefully to every comment. Her students expressed confidence that the training would help them in their future work.

"I'd also like to hear about the difficulties you face," Thuy added. "Funding, organization, lack of materials - or even the attitudes of local leaders. All of these affect how a library can function."

The room buzzed with energy. Then suddenly, a sharp knock broke the rhythm.

"Ms Thuy, the director has sent for you," said a clerk standing at the door.

Thuy quickly apologized to her students and took the note from the clerk's hand. One glance at the message and her heart sank. Something was wrong she could feel it.

"I'm sorry, everyone," she said softly. "An urgent matter has come up. Please continue your discussion the class monitor will record your comments and send them to me later."

The director's office was on the second floor of the building behind her classroom. As she climbed the stairs, her mind raced. Could this be about her husband?

Her palms were damp when she knocked on the office door.

"Come in," a voice called.

Thuy stepped inside.

"Good morning, sir. I received your note."

"Sit down," the director said, adjusting his glasses. "I have a few questions." He paused, then continued. "Do you know where your husband is? He hasn't been showing up at his office."

"No, sir," Thuy replied calmly. "He's on a work trip as assigned by his department."

The director nodded slowly. "From today, you'll be transferred to another unit. The board has decided to assign someone else to take over your class."

"Sir," Thuy said, trying to keep her voice steady, "I've been responsible for this course from the beginning. There's only one week left before it ends. Please allow me to finish what I started."

"This is a decision from the board," he said curtly. "It takes effect today. Your department head will inform you of your new assignment."

"I'd like to understand the reason," she pressed quietly. "Why such a sudden change when my work isn't yet complete?"

"You are expected to follow the directives of your superiors," he said coldly. "Please hand over your duties to the replacement."

Thuy knew there was no point in arguing. It was already decided. She rose, nodded politely and left the room.

That morning, teaching had been her one escape - her brief refuge from the chaos in her mind. Her students' energy had given her a sense of purpose. Now, even that had been taken away. The blow hit hard, leaving her hollow and lightheaded.

Taking a deep breath, Thuy composed herself and returned to the classroom. Standing before her students, she announced the news and said her goodbyes, her voice calm, though her heart trembled beneath the surface.

Back in the technical department, there was still no news. The head of the unit had no idea who would replace her. The day dragged on slowly, filled with confusion and unease.

That evening, Thuy and her daughter ate dinner earlier than usual. Since moving into the new apartment, life had grown quieter. There were no more pigs to feed, no chickens to tend, no vegetable patch to water everything they had was confined to one narrow room. At the collective housing, life had always been full of noise and activity. Here, time seemed to move differently slower, heavier.

Now, at least, Thuy had more time with her daughter. She helped Hien practice reading and writing, and sometimes they coloured pictures together. Little Hien was delighted by this new routine, often singing or telling stories about her friends at the nursery.

"Mum," Hien said, grinning mischievously as she sat on Thuy's lap, "I like it when you stay home with me. You don't have to go to work anymore, okay?"

Thuy smiled and kissed her daughter's forehead. "You're such a good girl. But Mum and Dad have to work so we can take care of the whole family. And you have to go to the nursery to play and learn with your friends, remember? We all have our jobs to do."

"I love you the most, Mum!" Hien said brightly.

After putting her child to bed, Thuy sat down to knit. The room was quiet, though from time to time she could hear faint voices drifting in from the neighbours. Her hands moved automatically; the rhythm of the needles came easily now. Her body worked, but her mind was far away.

The director's cold words from that morning still echoed in her ears. His tone, so distant and indifferent, had unsettled her deeply. He had once been kind - almost fatherly - but now his face seemed pale, heavy, withdrawn. Was he ill? Or was it something else?

He had asked about Binh. About her husband.

Thuy's heart tightened. Was this because of the war along the northern border? Because her husband was of Chinese descent? Was that enough to make her guilty by association? When had she become a victim of the war without even realizing it?

She had been forced to stop the work she loved most work she had poured her heart into. No explanation, only orders to obey. Her husband had abandoned her because she was Vietnamese. Now, because he was of Hoa descent, she was being punished for it.

Her thoughts spiraled endlessly. *What will happen tomorrow? What else could they take from me?*

Outside, the whole building seemed to be asleep. Only Thuy sat awake, knitting through the silence sweaters and hats to keep others warm through the winter. But who, she wondered, would keep her warm?

When the alarm clock finally rang, she could barely move. She woke Hien for nursery, though she herself wanted nothing more than to stay in bed. Something in her gut told her that this day would not be a good one.

She remembered the letter she had received a few days earlier from Phuong, her old school friend - a maths teacher in Dong Da district, Hanoi. Phuong had written with anger and despair.

Her husband, also of Hoa descent, had just been dismissed from his construction job for "political reasons." They had two small children and now no income. The school had not fired Phuong, but her teaching hours had been cut sharply. Thuy read the letter again and again, unable to shake the feeling that her own fate would soon mirror her friend's.

As she was gathering her books that morning, a clerk came to summon her once more. Her heart sank. The director again.

She walked toward his office, her steps slow, her pulse thudding in her ears. Standing at the door, she knocked lightly.

"Come in."

"Good morning, sir. You asked to see me?"

"Ms Thuy," the director began, "do you know where your husband is? He hasn't been at his office."

"My husband has been on a work trip since Monday morning."

"Tell me the truth. He didn't go on any work trip, your department head informed me. Where did he go?"

"I really don't know, sir," Thuy said, her voice trembling.

He stared at her for a moment, then spoke coldly. "Go back to your office. Think carefully. You can give me an answer later."

Thuy left, her knees weak. The moment she sat down, Ms Xoan from administration entered, holding a paper.

"There's an urgent matter," she said. "You've been asked to come see us immediately."

Thuy rose slowly, her swollen belly heavy, her body near its limit.

In the administrative room, three employees were chatting idly. Thuy nodded to them, then went straight to the desk of the department head.

"Good morning, sir. You needed to see me?"

"Ms Thuy, the board of directors has decided that you're to move again this week."

"But why?" Thuy's voice wavered. "I only moved into the new building a week ago."

"That's the order from above. I'm just carrying it out. Due to the 'political situation,' you must relocate immediately."

"Where am I supposed to go?" Thuy asked, exasperated. "I'm heavily pregnant and it's just me and my little girl."

"Where's your husband?"

"He's away on a work trip."

"Then why does the board say they don't know where he is?"

"How would I know? Just tell me where I'm supposed to move to?"

In the span of two weeks, Thuy had been forced to move twice. It was hard to believe but it was true. The weight of it all pressed down on her and her child, while her husband had vanished without a word. She couldn't confide in anyone, not even her father or siblings. They had no idea what she was going through.

The baby kicked and rolled restlessly. There was no way to refuse the orders of her superiors. Her life had become precarious, hollow and unbearably lonely. Still, she told herself to stay calm, she couldn't let her child sense her fear. Thuy was the only one left to protect her little girl.

She needed to plan the move. As she walked back to her room, her mind was racing, calculating what to do next.

The administrative manager led Thuy to a place about five hundred meters from the office. He pointed to a dilapidated thatched hut. The lime walls were cracked, stained and peeling. Inside, broken bricks and splintered wood lay scattered across the floor. The place looked like it had been abandoned for years.

"This is your new accommodation. You'll live here from now on," the manager said flatly.

"My family is supposed to live here?" Thuy's voice trembled. "This isn't a house. It's an abandoned storeroom!"

The man didn't respond. His task was done and he walked away, leaving her standing there alone. Thuy could barely believe her eyes but she had heard him clearly. This was the place they were giving her. A place no one else would dare to live in.

Next door was another decrepit building, once a warehouse for old books. Inside, shelves sagged under piles of torn, termite-eaten newspapers and magazines. Why hadn't they been burned or cleared out long ago? Thuy looked around, her heart sinking. The baby kicked hard again, dragging her back to the harsh reality.

Her first task was to clean. She went to ask her friends Ha and Hue for help. They sent their younger brothers to assist with the move. When the young men saw the state of the house, their faces darkened with anger.

"I'm just a lowly employee," Thuy said quietly. "All I can do is follow orders. I have no power, no one to turn to. For now, I just need to make this place livable."

Ha's gentle, usually soft-spoken brother suddenly raised his voice. "Don't worry, we'll help you and your daughter get settled. We won't let them treat you like this."

Thuy's eyes filled with tears. "I haven't even told my father yet. He'd only worry. And my colleagues..." she hesitated, "...they avoid me now. No one wants to be associated with me. I'm truly grateful to you all."

The three of them spent the entire day scrubbing, sweeping and clearing out the debris. The next morning, they borrowed a wooden ox-cart to move her belongings the bed, the cupboard, pots and basins. It took two strong men the whole day just to carry everything down from the third floor.

Using the spare wooden planks from the warehouse, they managed to build a small partition for bathing and cooking. At least this way, the house wouldn't reek of smoke and kerosene.

That afternoon, when Thuy picked up Hien from the nursery, the little girl stopped at the doorway of their new "home," staring wide-eyed.

"Mum! Is this where we live now? Why don't we go back to the other house?"

"That's right, my love. From now on, we'll live here. It's closer to where I work."

"I didn't like the old house anyway," Hien said cheerfully. "It was too tiring to climb all those stairs, Mum!"

Thuy smiled faintly, her heart aching. The house was barely large enough for a bed, a wardrobe and a few essentials. Still, transformed from an abandoned storeroom into something livable, she found herself almost *grateful* for the order - if only to stop moving.

A few people at the office knew she'd been granted emergency leave to relocate, yet no one came to help. Not a word of concern from the trade union or the women's association - though they were always quick to collect monthly dues.

That night, after bathing, Hien played with the doll her father had once bought her. Thuy cleaned a little more before lying down beside her child. Hien fell asleep easily, untroubled, wrapped in the innocence of childhood.

Thuy stared up at the roof. The wooden beams above were warped and faded, barely holding the frame together. Spiderwebs stretched across them like threads of neglect. From the next room came the constant rustling and squeaking of rats. Sometimes they scurried across the floor like shadows. A few even brushed against her feet through the mosquito net.

She shuddered, worried they might gnaw through the net. Were the rats angry that strangers had invaded their territory?

Exhausted, Thuy drifted into uneasy sleep only to wake with a start. A rat had nibbled at her toes. She gasped softly, pulling her feet in.

Another long night full of noise, fear and unanswered questions. What misfortune would come next?

Outside in the yard, the sun was already awake. Thuy got up to cook a small pot of porridge for breakfast. She hadn't had the appetite or strength to eat the night before, but this morning she felt hungry. The baby in her belly was kicking restlessly, asking for food. Thuy rubbed her belly gently and whispered, *"I'm sorry, baby."*

The new house was closer to both her office and Hien's nursery. After a quiet breakfast, Thuy took her daughter to school, then made her way to work a little earlier than usual.

A few people were already in the office. They looked up briefly, nodded without a word and went back to what they were doing. Thuy went straight to the department head's office. Nothing had changed since her two days off to move, only a few boxes of books were piled in the corner. She sat down, waiting. When the department head walked in, he spoke without preamble.

"The director wants to see you right away."

Again. Thuy stood up and walked slowly toward the director's office, her heart tightening with every step.

"Come in," came the same hoarse voice.

She opened the door and entered.

"Sit down, please. We need to talk."

Thuy lowered herself carefully onto the chair opposite the director.

"Your husband didn't go on the work trip with his colleagues," the director began. "He left without permission. That's a violation of regulations."

Thuy sat silently, unsure what to say. His tone hardened.

"According to the directive from higher authorities, all Vietnamese citizens of Chinese origin are now required to resign from their positions - including those in the Culture and Education sectors. They are to resettle and build new lives in the economic zones in Lam Dong Province."

He paused, then continued more sternly, "Your husband is of the Hoa people. That means the Board of Directors had planned to move your entire family to the new economic zone. But now that he has voluntarily left his job and because you are Vietnamese, you have two options."

He adjusted his glasses and looked her straight in the eye. "One - if you wish to continue working, you must file for divorce and give custody of your child to him. Two - if you refuse, you must submit your resignation. You have one week to decide."

For a long moment, Thuy couldn't hear anything. Her mind went blank. The words didn't make sense.

The director's hoarse voice cut through the fog, urging her to "think carefully."

She stood up in a daze and walked out, her body moving but her soul left behind.

Back in the office, everyone avoided her eyes. No one asked what had happened. She sat motionless at her desk, staring at nothing, until the end-of-day bell startled her back to reality. Someone had to remind her to go pick up her child.

As she left, a group of students from her short-term library course were walking toward her, laughing and chatting.

"Good afternoon, Teacher Thuy! We're having a little party to celebrate finishing the course won't you come join us?" a girl said brightly.

Thuy forced a smile, trying to keep her voice steady.

"Thank you, but I can't today. I wish you all the best."

She turned away quickly. Behind her, she could still hear laughter and whispers that cut through her like tiny knives. She kept her eyes on the ground and said nothing.

Thuy cycled to the nursery to pick up Hien. At home, as she prepared dinner, she could hear her daughter singing softly, brushing her doll's hair.

"Last night I dreamt I met Uncle Ho..." Hien paused. "Mum! Today my teacher taught me this song. But why do my classmates call me Vietnamese of Chinese origin? What does that mean, Mum?"

Thuy froze. A cold fear crawled up her spine. Even the children had begun to echo this cruel language. *My poor child,* she thought. *What else will we have to endure?*

She had believed she was the only one suffering this humiliation but now even her little girl was being branded and shamed.

She thought of Binh. *Where are you now? Do you even think of us? Do you know what we're going through because of you?*

She pulled Hien close and stroked her hair. "Your father is Chinese, that's why your friends say that. But it's okay. Mum loves you more than anything in the world, my darling."

Hien smiled, wrapping her small arms tightly around her mother's neck. "I love you the most, Mum!"

Thuy held her child, letting the warmth of that embrace steady her trembling heart.

The early summer heat was stifling, heavy in the air and pressing down on her like a weight. The tiny, narrow house felt suffocating and Thuy's head throbbed as if it might burst. She couldn't shake the director's words from that morning: *"You're the wife of a Chinese man... you must file for divorce... or resign."*

She turned restlessly in bed, thoughts circling around little Hien. Not only did she receive no sympathy or encouragement from anyone, but there were also those who seemed determined to make her life harder.

Next door, the rats were running wild again, scratching and squeaking as though taunting her. Did they sleep all day just to cause chaos at night? It was true - humans and rats could never share the same space.

*What answer should I give the director?* she thought. *How long will I even have this job?* The questions spun in her head until exhaustion finally pulled her into uneasy sleep.

When the sun rose, its warm light poured through the small window and onto her face. Thuy startled awake and turned to see Hien still fast asleep.

She got up, opened the door and let the morning sunlight flood the room. Taking a broom, she swept the dust from the doorway. Looking up, she saw Lien walking toward the market.

"Oh! Thuy, you live here?" Lien exclaimed in surprise. "I didn't know you'd moved!"

Lien was Thuy's younger cousin, who worked at the town post office.

"Good morning! I just moved here two days ago," Thuy replied. "Are you heading to the market already?"

"Yes, I'm buying some meat to make porridge for my little one. I'll come by later, okay?"

"Please do," said Thuy. "I actually have something I need to ask you."

Thuy planned to tell her cousin everything. She knew there were more obstacles ahead, and that peace was still far away. She would have to prepare and think carefully about her next steps.

After waking Hien, Thuy folded their blankets, washed her daughter's face and started to cook rice for breakfast. Just then, she heard someone calling from outside.

"Sister Thuy, it's me."

It was Lien.

"Come in," Thuy said quickly. "Let's talk before I have to leave for work."

Lien stepped inside and looked around the small, dimly lit room. Her expression turned worried.

"Why are you living here?" she asked.

"It's a long story," Thuy sighed. "I'll explain later. But I really need your help."

Lien reached into her basket and pulled out a small package wrapped in dried banana leaves.

"I bought sticky rice with mung beans for Hien's breakfast," she said, handing it to Thuy. "Now tell me what's going on? Does your father know you're here?"

"Aunty Lien brought you some sticky rice," Thuy said to her daughter. "Say thank you and eat by the door while mummy talks."

Hien smiled, said thank you politely and sat by the door with the warm package in her hands.

"You've probably heard about what's been happening between Vietnam and China lately?" Thuy began quietly.

"I've heard bits and pieces," said Lien. "But I don't know the details."

"Because Binh is Chinese," Thuy said, her voice trembling, "I've been accused of all sorts of things these past few weeks. They've already forced me to move twice. Yesterday, they demanded that I divorce him and hand Hien over to his family. If I refuse, I'll lose my job."

Lien's eyes widened. "That's terrible. What are you going to do?"

"I don't know who I can trust," Thuy whispered. "I'm being watched. I can't even tell my father, he'd only worry and there's nothing he could do."

"Tell me what you need," said Lien firmly. "I'll do whatever I can."

"You must promise to keep this secret from everyone," Thuy said. "Not even your husband and definitely not your coworkers."

"I understand," Lien nodded.

"When you're at work, please send a telegram to this address." Thuy handed her a small folded note with her sister-in-law's address in Hanoi written neatly on it. "You have to be very careful, if anyone finds out, it'll ruin everything."

"I'll be careful," Lien said with quiet determination.

"Send this message exactly as I say: *'Come back to collect me and Hien immediately.'* Can you do that?"

Lien looked at her cousin, eyes full of sympathy. "You're so close to giving birth... I can't believe you've had to go through all this alone. Of course, I'll help. I'll send it today and let you know as soon as I hear back."

She hugged Thuy tightly before leaving, whispering words of comfort. Hien gave her a cheerful wave goodbye and returned to her mother's side.

Thuy quickly dressed Hien for nursery, her mind already spinning with plans. There was no time to waste. She lifted her daughter onto the bicycle seat, steadying herself as she climbed on. Her belly was heavy, slowing her down, but she gritted her teeth and began to pedal slowly but determinedly, into another uncertain day.

When Thuy arrived at the office, she noticed that the head of the department hadn't assigned her any real work.

"Ms Thuy doesn't need to do technical cataloguing anymore. Come over here and tidy up this pile of new books," he said to the room without looking at her.

Thuy knew he was just following orders, doing his part to make her life harder. Still, it stung. Sorting books was work for new assistants, not for someone with her years of experience. She kept silent and did as she was told until the director's secretary appeared at the door and called her name.

Thuy had been expecting it. She calmly followed the secretary down the corridor, hearing the whispers and gossip rise behind her as soon as she left.

She stood at the director's door, waiting for that familiar hoarse voice.

"Come in."

"Have you made your decision?" he demanded. "Have you finished writing the divorce petition? Give it to me."

"I haven't written it," Thuy replied, her voice firm. "You can't force a husband and wife to divorce each other. It's unjust morally and legally."

The director's expression hardened. "Your husband is Chinese. He abandoned his job without permission. He's a traitor! You'd better think carefully. Come see me tomorrow. I'm already being lenient with you."

Thuy turned and walked out as quickly as she could. She didn't want to hear another word. Her anger burned hot beneath her ribs as she thought about his threats.

Back in the building, she passed groups of colleagues. No one spoke to her. They only glanced sideways, whispered among themselves, then turned away as if she carried some contagious disease.

These were the same people who used to coo over little Hien when Thuy brought her to the office. But she couldn't blame them. The system had made them this way afraid, careful, unwilling to be associated with anyone under suspicion. Thuy felt a sharp pain in her chest. She was utterly alone.

Right then, she knew what she had to do. She would write her resignation before they could fire her.

Later that day, Lien came by to tell her she had sent the telegram to Hanoi that morning. Now, all Thuy could do was wait for news from her husband.

In the office, she was no longer allowed to do professional work. Instead, she was ordered around like a janitor. Her colleagues avoided her eyes, their silence heavy and cruel. The air in the room felt stifling.

Stepping outside for a breath, a thought flashed through her mind she needed to withdraw all her savings before they froze her account.

On her way to the bank, she ran into Ha.

"Where are you going, Thuy?" Ha asked, concern in her voice. "What's happening now?"

Thuy rubbed her stomach, trying to hold back tears. She had been craving kindness for weeks and that one question broke her composure.

"The board of directors want me to divorce my husband and hand our daughter over to him to live in some 'new zone' for the Chinese. If I refuse, they'll force me out of my job. How will I raise two children with no income?"

Ha's eyes filled with pity and anger. "That's cruel. What are you going to do?"

"What do you think I should do?" Thuy asked, her voice trembling.

"There's a Chinese family living near me," Ha whispered. "They fled to Hai Phong yesterday, hoping to go abroad. The mother and two sons. The eldest was an army veteran, but they've been watching him since his discharge. He couldn't work anywhere."

Thuy nodded slowly. "So they ran away."

"Yes. I don't think they'll let you live in peace either."

"You're right," Thuy said quietly. "I'll resign. Staying is impossible. But please, don't tell anyone."

"Of course not. I wish I could help more, but you know how things are."

"I know. Just hearing your sympathy means a lot. Everyone at work looks at me like I'm a criminal. I don't even know what's going to happen to me and Hien."

Ha touched her arm gently. "You'll get through this, Thuy. Take care of your health and the baby."

They parted reluctantly.

Thuy went straight to the bank. It was nearly lunchtime. Behind the counter sat a young woman with a round, gentle face, focused on her paperwork.

"Hello," Thuy said softly.

"Hello, how can I help you?" the woman asked kindly.

"I'd like to withdraw from my savings account."

"Do you have your savings book and ID?"

Thuy handed them over. The woman flipped through the papers. "How much would you like to withdraw?"

"All of it, please."

"All of it?" the clerk looked up. "Then you won't receive any interest."

"I know, but my baby's due soon, I need this money," Thuy said quietly.

The transaction was completed, and she carefully slipped the cash into her pocket. Slowly, she stepped out of the bank into the blinding sun and made her way to pick up little Hien.

The midday heat was unbearable. The trees along the road drooped wearily and even beneath her conical hat, Thuy's face flushed red like a cooked prawn. Her steps were slow and heavy. The asphalt radiated a burnt, acrid smell that clung to the air. Everything around her seemed to press in suffocating her body and mind.

For lunch, Thuy cooked noodles and fed her daughter, all the while thinking about what needed to be sorted out quickly. The first issue was money. She needed as much as she could gather. Anything that could be sold - must be sold. But it had to be done quietly, so no one would suspect her intentions.

That afternoon at work, Thuy was again given odd jobs - meaningless tasks to humiliate her. She worked in silence, weighed down by anxiety. Her thoughts kept drifting to Binh - had he received the telegram yet? She decided she'd have to write her maternity leave application first, then her resignation straight after.

Overcome by the stifling heat, Thuy wandered to the doorway for some air. There, she saw Mrs Chin, the chief accountant, standing by the water jug.

"Hot day, isn't it, sister?" Thuy said, trying to start a conversation.

Mrs Chin, a tall, slim woman in her mid-thirties, with long black hair down to her waist, smiled kindly. Her daughter was the same age as Hien - the two used to play together whenever they came to the office.

"How are you, Thuy? When's the baby due?" she asked.

"It's nearly time now," Thuy replied.

"Your belly looks low, why don't you apply for maternity leave early?"

"There's still more than a month to go. Can I really ask that soon?"

"If you fill in the form, I'll arrange it for you," Chin said softly. "I understand what you're going through."

"Thank you. Will you be at work tomorrow?"

"Yes. And one more thing" Chin leaned closer and whispered, "We've got a lot of cash transactions right now. If you write the form quickly, I'll get it approved straight away."

Gratitude welled up in Thuy's chest. Finally, something seemed to be going her way. They parted, heading back to their offices in opposite directions. A cool breeze brushed her face, briefly lifting the oppressive heat of the afternoon.

When Thuy stepped back into her department, no one looked up. She sat down quietly and began writing her maternity leave form first, then her resignation letter.

As she wrote, her thoughts drifted to Dao - her old secondary school friend who had quit school early to help her parents on their farm. Thuy had seen her just last week at the market, selling vegetables. Dao's life hadn't been easy. Her brother had been in the army for nearly ten years with no word. Her fiancé, also a soldier and of Hoa descent had been discharged after the war and placed under constant surveillance. He was forbidden from leaving the district.

Dao had been forced by her Party unit to break off the engagement. As a Party member, she wasn't allowed to "violate Party policy." They saw her fiancé as the enemy and her as his accomplice. Dao hadn't dared to protest. To protect her family, she agreed. But her heart bled every day. Many Vietnamese women married to Chinese men were suffering the same fate just like Thuy.

When both forms were ready, Thuy carried them to the director's office and knocked.

"Who is it? Come in!"

"Good afternoon, Director."

"What do you want, Ms Thuy?" he asked without looking up from his papers.

Thuy stepped forward and placed the two forms on his desk. "Sir, these are my resignation and maternity leave applications."

He glanced over them briefly. "So, you've made up your mind?" His tone softened slightly. "Alright, the board and I will review your request. You'll have an official answer tomorrow."

"Sir," Thuy added calmly, "I'm close to giving birth, so I've also included my maternity leave form. I hope you'll take note that I've worked here for thirteen years."

"Don't worry. We'll consider it carefully," the director replied curtly.

Thuy left the office feeling oddly relieved. She didn't know what tomorrow would bring, but at least she had acted taken control of her fate. As she walked past the other departments, she caught glimpses of faces peeking out, then retreating. The whispers followed her, but she no longer cared. She kept her head high and walked straight on.

That evening, after dinner, the harsh sunlight faded behind the mountains. Streetlights flickered on, and a grey dusk settled over the town. Another lonely night began for Thuy. Though the heat of the day had eased, her white blouse was still damp with sweat. The small electric fan hummed, struggling to cool the room.

Determined to finish the last sweater in her batch, Thuy knitted steadily while little Hien sat at the table, tracing her letters - A, B, C - through tired yawns.

"It's bedtime, Hien," Thuy said gently. "You can write more tomorrow."

Obediently, the child lay down beside her mother. "Mum, sing the stork song."

In the dim light, the image of a young mother knitting beside her sleeping child was deeply tender - yet achingly lonely. The soft lullaby floated through the quiet night:

"...Ah... ah... the stork wades along the riverbank..."

The little stork soon drifted into dreams, but the mother remained awake wading through her own dark river of worries.

Then a sudden sound outside. A knock at the door. Another, softer this time.

"Who's there?" Thuy's voice trembled.

"It's me. Open the door," a whisper came through the crack.

"Who?"

"It's me, Hien's father. Open up, quickly."

Thuy froze, then recognised the voice. Her heart leapt. She rushed to unlock the door.

Binh slipped inside quickly. Thuy was both relieved and terrified. She glanced outside, then locked the door behind him.

"We've been waiting for you," she whispered. "Did you get my telegram?"

"Yes, I got it. The boat didn't have enough people to leave the port, so I came back to Hanoi. That's when I received your telegram. I took the night train as soon as I could. How have things been here?"

Thuy shook her head in disbelief. He had no idea. "Since the day you left, the Party has made everything difficult for me. They've questioned me about you. At work, they told me to divorce you and hand Hien over. They said I'd lose my job if I didn't follow their demands. We had to move again into this derelict building."

At that point, Thuy choked up and couldn't speak any more. Binh pulled his wife into his arms. "You can't stay here. We have to go to Hai Phong together. We can take a boat and escape. We'll need a lot of money and the right documents, but the boat needs more people before it sets off, so we can all go together. What do you think?"

"I've thought about that too. I've handed in my resignation and tomorrow I'll find someone to sell some of the things we have. I've withdrawn all the money from the bank. For now, you must stay here until everything is organised."

"Alright, I trust you. I know you'll handle everything discreetly."

That night, the couple whispered quietly to each other. From outside the building came only the rustling and scurrying of rats a good cover, since anyone spying would never suspect that inside were two frightened people nervously planning their escape.

The sky was still dark when Thuy cycled to Ha's house. It was only half a kilometre away, but she pedalled as fast as she could. Ha was preparing breakfast when she heard a knock at the door and an urgent voice.

"Sister Ha, please open the door for me!" Ha opened it, startled to see Thuy.

"Thuy? Are you alright?" Ha asked anxiously. "Let me in and I'll explain." The two of them stepped into the yard.

"Sister, I urgently need some cash. Some of the wood I left at your house was meant for a bed and a wardrobe, but now I have to sell it."

Ha wasn't surprised to hear this. "I was actually hoping you'd leave that wood with me. I didn't think you'd be using it any time soon, living where you are. I can buy it from you right now."

Thuy was so grateful for her friend's words. "Oh my God, thank you! I hope you understand. I really need the money today. Is that alright?"

"Don't worry, I understand. I'll withdraw the money later and bring it to you this afternoon."

"And please keep this between us?" Thuy added softly.

"I know, don't worry. How much do you need? I don't have much, but I'll help as much as I can." Thuy was deeply moved. "You've always been like a sister to me. After I lost my first child, you were always there for me. You've helped me through so many difficult times. I'll miss you terribly."

Thuy spoke through tears and sobs. Ha hugged her tightly, wanting to protect her like an older sister.

"Be strong. We understand each other that's enough. Now go home and get everything ready. Wipe your tears and don't let anyone see you cry, alright?" she said firmly, though her own eyes were full of tears.

Thuy obediently wiped her eyes and said goodbye to her friend. When she got home, Hien was playing with her father, chattering happily as she told him stories.

"Hien's a good girl and loves her mum and dad, doesn't she?" Thuy asked gently.

"Yes, I love you both very much."

"Then listen to me. Today you must stay home with your dad, but you two can't laugh or talk loudly, or they might take your dad away. Can you remember that?"

Hearing that her father might be taken away, Hien bowed her head in fear.

"I'll remember and I won't go to nursery today?"

"Yes, you'll stay at home. Mummy has something to do and will be back soon."

Pushing her bike out through the door, Thuy reminded her husband, "I'm going to the market to buy a few things. Don't forget to cook something for you and Hien."

"Alright, I won't."

In her mind, Thuy's plan was for the whole family to leave the next day. She bought some vegetables and a piece of pork. Then, at the grocery shop, she picked up six tins of condensed milk and gently rubbed her belly.

"Lie still and be good. I can't rest at all today, there's too much to worry about. I daren't even think about when I gave birth to your brother. The hospital was careless and irresponsible. They suffocated him before he was even born. It broke my heart, but I won't let anything bad happen to you."

Suddenly, the baby kicked hard. Thuy saw her stomach bulge and smiled sadly.

"Oh, are you blaming me? It wasn't my fault. How was I to know what was happening? I trusted the doctors and nurses at the hospital..." She rubbed her stomach to comfort the baby.

At the grocery shop, she spoke quietly to the woman behind the counter. They had known each other for some time, so Thuy sat beside her and agreed on what she could sell. She would bring the goods over later that day. The prices were low, but she needed the money quickly and had no choice.

Thuy had been saving all these Chinese goods at home - perfume, face cream, handkerchiefs all untouched, as she hadn't dared use them. Now, she couldn't take them with her anyway. There was also some beautiful blue wool she had planned to use to knit something for her baby, an antique tea set and a Chinese quilt. She would have to clean everything and sell it. Thuy wanted to give some of these things to Ha and Chin, both of whom had helped her so much.

As well as selling what she could to raise money, Thuy needed to have photos taken of herself and Hien, they would be required for their travel documents. She planned to ask her cousin's husband, who was a photographer, to take them straight away.

While walking and calculating everything in her head, Thuy returned home and saw Binh helping Hien change her clothes.

"Hien and I have eaten. There's a bowl of noodles on the table for you - you must be starving after running around all morning," Binh said kindly.

"I am tired and hungry. I bought a rice cake for Hien," Thuy replied, sitting down.

"After I eat, I'll go to the office to see if they've made a decision about my maternity leave. While I'm gone, could you check what things we could sell? I've found someone willing to buy them. If anyone asks why we're selling so much, just say we need the money for me to go back to my hometown to give birth."

Thuy paused to eat some noodles. "When I get back from the office, I'll take Hien to have our photos taken."

"Alright. Please be careful," Binh said.

When Thuy arrived at the office, she sensed that today was different. She greeted everyone as she walked in.

"Good morning, Ms Thuy. I heard you've asked for maternity leave, is that right?" the department head asked. News travels fast, Thuy thought.

"Yes, yesterday I handed the application to the director. My due date is very near and I'm feeling exhausted. I'll take my child to my parents' home so I can rest and be looked after before the birth."

As she spoke, the secretary entered. "Ms Thuy, the director would like to see you."

Thuy quietly made her way to the director's office, feeling calmer than she had in days. She knocked firmly on the door.

"Come in!"

Thuy opened the door. The director looked up and removed his glasses.

"Ah, Ms Thuy. The board of directors has reviewed your resignation request. They've agreed to grant you maternity leave and accept your resignation."

He handed Thuy two copies of the decision. "Now go to the finance department. Give this decision to the chief accountant for signing and approval, they'll issue your payment. Make sure to hand over any remaining work before you leave. The decision takes effect from today. You are no longer an officer of the Department of Culture."

These were the final words she would hear in the job she had worked twice as hard as anyone else to achieve. It felt like a stab of pain, but also a release. Thuy turned and walked away confident, calm and without regret.

There went thirteen years of work, thirteen years of her youth devoted to the local government and the socialist state, all ended because two neighbouring countries were fighting over something she could never understand. She was at least relieved that they had paid her at her seniority level and granted her maternity leave. Despite all their corruption, they'd done the right thing in the end.

Thuy went straight to the finance office in the next building. From a distance, she saw Chin standing by the door. "Thuy, did they give you the decision you wanted?" Chin asked with a smile.

"You know already?" Thuy asked in surprise. "News travels faster than lightning here!" She smiled and handed over the two documents.

Chin glanced at them, then took out a pen, wrote *'Agreed to pay the money'* across both papers and signed her name. "Now go to the cashier to collect the money."

Thuy thanked her and they agreed to meet during Chin's lunch break. Several people in the finance department asked about her resignation. She knew they didn't really care, they were just being nosy, as was often the way. Still, she kept a calm expression and chatted with them pleasantly.

Thuy wanted to say goodbye to her co-workers, even though she knew they weren't truly concerned. Some feigned surprise at her departure but didn't ask any real questions. Their indifference and coldness sent a shiver down her spine. Even so, she didn't have time to dwell on farewells; there was still much to do.

The midday heat was growing harsher, yet Thuy felt cold inside. She quickly cycled home to fetch the gift she'd prepared for Chin as a thank you and farewell. The heat rising from the asphalt burned her face, making her feel even more uncomfortable. It wasn't far, but every metre felt heavy.

When she arrived home, Binh was cooking rice and chatting in the kitchen with Hien. Hearing the door open, Hien ran out to greet her mother.

"The rice is almost ready we'll go once we've eaten," Binh said, looking up.

Thuy picked up the gift for Chin. "I've got to go now. I want to give this to Chin at work. If Hien's hungry, feed her first. I'll come back later and then I need to take her to get our photos done."

She hurried off, hoping to catch Chin during her lunch break. As she handed over the gift, Thuy could feel eyes on her. Someone even leaned in and asked quietly if she had anything to sell.

It was the same person who had been avoiding her for days, yet now they weren't ashamed to ask such a question. Thuy simply smiled and shook her head. They looked at her with disbelief, but she ignored them. She said goodbye to Chin, got on her bike and pedalled home, leaving the whispers behind.

They had a simple lunch in their run-down thatched house, but the atmosphere was different that day. Little Hien was cheerful, eating her meal and glancing happily between her parents.

"Eat up, Hien. Afterwards, I'll take you to Mr Tan's house for some photos," Thuy said gently.

Delighted, Hien ate quickly without needing further encouragement.

It was nearly one o'clock when mother and daughter left the house. The sun was fierce, but they couldn't wait. They rode the bicycle through the heat. The photos clearly showed their faces. According to the ID form, the background had to be plain. These photos would be handed to the boat owner. Here, unlike in government offices, no one asked questions, it was all business. Thuy felt a quiet relief at not having to make up excuses. By the time they returned home, the afternoon was already fading.

She had been on her feet all morning, going back and forth without rest and her belly now hung even lower. Lying down at last, Thuy finally felt the weight of her exhaustion.

"Get some rest. I'll call you when dinner's ready," Binh said as he left the room. "You can play with your doll, but be quiet so Mummy can sleep," he told his daughter.

Hien sat quietly beside her mother, hugging her doll. But before long, Thuy remembered another errand. She'd arranged to meet the woman from the grocery shop to sell some goods. So rest would have to wait. She began gathering the items together again. Later, when she returned, Binh wanted to know everything.

"How was it today?" Binh asked, seizing the moment.

"Very good. Work approved my maternity leave, and today was my last day there. I've got all the money we need to buy the boat tickets for me and Hien. The photos are done too." Thuy took a breath. "Tomorrow I'll ask around to see who might buy the bed. It's made of rosewood and still looks new we should get a good price for it. Our pair of water buckets were made from American plane wrecks; I'm sure they'll fetch decent money as well."

"Really?" Binh was surprised that anyone would want to buy their old buckets.

"At times like this, there's always someone willing to buy what others are selling. We just have to be careful with our money - once we've sold everything, that's all we'll have left."

Thuy looked closely at her husband as she spoke. "Tomorrow I'll buy more fabric to make nappies for the baby and I'll need some mosquito netting to use after the birth."

"Do you think we'll be ready to leave in a day or two?"

"Do you know exactly when the boat's leaving?" Thuy asked in return.

"The owner didn't give an exact date - just said it would set sail in about a week."

"Then we'll have to finish everything tomorrow. I want to go home and tell my father."

"I was thinking the same. He'll probably be very sad," Binh agreed, already imagining how heartbroken Thuy would be when she told him.

"Sister Thuy, are you home?" came a voice from outside. It was the woman from the grocery shop. Recognising Thu's voice, Thuy opened the door.

"Come in, please!"

The transaction was quick. One sold while the other examined the goods, mumbling and calculating their worth. Looking at the beautiful, carefully kept rolls of wool, Thuy felt a pang of sadness. She had once dreamed of knitting jumpers for herself and her children. Now she had to give up such small luxuries, clinging to the hope that one day she might have them again. Thu packed everything neatly into a large cloth bag.

"Can you take it all away tonight?" Thuy asked.

"Yes, I'd like to sell everything tomorrow, so don't worry, I'll take it home this evening."

Fortunately, Thu lived nearby, barely a kilometre away. Within an hour, everything was finished as planned. The house grew quiet again a heavy silence settled over them, each lost in thought. Thuy wondered what was going through Binh's mind. Little Hien whispered softly to her doll. As for Thuy, her head swirled with the day's events, her emotions tangled and heavy.

Heavily pregnant, she hadn't had a moment's peace. She forced herself to stay strong under the strain; her nerves were constantly on edge. Thuy sat still as wood, watching everything she owned slip from her hands. What would tomorrow bring?

"The food's ready, let's eat," Binh said, breaking her reverie.

Thuy blinked, coming back to herself. Hien looked up at her mother. "Daddy's calling, let's go and eat."

Looking at her daughter, Thuy returned to reality. Her heart ached with love. She had to endure for Hien's sake. The little girl took her mother's hand happily and went to sit at the table.

On the table sat a plate of boiled spinach, an omelette, and a small, faded bowl of salted roasted peanuts. A simple meal for the unfortunate family in their dilapidated house. The atmosphere was calm; they spoke quietly, as if trying to hide both their excitement and their unease.

Outside, the occasional gust of wind rustled the trees. The sky was pitch black, the silence broken only by the sound of leaves whispering. The final days before departure dragged on endlessly.

Later that evening, Thuy and Binh would take Hien to her grandfather's house. It was going to be one of the hardest conversations of Thuy's life. Even now, she could feel a lump rising in her throat and tears stinging her eyes.

The road to her father's house was about three kilometres long. Thuy had walked it countless times with her school friends. The road by the Gia Bay bridge over the Cau River still bore the scars left by American bombs. Back then, Thuy and her friends had been fearless, cycling past corpses, the wounded and scattered limbs without flinching, it had been a grimly normal sight.

Many roads had since been paved smooth, erasing the traces of war. Yet as Thuy walked this familiar path one last time, she was leaving her homeland because of another war.

Crossing the bridge, the banyan trees on both sides of the road swayed in the wind, as if waving goodbye. The dim streetlights reflected the silhouettes of Thuy, her husband and their baby girl. The road was deserted, with only the occasional passer-by. It was a dark, cold night and they were approaching Thuy's family home.

The thatched house with three rooms gradually appeared before them. It was the quietest corner of the town, far from the traffic. The three of them went into the backyard. The dog wagged his tail and ran around barking, recognising that they weren't strangers. Thuy's father came out, his smile showing how happy he was to see them.

"Dad, have you had dinner yet?" Thuy asked, then reminded her daughter, "Hien, what do you say when you see Grandpa?"

Little Hien said softly, "Hello, Grandpa."

Thuy's father looked at Hien and gently replied, "I had dinner a long time ago. Why have you come so late? Oh! Why does my puppy look so down?"

Binh greeted his father-in-law, parked the bike outside the house and then, with Thuy, walked inside. Grandfather and granddaughter held hands as they followed behind.

Thuy looked around and asked, "Is Aunty not home, Dad?"

Bay was Mr Lan's second wife. She came out of the kitchen and said quickly, "Sorry, I was tidying up. Have you come to visit us?"

Hien sat quietly on her grandpa's lap. Thuy replied in a sorrowful tone, "Yes, I have something to tell you both."

"Father, Aunty… I'm sure you've heard about the fighting between China and Vietnam at the border?"

"Yes, I've heard," Thuy's father said calmly. "Some of the Hoa families living around here have sold their belongings and moved to China."

Thuy continued, "The situation at my office is terrible. Because I'm married to a Chinese man, they've given me two choices: either our whole family must move to Lam Dong province in the South, where they're gathering all the Hoa people, or I have to divorce Binh and lose Hien."

She paused, her voice trembling. "We've decided what we're going to do. I've quit my job and we're going to take a boat from Hai Phong to go abroad."

Mr Lan couldn't believe his ears. Thuy looked at her father, waiting.

"But you're pregnant and almost due! Hien is still so young how can you cross the ocean by boat? Have you really thought this through?" Mr Lan said desperately.

Thuy stayed calm and tried to comfort her father. "I have to, Dad. There's no other choice. I could lose Hien. I have to go. Life here won't be the same if I stay. I'm sorry, Dad. Please try to understand. I've already prepared the money to pay the boat owner."

He knew his daughter's words were final. There was nothing he could say to change her mind. He just sat there, stunned, his eyes fixed blankly on Thuy. His voice broke.

"You're in trouble, but I can't help. I don't have any money to give you. *'The boats follow the rudders, the girls follow their husbands.'* I'm heartbroken... what will happen to you all?"

Seeing her father's eyes redden, Thuy felt deep pain and regret for leaving her old father behind. Her two younger brothers were still in the army, she didn't even know if they were alive and they had no idea what was happening to her. The room fell silent, heavy with sorrow. Bay sat still, not having said a word since she came in.

"So, when will you leave?" Mr Lan finally asked.

"Tomorrow morning. We'll have to leave early to reach the boat on time."

Mr Lan hugged little Hien tightly, not wanting to let go of his only grandchild. He knew he was already losing her.

They sat for a while longer, then Thuy asked her father and stepmother for permission to leave so they could prepare for the morning.

"Tomorrow morning, I'll be there to say goodbye," Mr Lan said solemnly.

Little Hien said goodbye to her grandpa. Thuy and her husband sadly pushed their bicycles away, waving goodbye to her father and stepmother. As Thuy walked, she looked back at the beloved house one last time. In her heart, she wondered when or if she would ever return to see her father and her childhood home again.

At nearly 5 o'clock in the morning, Thuy was ready to go. She knew she couldn't take much, but she packed all the essentials into a large, sturdy cloth bag. They also had one suitcase containing Hien's clothes, nappies for the baby and a few tins of *Ong Tho* milk for when the baby was born. The three of them went to the coach station in the centre of town. Their first stop would be Hanoi. The drizzling rain made the air even more stuffy and uncomfortable than they already felt. Thuy's father was waiting for them at the coach station.

At 6 o'clock, the first coach of the day departed for Hanoi. From afar, Thuy could see her father pacing back and forth impatiently. She felt deeply sorry for him. Binh carried the large cloth bag and in his other hand a small suitcase. Thuy held Hien's hand until Mr Lan hurried over to pick up his grandchild. Tears, mingling with the rain, ran down his face. It was the first time Thuy had ever seen her father cry. He had always been a strict parent, but one who showed his children great affection.

"You go in good health. Be a good girl and remember to listen to your parents," he said softly to Hien.

Seeing her grandfather's tears, Hien wiped them away with her small hand.

"Don't cry, Grandpa. I'm only going away for a few days, then I'll come back and bring you some sweets. You must be a good grandpa!" she said, trying to comfort him.

Mr Lan hugged Hien tightly to his chest, choking back sobs. "I know... yes... I know..." No one spoke for a while. They wanted to say so much, yet the words were caught in their throats.

"Dad, take care of yourself. We have to go now. I'll find a way to contact you and let you know where we end up," Thuy said.

Mr Lan looked at each of them in turn, as if he wanted to imprint the image of his children and grandchild forever in his mind.

There are farewells when you know you'll meet again but this farewell had no return date. The future ahead seemed dark and uncertain. What parting doesn't bring tears? What separation doesn't cause heartache? Who could say what hardships lay ahead?

The conductor urged everyone to board the coach quickly. Hands clasped together, Thuy pressed her lips tight, her eyes filling with tears as she looked at her father one last time. His image blurred through her tears, mixed with the rain. It was as if heaven itself understood and shared the sorrow of these poor souls. Binh said goodbye to his father-in-law and carrying the bag and suitcase, stepped onto the coach. Hien reluctantly let go of her grandfather's hand and followed her father.

As the coach began to move, Thuy's father stood motionless, like a wooden post. His face was etched with anguish. When Thuy was not yet sixteen, she had left home and her father to go to work. Now, she and her small family were going far away, leaving him once more. This time, Mr Lan did not know when - or if - she would return. Helpless and guilt-ridden, he stood there gently waving goodbye to his loved ones, whispering a prayer for his children and grandchild to be safe, lucky and to survive the trials ahead. Through the coach window, his figure gradually faded, disappearing behind the rows of banyan trees lining the road - the familiar streets and pathways that held the footprints of Thuy's student days, all fading from sight.

Farewell!

Goodbye, everyone!

Farewell, Mother's grave!

Goodbye to both happy and sad memories.

Thuy's heart ached, her mind a whirl of tangled thoughts.

***A day in mid-April 1979.***

-----

**Note:**

According to directives from the Lê Duẩn and Lê Đức Thọ groups in April 1979, Vietnamese citizens of Chinese origin - along with their spouses and children - were prohibited from working in seven sectors: Foreign Affairs, Culture and Education, Health Services, Transport, the Military, Food, and Economic.

# CHAPTER 4

## Hanoi Capital

### One day in mid-April 1979

*"The day begins and now let's see*
*what this new world will do for me!"*
***Jean Valjean, Les Misérables* by Victor Hugo**

The coach sped along the road, quickly passing rows of houses on either side. Thuy felt numb and motionless, watching the town she knew so well fall behind. A sense of loss came over her, as though she had left behind something precious. Regret began to take root.

Little Hien slept soundly in her father's arms. Binh glanced over at his wife from time to time, worried about Thuy's health and the baby she was carrying.

"Have a nap or you'll be tired. I'll wake you when we get to Hanoi," Binh said gently.

Thuy closed her eyes. The events of the past few days replayed in her mind like a film in slow motion. She was leaving her hometown - the place where she was born and grew up. She had to leave her father and siblings behind, not knowing where she was heading or when she might return. What would happen to them all now?

Lost in thought, Thuy drifted into a restless sleep, lulled by the steady hum of the engine on the deserted early-morning road. Around her, passengers leaned their heads against the windows and nodded off. Some were half awake, others deep in sleep, their mouths open, hands tightly gripping their bags.

Hien and her father had also dozed off. The driver slowly pressed the brake pedal, guiding the coach towards the station. Then, all at once, he braked sharply, the vehicle came to a complete stop. He let out a sigh of relief. He had made it to Hanoi safely and was ready to head home.

Like the others who had been dozing, Thuy woke with a start.

"We've arrived at Kim Lien Station, in Hanoi. Please collect your belongings and get off the coach," the conductor called out loudly.

The coach filled with noise and confusion. Everyone wanted to get off first pushing, shoving, fighting their way to the front. Courtesy and patience had vanished; people thought only of themselves as they trampled over others.

Thuy's pregnant belly made moving difficult, but in a coach packed with desperate people, no one had any privilege. A woman in her mid-thirties deliberately shoved Thuy aside. With legs as heavy as tree trunks, she tried to climb over her, accidentally hitting Thuy on the head with her bag.

"Hey you! Can't you watch where you're going?" Binh shouted, pushing the woman back. She ignored him, muttering a few insincere apologies as she continued forward.

Not wanting to cause a scene, Thuy let it go. Binh carried Hien down the steps of the coach, then reached up to help Thuy.

The three of them stood still, bewildered by the chaotic, bustling scene before them.

"Is Duc's house far from here?" Thuy asked, her eyes scanning the crowd.

"Not too far, but we can't walk it. I'll get a cyclo to take us."

They didn't have to look far - a group of cyclo drivers were already at the station, calling out to passengers and competing for fares.

Seeing the small family, one of the drivers hurried over. "Where are you heading, sir? Get in my cyclo. It's got new cushions, very comfortable for the lady and child."

"How much to Hang Bai? Two adults, one child. Luggage: one sack, one suitcase," Binh said firmly.

"Three dong, please."

"No, that's too much. It's a short distance," Binh replied.

"The lady's pregnant, so I'll have to go carefully. Two and a half dong, how about that?"

"Deal. Drive safely."

The driver knew he'd lose the fare if he didn't lower his price, so he agreed. It was work none of the other drivers had managed to get anyway.

Binh helped his wife into the cyclo, then lifted Hien onto his lap beside her. The driver placed the sack across the floor and slid the suitcase under Binh's feet.

"Ready? I'll set off now!"

The cyclo slowly left the station, merging with the flow of bicycles and workers heading into the city. The sound of bicycle bells, the rumble of cyclos and the cries of street vendors filled the air - the familiar, lively music of the capital.

"Hot dumplings here, who wants dumplings?"

"Mung bean sticky rice, hot and fresh!"

"Crispy bread rolls, still warm - come and get some!"

"Excuse me, driver," Thuy said, turning back to look at him. "Could you stop for just a minute, please?"

Looking over to the pavement, Thuy noticed a few sticky rice sellers and waved to one of them.

"Hello! I'd like three portions of mung bean sticky rice, please," she said, taking some money from her pocket.

Binh accepted the three parcels of sticky rice, handing one to Hien first and then to Thuy.

The cyclo moved off again. Little Hien held her sticky rice carefully, but her curious eyes wandered everywhere - like a small bird discovering a vast new world. People bustled about, walking, selling, carrying sacks of goods. Everyone seemed in a hurry, and all sorts of sounds merged into a lively, chaotic symphony.

It was Hien's first time in Hanoi. Everything she saw was strange and exciting compared to her hometown. She watched in amazement as a tram passed by, gliding along without the roar of an engine. When the tram reached a busy area, the driver pulled a rope and a bell clanged to warn people ahead. The ringing sound added yet more noise to the already bustling streets. Hien was delighted and laughed out loud.

Thuy looked at her daughter and smiled, suddenly recalling her own years studying in Hanoi. Every month, after receiving their stipends, she and her classmates would go to Dong Xuan Market to eat *bun cha* - rice noodles with grilled pork - or noodles with large edible snails. Thuy had been addicted to those dishes.

There was also a time when her classmates dared one another to jump onto the tram without paying. Thuy would run behind and grab the door handle to leap on - she had to be quick and time it perfectly or she'd miss it.

At the next stop, whoever managed to jump on and off first was the winner, earning a free bowl of *bun cha*. Thuy still remembered those mischievous days, chuckling to herself at the thought of her carefree student life.

Hien was still staring intently at the tram and pointed to the tracks ahead.

"Mum, look! Two black snakes are chasing the tram!" she cried.

"Snakes? Where?" Thuy asked, following her daughter's gaze.

"There - those two snakes!"

Thuy laughed softly. "My clever girl, those are the iron rails. They help the tram's wheels run straight and not lose their way."

"They look just like snakes, Mum," Hien said in awe. The way the tram wheels gripped the rails made them seem like two black snakes slithering along the road.

"Mum, look! There's a little house in the middle of the lake! Does anyone live there?" Hien called out excitedly as they passed Hoan Kiem Lake.

"That's the Turtle Tower, not a house. No one lives there - there's only an altar inside," Thuy explained with a smile.

"Mum! Look, there's a small red bridge over there! It's prettier than the one near Grandpa's house. What's it called?"

"That's The Huc Bridge. It's made of wood. What does it look like to you?"

Hien narrowed her eyes, thinking. "I think it looks like the red dragon from the fairy tale - the one that was sleeping."

"Oh, my little artist," Thuy said fondly. "Many people say The Huc Bridge looks like a strip of soft red silk lying across the corner of Hoan Kiem Lake." She gently stroked her daughter's hair.

"I want to go there to play! Have you been, Mum?"

"Yes, I had and I'll take you another time. But for now, we must go to Aunty Duc's house first."

Thuy looked again toward The Huc Bridge. Hoan Kiem Lake, in the early summer morning, was peaceful and still. A thin mist hovered above the water's surface and the willow trees on both banks leaned gracefully, their reflections shimmering below. The red bridge connected the lakeside to the small, charming island where the sacred Ngoc Son Temple stood.

Back when she was studying in Hanoi, Thuy and her classmates would visit Ngoc Son Temple before exams to pray for luck. They half believed and half doubted whether it truly worked, but it was worth going just to be surrounded by the calm, natural beauty.

As the cyclo circled the lake, the mossy green of the water blended with the bridge's bright red, creating a mysterious and poetic harmony. Thuy's thoughts began to drift uneasily. She was gazing at the blue lake today, but by tomorrow she would be looking at the vast blue of the ocean. Where would it take them?

The cyclo driver kept pedalling steadily along the lakeside. A few people were exercising on the grass, others strolling by the water's edge. Nearby, a few tea stalls had been set up with small tables and tiny wooden stools for those enjoying their morning tea -

often accompanied by a few puffs from a bamboo water pipe.

Thuy imagined the bitter taste of green tea on the tip of her tongue, slowly turning sweet as it went down. She could almost hear the bubbling sound as someone drew on the water pipe, then the soft plume of smoke rising into the air. The smoker's eyes would glaze over as they looked out across the calm lake, perhaps remembering happy, glorious times gone by and momentarily forgetting the hardship of the present.

Thuy thought of her father again. If he lived nearby, he would surely enjoy sitting by the lake with his old friends, sipping tea and reminiscing about the past.

Blending into the crowd, the cyclo continued along the busy street, eventually rolling past the Trang Tien General Store. The driver slowed his pace, giving Hien the chance to take in all the sights and sounds. She spotted wooden dolls dressed in fine suits and elegant ladies in flowing *áo dài**[1] beautiful, graceful like figures in a painting.

There was a little girl in a colourful floral dress standing near the entrance. Behind the counter, inside the glass cabinet, were displays of sample goods bright fabrics, household items and gleaming electric lights.

"Mum, that shop is so big and beautiful, isn't it? There must be lots of lovely clothes and pretty dolls inside. Have you ever been in, Mum?" Hien asked excitedly.

"I had, but I was just a poor student then and I couldn't afford to spend my money on pretty clothes," Thuy replied gently. "I had to save for food! This store is for people in Hanoi who have ration coupons, my dear."

Hien's face fell slightly at her mother's words. She had been hoping to hear about all the beautiful things her mother might have bought there.

Thuy's mind drifted back more than a decade, to when she was sixteen and had only just begun working at the library. She had travelled to Hanoi with Minh, her team leader, to buy books. The city had been so crowded people and vehicles jostling everywhere. Their mission was to buy new titles for the school library. There was the main Trang Tien Bookshop, but also many small ones scattered nearby. It had been hard work finding and selecting the right books to take home.

Thuy remembered stopping outside the general store, curious about what was inside, but never daring to step in. Shopping for pleasure had been an unfamiliar concept to her then. There was always an invisible divide between the people of the capital and those from the provinces.

Another memory surfaced. Once, when Thuy had come to Hanoi with a delegation from the Culture Department, they had gone to the Trang Tien General Store during their lunch break, just to pass the time. Two of the young men in the group whispered together in a corner, nodding and grinning as if plotting something secret.

One of them was Vinh, a Muong man - a talented guitarist and singer from the provincial art troupe. He wore an indigo scarf tied around his head and pulled down the embroidered sleeves of his jacket, wanting to appear distinctly "from out of town".

Vinh and his friend Thang wandered about, peering into the glass display cases. One of the shop assistants noticed Vinh's innocent, open expression and began to watch him. He stood in front of her counter, staring silently. Wherever she went, he followed. When she stopped, so did he. It began to irritate her.

"Are you mad? Why do you keep following me?" she snapped.

Vinh froze, his face blank as if he hadn't understood. He gestured for Thang to come over, and the two exchanged a few words in their ethnic language.

"Sorry, miss! He can't speak or understand the common language," Thang explained with an apologetic smile.

"Who is he and where's he from?"

"He's from Ha Giang, up in the rocky mountains. It's his first time in Hanoi today."

The shop assistant seemed to soften a little.

"So, what does he like? What does he want to buy?" she asked.

The two men whispered again. Vinh nodded and pointed towards the counter. The girl followed the direction of his hand and gestured towards a bar of fragrant soap.

"This one?" she asked.

Vinh shook his head. Thang also shook his.

"Or perhaps this? To make a dress for your sweetheart?" she teased, pointing at some floral fabric.

Again, Vinh shook his head. Patiently, she pointed to each item in turn, but he continued to refuse, his head moving from side to side.

"Well then, what do you want?" she said at last, exasperated.

The two exchanged more hurried whispers in their own language.

"He's seen that pretty box with the picture of Dien Bien Phu on it," Thang said finally, "and he wants to know if he can buy it."

The girl laughed. "He didn't tell me that, he's just been following me around and staring! I was getting embarrassed."

"Could you please ask him properly what he wants to buy?"

"He says he wants a pack of Dien Bien cigarettes," Thang translated.

"No, no," the girl said, shaking her head. "You need a Hanoi coupon and an introduction letter to buy those."

"Then never mind," Thang said cheerfully. "He's from the highlands, he only wanted to buy it to see what it was like. He doesn't even smoke cigarettes. He smokes home-grown opium!"

Thang wandered off to look around, leaving Vinh still standing in front of the counter, staring at the girl until she grew irritated again.

"Excuse me, sir, could you please help me out here?" she called after Thang.

Thang returned with a grin.

"Well," she sighed, "if heaven doesn't outdo the earth, then the earth must outdo heaven! All right, I'll sell him one pack. But please tell him to go elsewhere afterwards."

The two men muttered a few more words in their language and Vinh nodded.

The salesgirl took out a packet of Dien Bien cigarettes and handed it to him, but Vinh shook his head again and pointed at another packet.

"No, no," she explained, "the silver packet is the premium brand."

Thang translated, but Vinh still pointed stubbornly at the silver ones.

Annoyed but resigned, the girl gave in and handed him a silver packet. Then Vinh held up two fingers.

"No, just one pack," she said quickly.

"He wants two," Thang interjected. "He says they're souvenirs for his wife. Not for smoking - just because he likes the packaging."

"The mountain people love their wives dearly wherever they go, they always want to bring something home to share with them."

"Alright then, here you are, two packs of cigarettes. That'll be one dong and twenty cents," the shop assistant said briskly, eager to be rid of him.

Vinh pulled a handful of crumpled notes from his pocket and laid them on the counter for her to count. He placed the two packets carefully into his woven bag, smiling with satisfaction. Before leaving the general store, he took out one of the packs and handed it to Thang.

"Thank you very much, young lady," Vinh said in perfect Vietnamese.

The two young men had fooled the salesgirl completely with their act. When they stepped outside, the rest of the group burst into laughter. The girl inside was probably laughing at herself too. Vinh and Thang hugged each other, laughing heartily proud of their mischief and their small victory.

It had been a carefree moment in a simpler time, before responsibility weighed heavily on their shoulders. Remembering it now brought Thuy a few minutes of lightness, a brief escape from her anxious thoughts.

"We're here, love, this is Duc's house," Binh announced, pulling Thuy back to the present.

The cyclo stopped at the top of Hang Bai Street. It was a wide avenue lined with two-storey houses, all built in the same style and painted a faded yellow.

Binh climbed down first, lifted out the cloth sack and suitcase and set them on the pavement. Then he helped Hien down before offering his hand to Thuy.

Most of the houses along the street doubled as small shops. Some sold soft drinks, others tea or groceries, with makeshift stalls spilling out onto the pavement. Thuy looked around uneasily and shivered; city life felt overwhelming and unfamiliar.

Binh led his wife and daughter to a house with a weathered brown door, half open, half shut. He knocked and called out, "Hello! Is anyone home?"

A head popped out from behind the door. "Ah, you're here already! Come in!"

Inside, Thuy heard the sound of hurried movement - things being tidied away. Binh's younger brother-in-law was clearing up, stacking bags and boxes. He looked up and nodded politely.

"Hello! Have you just arrived?" he asked.

The house was cluttered with black bags and old handbags. There wasn't a table, chair, bed or wardrobe in sight. Thuy stood awkwardly, unsure where to sit or even stand. Feeling faint and tired from the journey, she finally spoke.

"We came by coach. We just wanted to stop by, see you all and ask what's happening with the boat."

"You'll probably go to Hai Phong first," said Binh's younger sister, still bustling around the house. "If there are enough people, the boat should leave as planned. We still have lots to sort out here, so we might have to wait for another boat later."

Thuy could sense her sister-in-law's coldness immediately. She turned to Binh, who had been standing silently since they entered, observing without a word.

"They're busy, let's go to the station and get the train to Hai Phong," Thuy suggested quietly.

Binh nodded in agreement and reached for Hien's hand. As they stepped outside, Duc followed them to the door but said nothing. Once they were out on the street, he shut the door behind them and called out, "Try to leave right away if you want to catch the noon train!"

Little Hien looked tired and droopy-eyed, her face pale with sleepiness. Thuy's heart ached for her. She had thought that once they reached the house - after a journey of nearly a hundred kilometres - they could rest for a while, maybe have something to eat or drink and discuss the boat trip in peace.

Instead, she was both hungry and parched. The weight in her belly pressed heavily and exhaustion made her limbs ache. But there was no choice; they had to keep moving. Binh walked beside her silently, his head bowed. Thuy couldn't tell whether he felt ashamed of his sister's coldness or was simply lost for words.

Her father's voice echoed in her mind: *"My child, wherever you go, you must think of yourself first. No one will love you more than you love yourself."*

Tears pricked her eyes. She missed her father dearly and wished her younger brother were with them now.

A cyclo bell jingled in the distance. Binh raised his hand to hail the driver.

"Where to, sir?"

"Hang Co train station, how much?"

"Two dong," the driver replied.

Binh nodded without bargaining and they climbed in, arranging their bags around them.

Thuy was surprised he hadn't tried to haggle; perhaps he just wanted to get away quickly after their frosty reception.

The young cyclo driver pedalled hard and before long they reached Hang Co Station. Outside, the scene was crowded and noisy trams rattled past, people hurried in every direction and two trams in the middle of the road had stopped to let each other pass.

The cyclo came to a halt and Binh unloaded the bags. After paying the driver, Thuy said wearily, "Let's find a tea stall. I'm so thirsty, you and the child must be too."

Hang Co Train Station had been built by the French and opened in 1902. The colonial government had built it as part of its network to aid the exploitation of Indochina. After reunification in 1975, it had been renamed Hanoi Train Station.

It was an impressive two-storey building large and imposing. On the front façade, big concrete letters spelled out *Ga Ha Noi* - *Hanoi Station* - and above them hung a huge round clock, over a metre wide, its hands marking the steady passage of another day.

Thuy looked up at the clock, it was 11.32 am. In front of the station, there were crowds of people, motorbikes, bicycles, cyclos and trucks, all on their own little missions. The rich were dressed in luxurious, formal clothing, carrying bulging suitcases, while the hired workers wore old, faded clothes and carried goods for sale.

People bustled about with baskets of food, cages of chickens, ducks and pigs, all preparing to board the train. Occasionally, beggars in tattered, dirty clothing held out their conical hats, pleading for a few coins.

"Ladies and gentlemen, please give this humble person a few cents or a dime."

The scene at the station was constant, unending motion.

Spotting a tea stall at the right-hand corner of the station, Thuy led little Hien over. Binh followed behind, carrying their two bags. The tea stall lady smiled warmly, fanning her face with her hand as sweat dripped down.

"You two must have come a long way. Your wife looks exhausted - is she close to giving birth?"

"We're going to Hai Phong, to my mother's hometown, for the birth," Thuy said with a forced smile.

"It takes ages to queue for tickets buying from scalpers will be faster and cheaper," the tea lady said sympathetically.

"No, thank you. Please just give us some fresh tea and some bread," Binh replied.

"Could I buy some extra green tea or some boiled water to cool down? I can put it in a flask to drink along the way," Thuy asked, handing over her flask.

"Yes, right away."

"Is there a *phở* shop nearby, madam?"

"Yes, there are two or three across the street, but they're very expensive."

Thuy took back her flask, paid the lady, then turned to Hien.

"Daughter, do you want to eat the bread now or have *phở* later?"

"Mum, I need to pee," Hien whispered.

Thuy stroked her hair, seeing sweat covering the little girl's forehead. Hien had been obedient all morning, never complaining once.

"My good girl," Thuy said softly, "I know you're tired and sleepy. We'll go inside and find somewhere for you to pee. You can wash your face and cool down too, and then we'll wait for your father to buy the tickets."

She was comforting not only her child, but herself as well. Thuy led Hien inside the station, with Binh following behind, carrying the bags. The ticket counter had three windows, each with long queues. Binh chose one and joined the line while Thuy and Hien went to the toilet.

There were plenty of stalls, so they didn't have to wait long. When they came out, they saw Binh near the ticket booth, with only a few people left ahead of him.

Thuy looked around for somewhere to sit. The waiting area had several rows of long wooden benches, their backs leaning against each other. Some people were sleeping, some lying down with their heads resting on bags, others simply sitting on the floor.

Thuy noticed a woman breastfeeding her baby on the ground, another child beside her crying loudly. The baby's wailing mixed with the chatter and laughter of several men - the noise was endless.

Then Thuy saw two people stand and leave from a back row of benches, so she quickly led Hien over to the empty seats. At last, she could stretch her legs, lean back and take a deep breath to ease her fatigue.

About fifteen minutes later, Binh held up two tickets and waved them at her. "I've bought two tickets to Hai Phong on the two o'clock train. Children under five don't need a ticket."

Thuy breathed a sigh of relief at least the next stage of their journey was secured.

"It's still early," she said. "Let's go find some rice or *phở*. We're all hungry. We can save the bread for dinner. What do you think?" Binh nodded.

"I think Hien's hungry and sleepy too. I just need the loo, then we can go."

Hearing there'd be *phở* soon, Hien perked up immediately.

By now, the noon sun was fierce. There was no shade, only dry, dusty, stifling air. The heat shimmered so strongly that the station clock's numbers blurred.

Thuy and Binh took Hien across the road, where tea stalls, bread stalls and small restaurants lined the pavement, all bustling with customers. They stepped into the nearest restaurant, found an empty table and ordered straight away.

The menu on the wall listed dishes like fried rice, plain rice, braised pork with tofu, vegetable soup, and stir-fried greens, each with its price clearly shown.

Thuy turned to her daughter. "What would you like to eat, darling?"

"Mum, I want to eat everything! But *phở* is what I like best, I'm bored of sticky rice."

"Then let's go to a *phở* place, this one doesn't sell it."

Thuy smiled apologetically at the waiter. "Sorry, the child wants *phở*."

They went next door to a quieter *phở* restaurant and sat down. The menu was full of tempting dishes, but the prices were high. Thuy hesitated, asking Binh what he thought.

"It's up to you whatever you order, I'll eat it," he said kindly. "We've saved for this trip. I understand you and our child have suffered and starved enough. Let's eat properly today. After this meal, we'll say goodbye to this place."

"Alright then," Thuy decided. "Three bowls of *phở* chicken and pork. We'll eat quickly and catch the train."

After finishing, they returned to the station. The clock now showed 1.20 pm. They went straight to the platforms, where crowds were already gathering.

Everyone fidgeted, eager to be first through the

gate to claim a good seat. Not all were fleeing the country some were simply visiting family, others on business, or travelling with spouses and children.

Among them were the *train traders,* women who carried large sacks balanced on poles, filled with goods to sell at each destination. They were strong, quick and fierce, their movements sharp and their voices loud, like wild creatures fighting for space.

Seeing them, Thuy, heavily pregnant and holding Hien's hand, stepped aside. Binh moved ahead to shield them.

Only five minutes remained until the gates opened, but the crowd was already pushing and shoving, tempers flaring, voices rising in a clash of accents and tones. It was a wall of sound - shrill, rough and restless.

Then came the long whistle of the train, like a signal summoning everyone forward. The crowd surged again, but suddenly a loudspeaker announcement crackled overhead and people fell quiet.

"Attention, attention! Passengers, please have your tickets ready. The station will open shortly. Be aware that there are pickpockets. Please take care of your belongings, documents and money."

"Mum, what did she say? Can we go yet?"

"Shh, listen to the announcement." Thuy strained to hear, but the speaker crackled with static, the words muffled - that indistinct, echoing sound only ever heard in stations.

Before the gates were even fully open, the crowd surged like a flood, sweeping Thuy and her daughter along. Young people rushed ahead; the elderly, children and those carrying heavy loads were left behind.

The train had no assigned seats whoever boarded first got the best ones. Thuy's family were lucky to get on at all amidst the chaos.

Binh ran ahead, finding a small compartment with two seats facing each other by the window. He quickly placed their bag and suitcase on the seats to reserve them.

A man in his forties, wearing a faded army uniform and carrying a heavy backpack, looked around wearily for somewhere to sit. He was limping slightly, his face dripping with sweat.

"Hello, soldier! Come and sit here," Thuy called out.

He turned, surprised, seeing a pregnant woman waving him over. He hobbled closer.

"You don't have a seat yet, do you? You can sit next to my little girl," Thuy said, pointing to the seat beside Hien.

He hesitated. "But what about your family? Will there be enough room?"

"Don't worry," said Binh kindly. "There are only three of us. I'll put our things in the luggage rack."

The soldier was touched. He shook Binh's hand repeatedly, thanking him rare words amidst the clamour of people boarding.

From that moment on, the journey to Hai Phong had an extra companion someone to share stories with and lighten the road ahead. At first, conversation was shy and polite, but soon they were chatting easily. Even little Hien joined in, her sweet, curious face making everyone smile.

"I was sent with my unit to Battlefield B at the end of 1967," the man - Tuan - began, glancing at Hien. "My daughter was three then, about your girl's age.

"After the Mau Than Lunar New Year Offensive in 1968, I was moved from one unit to another. I never had a chance to write or visit home. Then I was injured and sent to a camp for wounded soldiers. When I was discharged, I only had one leg left. I don't even know if my daughter will recognise me after twelve years."

He looked out of the window, his expression distant and troubled. Thuy thought of her two younger brothers in the army and how she hadn't been able to say goodbye.

"Don't worry, sir," she said softly. "I'm sure your family will be overjoyed to see you. After so many years apart, love will make up for everything. The only sadness is not knowing when this war will finally end."

The atmosphere changed with the telling of the soldier's story, until Hien suddenly got up, full of excitement.

"Mum! Dad! Our train's crossing the river, it's on the bridge! Wow!" Hien pressed her face against the window.

"Why's the river water so red, Mum?"

This made Tuan smile. He held Hien tightly, afraid she might get too excited and stick her head out of the window.

"Our train's going over the Long Bien Bridge. Below us is the Red River, my dear," Tuan explained.

"Why's it called the Red River, Uncle?" Hien asked, turning around.

"You're wondering why the river water's red?"

"The river near my grandfather's house isn't red. Someone must have been naughty and spilled red ink into this one, Uncle," Hien said, frowning, her small eyebrows forming a question mark.

"The Red River gets its name from the distinctive red alluvial colour of the water, my dear," Tuan said, patting Hien's head.

"The river's so big and wide, is it long too?"

"The Red River is 1,149 kilometres long. It begins in the Yuanshan Mountains in China, but only 510 kilometres flow through Vietnam."

"Wow, how do you know all that? My teacher didn't tell us any of this in class," Hien wondered.

"Sit still and don't bother Uncle Tuan too much, he'll get tired," Thuy said, thinking her daughter was asking too many questions.

"It's all right," Tuan replied cheerfully. "When you grow up, you'll learn a lot and know even more! It's a shame that when my daughter was your age, I wasn't at home to talk to her or teach her these things."

Thuy's thoughts began to drift. She remembered when she was still at school and, because of the war, the students had to evacuate to Hung Yen Province. They all stayed in people's homes for five months. Thuy and her classmates used to go down to the Dang Giang River to wash their clothes. She once had a white shirt her father had made her for Tet, but it ended up being dyed by the river water. The river's red sediment had stained it permanently. She couldn't wear that shirt again and hadn't dared tell her father. The memory remained vivid.

The train continued over Long Bien Bridge and into Gia Lam District. Thuy's aunt lived there - her father's younger sister. When Thuy was little, she and her three siblings would stay with their aunt for several months during the summer holidays. There had been no chance to say goodbye to her aunt back then and she hadn't known when - or if - she would ever see her again.

By now, people were growing tired of talking and wanted to close their eyes and rest. Each time the train approached a station, it whistled three times to alert passengers and staff. The train would blow its horn, releasing hot air into the sky, and a column of white steam would rise to cover the roof of the entire train. Anyone who stuck their head out of a window would be hit by the steam.

Inside the carriage, a child of about eleven or twelve walked down the aisle carrying an aluminium kettle and a few china bowls. They were selling green tea to passengers. It was easy to sell tea in such hot weather everyone was thirsty and needed refreshment. In no time, the kettle was empty, and the child could proudly tell their parents how well they'd done.

Little Hien dozed off with her head resting on Tuan's lap. The whistle sounded to announce Cam Giang Station, waking her up. The area was famous for its boiled water spinach served with Bần soy sauce*3 delicious even when there wasn't much rice to eat.

At each stop, the train waited two to five minutes, just long enough for passengers to get on or off with all their belongings. The station staff wore green uniforms and caps, with a red armband on their right arm marked with the white letters NVNG*4. Each staff member held a blue-and-white painted baton in one hand and a small red triangular flag in the other. They would blow their whistle to signal the train was ready to depart. Little Hien looked down and saw them waving their flags and blowing their whistles.

"Mum! Which station are we at?"

Just then, a young woman in green clothes holding a loudspeaker made an announcement:

"The train has arrived at Hai Duong Station. We will stop here for thirty minutes to take on water and supplies. You may get off to buy food and drinks or use the restroom."

Everyone stood up, preparing to disembark. Once again, there was jostling as people tried to be first off. It was the perfect time for thieves when people were distracted and careless with their belongings.

"Do you two want to get off to eat or go to the toilet?" Binh asked his family.

Thuy shook her head, then looked at Hien. "Do you need the toilet?"

"I don't want to. The restroom's really dirty," Hien said, frowning.

"Then we'll stay on the train. Everyone else can get off."

Thuy turned to Tuan to ask if he wanted to get off, but he also shook his head, saying it was difficult to move around much with only one leg. Thuy knew she could always call the street vendors over to the window if they needed anything.

Hai Duong's sweet speciality was the Golden Dragon Brand green bean and sugar cake. The finely ground green bean filling was smooth and melted on the tongue. Some people preferred to eat bánh chưng, but this station was also famous for its delicious bánh gai.*[5] When Thuy was a little girl and her grandmother came to visit from the countryside, she always brought dozens of bánh gai - the kind of cake every child loved.

Hien looked out of the window again. She could see people hurrying to the restroom. Many of the vendors were girls around twelve or thirteen, clutching baskets against their ribs filled with all kinds of cakes, calling out to sell to the new arrivals. Thuy waved one of them over, she wanted to buy a bánh chưng and a mung bean cake.

"Mum! Can you buy me that box of mung bean cakes with the beautiful Golden Dragon label?" Hien said excitedly when she saw the packets in the baskets.

Tuan also called to one of the girls. "Four bánh chưng and two boxes of Golden Dragon Brand mung bean cakes, please," he said.

"You're alone, why do you need to buy so much?" Hien asked curiously.

Thuy gave her a warning look.

"It's not all for me," Tuan replied with a slight awkwardness. "They're for my family. I haven't seen them for years and want to bring them a gift."

The train blew its whistle a few more times and slowly began to move. Those still in the restrooms ran out and jumped onto the steps, just managing to pull themselves aboard.

Through the windows, vendors kept trying to sell their goods, often taking passengers' money but delaying handing over the items. As the train gathered speed, the vendors would pretend they couldn't catch up, waving the cakes in the air. Passengers would lean out of the windows, reaching for their purchases, but the food always stayed just out of reach. Once the train was far enough away, the vendors would laugh and wave the cakes triumphantly.

Sometimes, even those who managed to grab their cakes would peel off the green leaves only to find a lump of mud inside. There were many ways to cheat people on a passing train. It had happened to Thuy too, when she opened her packet, there was a piece of clay instead of bánh chưng. Thuy smiled, though she also felt ashamed and pity for those miserable people who had to cheat for a living. Life was hard and they were deprived; perhaps, in their own way, they were just trying to take a little more than they were given.

The local authorities couldn't resolve the situation on the train platforms, and even after reports appeared in the newspapers, the vendors continued their thriving scams.

Little Hien, watching all the commotion among the passengers, saw a woman running out of the restroom holding up her trousers. Hien laughed and shouted to her parents that she could see the woman's bottom!

Again, the noise level inside the carriages rose. People were complaining about lost bags or missing money. Arguments began to break out.

Suddenly, a middle aged woman wearing a brown blouse and black trousers, and walking with a limp, hurried down the train. Her eyes darted about as she muttered under her breath.

"Oh my God! The wrong carriage!" she cried.

"Where's your seat?" a man asked.

She began to sob in panic. "I needed the toilet, so I ran straight off the train at the station. I didn't think to remember which carriage I was in!" She frantically searched the seats with her eyes.

"The carriage I was sitting in wasn't like this one. There were two long rows of benches on either side, space down the middle for bags and poles belonging to those women who sell at the market. I had six or seven big hens in a cage!" she said desperately.

"Was there anyone with you?"

"Do you remember anyone who was sitting near you?" people asked, trying to help. Then someone spoke up, seemingly knowing where she'd gone wrong.

"Oh no, your seats are in the freight carriage - the merchants' coach, full of goods and supplies. You'll need to ask the train staff where that carriage is. You might find your chickens there."

Everyone laughed, subconsciously and without malice, but it still stung. The woman was distraught at the thought of losing all her belongings.

Little Hien had been standing on a chair, watching everything unfold, holding onto Tuan's shoulder.

"Mum! She's so old but she still got lost, huh?"

"You shouldn't talk about grown-up matters. Sit back down," Thuy scolded gently.

Hien sat obediently, saying no more.

From the far end of the carriage came the sound of an erhu*6 someone was singing too. Hien fidgeted, looked up at her mother and asked what was happening.

The singing came closer. A woman and her young son were performing folk songs. The mother, about forty years old, wore sunglasses, but on closer look, long scars could be seen where her eyes should have been. She played the erhu with one hand, led by a boy of about eight or nine. His trousers were torn, one leg longer than the other. He clutched his mother's sleeve with one hand and held out an old conical hat with the other, asking for money. The blind woman sang and played, her voice carrying a sad story about her family:

*"From the day when you walked away,*
*You left your son and he lost his way.*
*Your son was hungry and cold,*
*We were craving for food.*

*Your son led me by his cold hands,*
*To wherever we could go to beg.*
*Why are our lives so miserable?*
*Asking God, but he is silent.*
*Asking Buddha, but no answer.*
*Please, ladies and gentlemen, help us.*
*From the day when you stepped away,*
*Your son you left at home with me.*
*Your son, hungry and craving,*
*Led me everywhere to beg.*
*You went to fight far away,*
*Leaving your old parents for me to care for.*
*Months and years have gone by - I waited.*
*Your parents passed away…*
*But I never heard from you.*
*Where were you? Where…?"*

The blind woman paused and spoke to the carriage.

*"I ask you, gentlemen, is that good?*
*I ask you, ladies, do you understand my pain?"*

Her song was slow and mournful, lamenting the fate of blindness - a widowed mother and her orphaned child, hungry and destitute.

"I beg you, ladies and gentlemen, take pity on me and my son. Pray to Buddha and you may be blessed. Please spare a few coins, have mercy on us," she pleaded.

Thuy bent down to find some coins in her pocket and dropped them into the boy's hat. Tuan, with tears in his eyes, took money from his shirt pocket and added it too. The child, his face dirty but his eyes wide with gratitude, thanked them softly.

The mother continued playing as she moved down the carriage. People dropped bananas and sticky rice cakes into the hat. The music and the silhouettes of the mother and son slowly faded into the next carriage.

-----

The train rumbled steadily on. The rhythmic sound lulled passengers to sleep, and calm returned after the earlier chaos. Passing Thuong Ly Station and approaching Hai Phong, the train began to slow. Before it reached Cau Dat Street, a station guard blew his whistle and waved his flag to stop pedestrians. He pulled the barrier across to hold back the traffic and the crowd. As the train neared, it blew its whistle three times to signal its arrival.

They had reached their final destination - Hai Phong Station.

Hai Phong! Hai Phong! The City of Red Flamboyants! This was the last stop on Railway Line No. 5 from Hanoi.

As soon as the train passed Cau Dat Street, passengers rushed to gather their belongings. People jostled, argued and pushed - an old habit that seemed impossible to break.

Binh stood up, reached for the luggage from the overhead rack, picked up little Hien and sat beside Thuy. They looked at each other, signalling to wait until the crowd cleared. Tuan sat quietly with them; the four of them waited calmly for everyone else to disembark first.

"Goodbye, little friend. See you again soon. Wishing everyone good health and peace," Tuan said, patting Hien's head.

Thuy smiled. Binh and Tuan stood and shook hands before saying their goodbyes. Tuan stepped back to let Binh get off first with their bags. Thuy led Hien to the door, where Binh took the child's hand as she gripped the iron bar of the train door and stepped carefully down onto the platform.

The crowd hurried through the ticket gate and once outside on Ga Street (Station Street), everyone dispersed in different directions.

A strange feeling washed over Thuy as she stepped off the train at Hai Phong Station. It was nothing like the times she had travelled home before. She understood that from this moment on, the road ahead would be filled with uncertainty.

-----

**Notes:**

*[1]Áo dài – The Vietnamese national dress, symbolising grace and cultural pride. Recognised for its simple elegance, it embodies both tradition and modern sensibility.

*[2] B is a battlefield in south Vietnam.

*[3] Bần soy sauce – A speciality soy sauce from Bần craft village in Hưng Yên Province.

*[4] *NVNG* – Short for *Nhân Viên Nhà Ga,* meaning "station staff".

*[5] *Bánh gai* – Sticky rice flour cake with mung bean and coconut filling.

*[6] *Erhu* – A traditional Chinese two-stringed bowed instrument.

# CHAPTER 5

## Hai Phong City

*Undoubtedly they seemed very depraved, very corrupt, very vile, very hateful even-but people rarely fall without becoming degraded.*

**Victor Hugo**

Thuy, with her husband and child trudged along to the ticket gate. They were the last ones to leave the platform. It was 6.30 pm and everyone else had gone already.

Hai Phong train station was built by the French colonial government in 1902. It had a European style, big, beautiful and spacious, just a bit smaller than Hanoi station.

Thuy's body ached. She was tired and numb after a long four hours journey sitting on the train's wooden benches. She was in no mood to appreciate the beautiful architecture of the building. Little Hien was also indifferent. Her head was down and she slowly dragged her feet behind her mother.

"I think we need to get something to eat. Then we can get another cyclo to where we're staying." Thuy said to Binh.

The station was bustling with people and vehicles like any other in the country, but during rush hour, the road was even more crowded and noisy. As Thuy's family exited the station, they could see a row of small restaurants opposite them. Binh led the way to the nearest one.

The owner of the restaurant was plump, strong and healthy. She stood next to a large table, holding a cleaver in her hand. The menu displayed at the window listed, boiled rice, boiled water-spinach, vegetable soup, pork and fish.

Thuy and Hien went inside to find seats. There were only six tables. Some of them were occupied, but you could see that they would all fill up quickly with people. Thuy took up space at one of the empty tables.

"They have rice and vegetable soup, braised meat, fried fish, what do you want to eat?" Binh asked Thuy.

Thuy looked at Hien. Her little kitten sat still, not moving. She knew Hien was exhausted.

"I'm very tired. Just order some rice, a bowl of vegetable soup to cool us down and a salty dish. What do you think?" Thuy replied.

Binh nodded in agreement with his wife, and ordered their meal at the counter.

It wasn't long before the restaurant was full. It was the first one you could see standing outside the station, so the tables were never empty for long. The owner was always busy, but she only got help later in the day when her husband arrived. Thuy's family had a satisfying meal after a day of traveling to many places.

When they had finished Binh waved to a cyclo to grab his attention. the man quickly pedalled over. He had dark skin and was strong and healthy looking and stopped in front of them.

"Where do you want to go?"

"Take us to Mrs Fat's boarding house, Quang Trung Street." Binh answered.

"Yes, I know Mrs Fat house. For three people, bags and suitcases, give me two dong."

"It's only early evening and you want to kill me off. I'll pay one and a half dong, but you have to drive carefully. My wife is heavily pregnant and have a small child. If you can do this, then let's go, otherwise I'll call another one." Binh said firmly.

The cyclo driver silently pedalled closer to where Thuy and her child were standing. The family had gotten on a cyclo several times that day and Thuy wondered if this would be the last time they would haggle for a ride.

Hai Phong station gradually receded behind them. As the cyclo turned to Cau Dat Street, where all the street lights and shops were lit up for the night.

At the top of the street was the Cong Nhan movie theatre. There must have been a new movie on. Both sides of the wall were covered in posters advertising the film, along with pictures of the actors. It was an escape to another life and that was attractive to the people of the city.

In front of the cinema theatre, there were children selling roasted peanuts, roasted corn and melon seeds. These were theatre snacks.

Little Hien was more awake now, but oddly she wasn't interested in the theatre and its posters. The cyclo turned left and went straight to Quang Trung Street, near the Sat market. Along the way there were many people spreading mats on the sidewalk.

"Hello! Driver, why are there so many people lying on the sidewalk?" Thuy asked.

"Many people are coming to Hai Phong these days, madam. They sleep in parks, churches, pagodas, temples and shrines, it looks so miserable." The cyclo man replied, still pedalling.

"Do you know why?"

"I live near some Chinese families and they have been afraid since the outbreak of war between China and Vietnam at the borders. They are trying to flee the country." He answered solemnly.

Thuy felt sad, thinking about her situation, yet the country carried on in a pretence of stability.

"So, you are Vietnamese?" Thuy was interested in knowing more.

"Yes, I am! But that is all I know, it is best to keep quiet. I live in Hai Phong and I heard about the Vietnamese family who fled with the Chinese on a boat. They were caught by the coast guards and put into prison. The whole family was monitored. This is their life now, they're not going to have a peaceful future."

Binh looked at his wife and shook his head, indicating not to ask any more questions. They were all quiet from that point onwards.

Thuy remembered what had happened to her only a couple of months ago, and became more and more restless and worried.

From January 1979, a month before the war, the Dong Dang, Lao Cai and Mong Cai border gates were closed, so everyone ran to Hai Phong. Like Binh's relatives who also fled their homes because of the war. The Chinese people from the northern borders flocked to Hai Phong in their hundreds. It was the port to go to escape the country. However, Hai Phong had very few hostels or places to rent and almost no hotels, so people just slept rough on the streets, parks, churches, temples. Anywhere there was space, until it was their time to go. Even the roads were lined with homeless families, from new born babies and young infants to frail great grandparents. Human waste built up beneath trees and there was rubbish everywhere. It was another dreadful side to war.

Thuy was lost in thought when suddenly the sound of the cyclo driver rang out. "We've arrived at Mrs Fat's boarding house!" The car stopped in front of a row of thatched roof brick houses. From the outside you couldn't tell that there was an inn on the row.

Binh had been renting it and staying there since last week, so they were the lucky ones who had shelter for the night.

"It's Quang Trung Street, honey! Fat lady's boarding house is here." Binh said, reading his wife's anxious look.

The driver held the cyclo still for Binh and his family to get off. In front of the row of houses were people lying and sitting, adults and children, old and young. Thuy took little Hien and hurriedly followed Binh past all the bodies. There was a piece of wood about two hand spans wide, hanging in front of the house. The word 'hostel' was scrawled on the piece of wood like a child's handwriting. They all stood in front of a bamboo woven door.

"Hello! Mrs Fat, open the door for me! It's Binh!"

The sound of slippers clattered from inside the house. A big woman, almost barrel shaped and about thirty-five to forty years old opened the door.

"Who is this, Binh?" Mrs Fat asked, standing centre of the entrance.

"This is my wife! Her name is Thuy and our beloved daughter, Hien." Binh happily replied.

As if on cue, little Hien bowed her head to the woman. "Hello, Grandma." Hien said softly.

This pleased Mrs Fat and her face brightened. "Wow, Binh's daughter is so polite. Grandma welcomes you."

Thuy said hello to the woman as well and then they were all invited inside. Binh walked in with their bag, while Thuy held Hien's hand and followed behind him. The woman then closed and bolted the door.

"So, Binh, is the plan still for your family to stay here?" Mrs Fat looked at Binh and continued. "I haven't arranged a room yet."

"I wanted to discuss this with you. I would like my wife and child to stay here until the day our boat sets sail. If there isn't a bigger room, could we have a double bed to replace the current one, madam." Binh asked in his polite voice.

"Okay, tonight I can give you a double bed. Then tomorrow, when someone checks out, I can give your family a bigger room, but it will cost more, as there are now three of you."

"I will pay more but you must let me cook and use the bath. My wife is heavily pregnant, so we can't eat out every day. I have been your long-time guest, so perhaps you can give me these extras?" Binh was cautious asking this.

"Hmm, you are cheeky. Can't you see how many people have to sleep on the streets?"

Binh remembered that Mrs Fat admired his sister.

"Maybe tomorrow my younger sister will bring you some goods." Binh said, trying to finalise the deal. Hearing that Mrs Fat's face brightened up and she agreed to everything. Life is like this:

*'Money makes profit,*
*Smile like a blooming flower.*
*No money, no profit,*
*Frown like a monkey smelling shrimp paste.'*

There were three or four bedrooms that were rented in this hostel. Binh took Thuy and Hien inside his room. It was a small room with a single bed, which really looked like a bamboo bench. Small strips of bamboo had been woven in rows and were worn smooth and pale brown from the sweat of hundreds of people lying on them. An old flower mat had been rolled up at the head of the bed, which was spread out at night for some cushioning.

In the corner of the room was a small table and two rickety wooden chairs. That room cost one dong a night, but now with Thuy and Hien occupying the room as well, it would be two dong. A happy outcome for Mrs Fat, even if she had to place a double bed in there for the night. It was a simple and sparse room, but Thuy knew they were the lucky ones. They had shelter and the family were all together. In a small corner in the inn, there was a water tap used for showering. Thuy and Hien were able to clean themselves of the day's dirt and grime. After a long day of traveling, the cool water gave them a new lease of life, a fresh start. The shower wakes little Hien up and she starts to take in this new environment. When they are done, mother and child return to the room and then it's Binh's turn to freshen up.

The double bed that has replaced the bamboo one is bigger and studier than the previous one. Hien climbs onto the bed and lies down straight away. She is exhausted. Thuy lies down next to her child, feeling like she has not been this comfortable in a long time. So, the first day of their travels to a new life ends. Homeless in their native land.

Tomorrow, Binh would check on the preparations for the boat's departure. He would have to hand over the money and documents to the boat owner and all the paperwork would be the owner's responsibility.

According to Binh, the Chinese and their families will be approved quickly and will leave openly due to government policy. Vietnamese people who want to leave must have fake documents or make their escape secretly.

Thuy and Hien sleep soundly despite the dirty bed and rough bedding. The only thing that concerned Binh was when the boat would set sail. When he left Hai Phong to collect his wife and child, his thoughts had constantly been on the boat and the hope that they would be able to sail on it within days of arriving. Thuy had arranged everything up to this point and it was the way it had and always would be.

When he received Thuy's telegram to come home to pick them up, Binh was both worried and anxious about where the money would come from to take them with him on the boat. He didn't have any. When he told his sister Duc about the telegram and his concerns, she had the answer. "You must go back to pick her up tonight. She must have money if she wants you to go and pick them up." Duc said confidently.

Binh was surprised by this assumption. "Why did you tell me the other day to go alone? You said Thuy was Vietnamese, so staying wasn't going to kill her?"

"The boat won't leave until there are enough passengers. Phuong is still waiting, so she can earn more money. If you get your wife, that means there are more passengers for Phuong. They will respect you more. There's nothing to lose."

Binh was inherently a gentle and honest man, although unable to make his own decisions. He knew his young sister wasn't very kind to his wife. People often said 'poor is mean, mean goes with inferiority'. So Binh just silently listened and did as Duc said.

The next morning, Binh told his wife his plans of meeting the boat owner to provide them with documents and money. "What are you going to do today?" Binh asked Thuy.

"This morning I want to go to the market to buy a kerosene stove and food to cook here. We've got this room for a couple of days while we wait for the boat to depart. I think we can save money by cooking here rather than eating out." Thuy replied and encouraged Binh to start his day out.

Mid-summer weather and the air was cool in the early evening. There was a taste of the sea in the breeze, but also the scent of the trees and grass mixed with the smells spewing from the cement factories.

The women from the sanitation company had cleaned up the trash along the road. Yesterday it was flooded with urine and human faeces, which blocked the sewers. The smell was overwhelming. The local government tried to move those sleeping rough on, but they always came back. The clean-up was only temporary and Hai Phong was going to remain a city of chaos for the time being.

There were many big public faucet-taps on the street. Most were roughly one hundred meters apart. People would queue up with their buckets to retrieve water. Those who had time in the day were willing to wait in line, and those that didn't had to fetch water in the evening.

There was always a folk song singer performing near these taps. Women with strong voices and big lungs. They would also use their voices to shout and curse at each other, squabbling over the water.

Fortunately, there was a street tap just opposite the boarding house where Thuy was staying. She could wash some clothes today. Little Hien was still sleeping soundly, while her parents readied themselves for the day. She was young so didn't have any worries, just as long as her parents were with her.

Mrs Fat said the Sat market sold everything from A to Z. Thuy wanted to go to the market early to make sure she got what was needed. For a while though, she sat watching her child sleep, not wanting to wake her up. Thuy's mind was anxious with questions. Were there enough papers and money? Would it be straightforward to leave? When would the boat set sail? What was happening with her father and siblings now? She knew that the immediate future would be difficult, but where were they going to end up?

She had had two difficult labours previously. What would happen this time without a doctor or midwife? She and the new-born might not be safe, but there was no turning back now.

Phuong was a native of Hai Phong and an entrepreneur. She colluded with the people who liquidated old and unused fishing boats from fishing cooperatives in Quang Ninh. She would buy them at very cheap prices and repair them, whatever was needed to attract customers who would pay a high price.

Binh hoped that his young sister, who knew Phuong, would sell tickets to his wife and child at a reasonable price. When he arrived, Phuong was having breakfast with a few people. At first glance, he assessed what type of character Phuong was; a cunning and ambitious business woman. She had an arrogant air about her and her shocking curly hair added to this.

"Mr Binh, come in and have breakfast with me." Phuong said with a big grin.

"Thank you, but I've already had breakfast. How is the boat getting on?" Binh asked impatiently.

Phuong sat sipping a cup of black coffee, holding a cigarette and flicking the ash on the ground. "Not done yet, we will leave in the next few days. How are you?"

"Yesterday I picked up my wife and child. I want to register them for travel on the same boat as me. My daughter is just three years old."

"Do you have all the documents and photos? It's not a problem to take your wife and child. That will be the price of two more tickets and you'll have to pay in full today." She smiled like a snake about to devour its prey.

"Please understand our situation. My wife worked for the government, we don't have that much money. She is also pregnant and our child is just three years old. Could you charge me for just one ticket?"

"How many months has she been pregnant?"

"Eight months."

"Actually, I should charge you for the baby in her belly too, but out of respect for Duc's acquaintance, I will only charge you for the price of two more tickets. Which is a great deal, five thousand dong. Can you pay that all today?" Phuong said in a cold voice.

Knowing that he could not negotiate any further with this calculating, iron-hearted woman, Binh handed over the papers and slowly counted out 5,000*[1] dong. Phuong slowly counted the money herself and checked all the documents.

"You can rest assured and go home. In a few days, I will send someone to notify you of the boat's departure date and time." She said in the same cold voice.

Binh left quietly. His mind was in turmoil, wondering how many more days he would have to wait. Thuy's belly was getting bigger and heavier, if they had to wait much longer, it might be too late.

Binh returned to the hostel. Thuy and little Hien had just returned from the market themselves.

Thuy didn't want to carry too much, but still managed to buy a kerosene stove, two litres of fuel oil, a piece of pork, some chrysanthemum greens, a packet of salt and a small bottle of fish sauce. This was just for their stay in the hostel.

"What is the plan with the boat?" Thuy asked immediately.

Binh knew his wife was anxious and worried. "Everything is fine, I met the boat owner, gave her the money and papers. The boat isn't ready to sail yet though. We'll have to keep on waiting until we hear from them." Binh replied calmly.

"How much was the boat fee and were the documents enough?" "There is still some money left." Binh gave the rest of the money to his wife and explained further. "That cunning Phuong, when she found out you were pregnant, she said she should charge us a ticket for the unborn baby! Our daughter is only three years old, but she still charged us for her ticket. I had to pay for two more tickets. Five thousand dong in total. She wouldn't reduce it even by a penny. She is truly an infamous woman in this business."

"They are business women. Money is the most important thing to them. There are no loyalties, no love or friendships with those people. Even with your sister, who she's known for many years, has no effect on her decisions. You know the saying, 'the more familiar you are, the more they will do you over.'" Thuy sighed. "Knowing that we are in this situation, when given the opportunity to squeeze, she squeezed as tightly as she could, without mercy."

Everything seemed to be going as planned. They had a place to stay and the boat fare was paid for. All that was left to do was wait. With only a little money left, Thuy knew she had to save and spend sparingly. None of them knew how long they would have to wait and in a strange place with no relatives, who could she rely on?

That afternoon though, Binh's younger sister, Duc, came along with four adults and a little girl about seven years old. Everyone went inside the house. Mrs Fat had been expecting them.

"Five more people? You have to rent an extra room then." Mrs Fat said, looking at all the faces.

Everyone looked at each other, no one said anything.

"They are all my relatives and have been on the move for many months now. They don't have much money and can't afford another room. Please show some mercy and let them share a room with my brother. Only an extra bed for the women and child. The men can sleep on the floor. In a few days the boat will set sail and they will all be gone." Duc said persuasively.

She spoke non-stop, without asking Thuy and her brother if they agreed to let them stay in the same room. Thuy looked over at Binh angrily, but he stood still, not saying a word. It's not that Thuy didn't understand the situation, but Duc's attitude put Thuy in a passive position.

Little Hien saw that there was another girl, so she approached her and started asking her questions.

"Okay, I'll give you a discount of one dong. But you all have to go to the public bathhouse, you can't bathe here, only Thuy and her daughter can. So, for the five extra people you have to pay me four dong a day now. Who is going to pay?" Mrs Fat demanded.

Duc looked at her relatives with a questioning look, but they all silently bowed their heads. So Duc took out money from her pocket and gave it to Mrs Fat, "I will give you 28 dong for five people, for seven days. Please write me a receipt."

Thuy observed this transaction and could see clearly the type of future she would have with these people. She didn't even know their names or how they were related to Binh.

After reaching an agreement with the landlady, Duc and the others went out. In the room, only the couple Binh and Hien were left behind. Thuy couldn't keep quiet any longer.

"How are you related to those people, Binh? Why does Duc think she can just bring these people to stay in this small room with us? She didn't even ask us for our opinion! And you are still silent. She treats me very badly, like I am an outsider." Thuy was angry and upset, but needed to get it all out. "We don't know how long before the boat sets sail and I've paid for the fare now."

"I didn't know she was going to do that." Binh grumbled. "I only knew when you knew."

"Tell me clearly, what is their relationship to you?"

"Two of them are the niece and nephew of Duc's husband, I don't really know them. The child must be theirs. The other two are from Duc's side of the family. Linh is my niece and Thinh is my nephew. I am the elder brother, so I have to help, what do you want me to do?"

Hearing her husband explain it that way, Thuy also found it difficult to decide. If it was her family, she couldn't turn them away either. However, she was more worried about her and her child and not knowing who to rely on. This incident made her feel truly alone in her husband's family.

Binh, Thuy and Hien also left the hostel soon after Duc's arrival. They returned in the evening. During that time Mrs Fat had added to their room, a large bed and two single mats. The mats were for the two young men to lie down on.

At the beginning of the night, Hoa and her daughter, Huong and Linh all slept on the bed. Tuan and Thinh, Hoa's younger brothers, occupied the two mats on the floor. They were young men, but they had never really had official jobs. They were always smuggling goods in the northern border areas. They never had an education, so their lives were spent struggling to make a living.

After two days, Thuy understood that they were only adding to her burden and she could not expect any help from them. They averted their eyes when help was needed and were oblivious to the idea that Thuy was pregnant.

In the morning, they all went out together and in the evening they came back tired, throwing their dirty clothes everywhere. Only little Hien was happy to have Huong to play with. She clung to her, so Thuy cooked for her too. Gradually though, Hoa and Thinh also sat down to eat, without any invitation. They did this so naturally as though this was the normal family meal routine. Thuy ended up with little food herself as there wasn't enough to go around, but they had no shame.

-----

There was always a queue at the public faucet tap. Thuy would watch the line and then when it got quiet, she quickly crossed the road to wash her clothes. Her belly was getting bigger and bigger, which made sitting on the small, low chair difficult. Anyone with any compassion would have helped Thuy do this task, but Hoa was cold and didn't say a word and then eventually just threw in her clothes and her child's clothes on top of Thuy's pile to wash.

Binh always went out with his relatives. He left his wife and child behind in the inn. He didn't show any care or consideration. Thuy silently endured. There was never a time to be able to talk to him alone, without dozens of ears listening in.

A week passed and still there was no news about the boat. Early one morning, as Thuy's patient was wearing thin.

"What is happening with the boat?"

"Still no news!" Binh snapped back at his wife. "I go out there every day to check on the situation. Why are you asking so many questions?!"

"I'm asking just so I know what's going on. I'm at home, so what do I know, unless you tell me." Thuy said as calmly as possible. "Last week, Fat asked for your cousin's rent."

"Okay, let me figure it out. You still have money though, so can you pay their rent first?"

Then it was Thuy's turn to snap. "You said you would work this all out yourself? Now you're asking me to pay their rent? Where do you think the money is coming from?" She was furious now and it all came out. "How have your wife and child been this week? You've paid us no attention. You don't even know how miserable it is of us. Hien is still young, but I'm now also looking after that seven years old girl! My belly is getting heavier and heavier, making it difficult for me to move around, but you don't see how your cousins make me wait on them. They do nothing to help me and now you want me to pay for their rent!?"

"Why do you talk so much?" Binh was annoyed, but also slightly embarrassed.

"You're always out and this is the first time I've shared with you how hard I am finding this situation and all you can say is that I talk too much? You refuse to see what is happening. No one seems to care about me and my child, so from today onwards, I will only take care of myself and Hien. I'm not strong enough to take care of all of you." Those were Thuy's final words.

After talking to Binh, Thuy knew she had to be calmer and more resilient. Her father had said to her, *'when you get married, you have to follow your husband, but remember no one loves you more than you love yourself.'* This was now truer than ever.

For many years, Thuy had to fend for herself and her family and now, even though she had a husband, she felt like a single mother. Being married to a Chinese man when the war broke out, meant you could not live a peaceful life. Now she was fleeing the country where she was born, taking her child with her to follow this man. Thuy found herself alone and isolated in her husband's world and she was beginning to wonder whether she had made the right decision. With each passing day Thuy felt physically and emotionally exhausted. She had no energy to care and made her annoyance with Binh's relatives obvious.

Mrs Fat no longer hounded her for rent and Thuy didn't care who paid. Binh and his relatives still left in the morning and returned in the evening, but they no longer ate at the hostel. Little Hien and Huong played together every day, so Thuy helped to take care of her. She hoped that everything would be peaceful until the day the small boat set sail.

-----

At the public faucet tap, while Thuy was washing clothes, she was able to listen in on the women's gossip. She learnt more of the situation in Hai Phong. The Hoa people continued to run to Hai

Phong to find ways to go abroad, among them were many families with Vietnamese husbands or wives. During this time, many Vietnamese also took the chance to flee this oppressive government and pursue a more prosperous life. They made fake papers and took on Chinese names. They bribed officers in the Foreign Police Department, who had connections to boat owners. Some people got away with it, but those that didn't were arrested and brought to court. Their sentences could be as long as three years in prison. This never discouraged others to try to escape, everyone wanted a better life.

Thuy remembered a proverb, 'Good land, birds flock.' So, why did so many Vietnamese people who were born and raised here not want to stay on the land left by their ancestors? Why were they not afraid of fleeing? Was this land no longer good, it made the innocent birds fly away?

One morning Binh and three of the others went out in a hurry. Thuy didn't understand why, but when they got back in the afternoon, Binh looked excited.

"There is good news, tomorrow morning we must gather at May Chai wharf to get on the boat. You get us all packed, we have to be at the meeting point at 5 am." He told his wife.

This was what they had been waiting for.

"Which foods can we bring?" Thuy asked.

"Aunty, we have paid enough money, the boat owner must feed us during the trip to Hong Kong." Linh answered for Binh.

"Aunty worries too much. There is no need to buy anything to take."

Everyone's minds were restless. They were all indescribably excited about the upcoming trip.

Thuy was excited too, but also felt uneasy. She told Binh to go to the market to buy a five litres water container and a few bags of dry food. "We have a little girl and no one really knows what it will be like on the boat, so just in case she gets hungry or thirsty, I have something to give her." She only whispered this.

The boat owner didn't want people bringing many things onto the boat. They were worried about the weight. Thuy had heard some of the women at the public taps talking about bringing big jugs of fresh water to drink and some dry food just in case.

Thuy had never been out on the sea before. She couldn't really imagine what it would be like and didn't know how to prepare for it. Binh and his nephews knew nothing, but they were young, so didn't have anything to worry about. Binh listened to his wife and went out to buy provisions she had requested.

That night, in the rented room, you could hear whispering all night. It was probably the last chance to get a good night's sleep until they were on land again, but people couldn't sleep. There was too much to think about.

At 4 o'clock in the morning, Binh called three cyclo drivers to come to the inn. It was still dark and people's faces were not visible.

After paying for Mrs Fat's room, Binh and his nephews quickly carried their personal belongings and went out of the door. Thuy and Huong held little Hien's hand and followed behind them.

In front of the inn, the cyclo drivers were waiting.

"Where are you all going?" One driver asked.

"Take us to May Chai wharf, as fast as you can."

"It's a long way from here to there and you want us to pedal fast. Give us 15 dong per cyclo." The bony face driver said coldly.

"You're taking advantage of us! We're all Vietnamese people in a difficult situation, 15 is too much!" Binh said half annoyed, half pleading.

"Well, you have plenty of money to run away, why are you haggling over a few coins? You know there are no customers from May Chai wharf to come back." Another cyclo driver laughed.

"We all have our own hardships. 12 dong 50 cents each then?" Binh firmly said.

The cyclo drivers looked at each other and nodded, pulled their vehicles closer to the sidewalk, and everyone quickly got on. The drivers started pedalling towards May Chai wharf. On the road, there were already a few women carrying goods to sell at the market.

Near the boat dock, many people were seen carrying bags, their faces full of fear, looking for the boat owner. Everyone got off the cyclo at nearly 7 a.m. The sun was high in the sky, casting golden rays of light on the river. There were shadows of wooden boats moored along the shore.

The May Chai Wharf was bare without a single tree and the early summer sun was starting to become harsh. The meeting point was exposed to the heat, as hundreds of people stood in groups waiting. Binh knew where Phuong's boat was, so they went straight there.

At the front of the wharf, three police officers in yellow uniforms were present. There was a square table and two chairs neatly placed across the entrance, close to the gangway and a large umbrella shaded the officers from the sun.

Captain Hung sat in the middle. A lieutenant sat next to him with a list on the table and a pen neatly placed in front of him. The boat was anchored a few meters from the shore. There was a wooden plank that connected the bow of the boat and the bank near the gangway. Another lieutenant stood right at the head of the dock, holding a list of names of people leaving the country that the boat owner had submitted in advance.

Phuong's boat was ordered to leave first, everyone lined up and the lieutenant read the name of each household head. They then had to reply in a loud voice, 'Yes! I am here!'

All the family members followed the household head to Captain Hung. They had to hand over all their documents; exit papers, household registration book, rice book, food stamps, cloth coupons, ID cards. The lieutenant next to Hung, would then look at the document before throwing it into the basket on the ground. He did it as though these were just scrap of papers. Then the two of them would whisper to each other, before the captain nodded to signal permission to board the boat.

"Truong Van Binh." The police lieutenant called. Binh stepped forward.

"Yes, that is me." Binh handed the papers over.

"How many people are there in your family?" The lieutenant asked.

Binh turned around and pointed at Thuy and his child standing behind him.

"There are three people in my family. I am the head of the household and that is my wife and my daughter."

The police officer looked at the list and read the names. "Le Thi Thuy, little girl Truong Thi Hien." Thuy knew he was going to say her name, but it still startled her to hear it. She handed over her papers.

Holding the ID card in his hand, he looked at Thuy very carefully.

"Are you Le Thi Thuy? Vietnamese? Are you this man's wife?" He asked clinically.

"Yes, it's clearly written on the paper."

He looked at Thuy once more with a cold gaze, threw the papers on the ground and pressed the tip of his leather shoe on her ID paper. He did this with anger, rubbing the paper into the ground. Even when the paper was torn and flattened under his feet, he still didn't stop. Thuy felt her heart ache, but told herself to restrain from saying anything and just endure the humiliation. Thuy thought, from that point on, she probably wouldn't be able to return to Vietnam. Captain Hung waved his hand and said loudly to let them get onboard.

The lieutenant gave a nod which meant they could get on the boat. Holding her daughter's hand and walking behind Binh, she slowly waded through the slimy mud to get to the plank. Nearing the boat, she could hear people whispering below, how sorry they felt for her, especially being so pregnant. She heard someone else ask, what would happen to her now she's following her husband to get away from this country.

*Hold a daughter's hand,*
*Pregnant wife follows her husband.*
*Feet stepping onto the boat,*
*Tears blend with the sea.*

Thuy walked with the sound of people talking below her. Binh's relatives continued to be called by their names. Binh walked ahead carrying their bag and suitcase, while Thuy held their daughter's hand and stepped inside the boat. From that moment onwards, they had no identity papers, no name and were no longer Vietnamese citizens. They had given up everything, to leave forever, away from this S-shaped land.

----

**Note**

*1 - 5000 dong; At that time, a doctor's salary was 70 dong a month.

# CHAPTER 6

## Bĕihăi Bay, China

*Since governments take the right of death over their people, it is not astonishing if the people sometimes take the right of death over governments.*

**Guy de Maupassant**

Thuy and her husband boarded the boat and saw a group of people huddled near the back of the cabin. More passengers continued to board Phuong's boat mostly families: husbands, wives, and children. The oldest was around fifty. Some families had as many as four children. Outside, the sun still blazed, and the voices of policemen calling out names for the next boat drifted through the hot air.

After 2 pm Phuong's boat completed its exit procedures. They waited for the tide to come in before they could raise anchor and set sail. A barge carrying five people including three police officers from the Immigration Department pulled up alongside the boat. They threw a rope to the owner, and the captain tied it securely.

Around 3 pm, the police barge began towing Phuong's boat away from May Chai Wharf toward

Dai Viet seaport. People whispered to one another, their faces filled with confusion and fear. Hearing the water rushing outside, they knew the boat was moving slowly leaving May Chai Wharf, slowly pulling away from Vietnam. The feeling was indescribable. They hadn't yet left Hai Phong waters, but there was no turning back.

The air grew heavy and tense. No one spoke. The only sounds were the occasional coughs. The children, too frightened to cry, slept quietly beside their families. The silence was suffocating.

There were 145 people on board. It was May, but the air was stiflingly hot, thick with everyone's breath. For more than a day, the barge towed the boat through the Cat Hai islands, past Cat Bạ and into Ha Long Bay. Around 7 pm the next day, they reached Ngoc Island, near buoy number Zero - the border of Vietnam's territorial waters. The police prepared to cut the tow rope and push the boat out into the East Sea. Their duty was done. Everyone stood at the stern, watching the barge.

Before turning back toward the mainland, Captain Hung looked at the passengers and shouted mockingly, "Good luck, everyone and enjoy your meals with plenty of fish!"

It sounded cruel and bitter, filled with resentment and pain. Suddenly, a voice from the crowd - half

Cantonese, half Vietnamese - called out, "I wonder who will eat whom?"

Silence fell. Thuy didn't understand the meaning, but soon people began whispering to be careful with their words. Rumours spread that there were police informants among them.

The barge slowly moved back toward the open sea. From the deck, its silhouette faded into the darkness. People stood watching the mainland disappear into the distance.

**Goodbye, Vietnam.**

**Goodbye to the land where we were born and raised.**

**Farewell!**

**Goodbye to it all to joy and sorrow alike.**

A deep, aching sadness was visible in everyone's eyes. They were truly leaving everything behind family, friends, loved ones. There was little hope of ever seeing them again. No one cried out loud; only quiet sobs, choked breaths and tears that fell silently like drops of blood from the hearts of innocent people.

All around them was darkness, the deep blue of the sea blending with the darkening sky. The vast ocean dwarfed the small boat, as fragile and lonely as a drifting leaf. Some passengers had lived near the sea in Vietnam, but for others like Thuy's family, who came from the delta, the midlands or the mountains, this was their first encounter with the open sea. The boat drifted on, carrying the fearful, lonely thoughts of those aboard.

-----

The boat was about 18 meters long and only four meters wide. Its hold was divided into two levels - the upper for people and the lower for supplies: food, firewood and coal.

A few young men on board were "reluctant sailors." They were fishermen from a Quang Ninh family, the parents in their fifties, with seven sons ranging from sixteen to thirty. Ten adults and two small children under five. They had paid only a few hundred dong and an old Soviet watch for passage a low price compared to others, but in exchange, the sons had to help crew the boat.

Most passengers were women and children. Men made up less than a third of the total. Each family occupied a small space in the upper hold, just large enough to spread out a mat to sit or lie on. Thuy's family of three shared one spot, though her husband, Binh, spent most of his time up on deck, giving Thuy room to stretch her legs with her feet resting on their bag.

Men were scattered across the floor, talking quietly or lying down. At the back of the boat was the toilet, a "room for prestige," they called it a small enclosure made of bamboo panels with a wooden plank across it, where waste fell straight into the sea.

At dusk, the boat sailed on with the wind. The owner trusted the captain, who had made the voyage to Hong Kong many times before and so allowed them to travel through the night.

Thuy and her child lay beside a family of five: a Chinese man and his Vietnamese wife, their 18-year-old daughter, 16 -year-old son and the man's elderly mother, around sixty. The husband had once been a deputy secretary of the Hanoi Youth Union, forced to resign; his wife, a textile worker at the March 8 Textile Factory, had been fired. Harassed by the local authorities, they fled to Hai Phong with his mother like so many other ethnic Chinese families seeking to escape.

Most of the passengers were ethnic Chinese, many from large extended families with grandparents, parents, uncles, aunts and children. They came from Lang Son, Cao Bang, Lao Cai, Hanoi, Hai Phong, but mostly from Quang Ninh. There were also a few families like Thuy's neighbours: Chinese husbands with Vietnamese wives, from all walks of life, now sharing the same boat, the same fate and the same fragile hope of reaching Hong Kong safely.

-----

Everyone was dozing. The cabin was silent except for the occasional low snore drifting through the air. Everything was calm until suddenly, the boat lurched and tilted as if something had struck its side. Then came the rain, pouring down like a waterfall.

The wind howled in fierce gusts and the waves slammed hard against the hull. The boat tilted, leapt, and slid, tossing violently from side to side as if spinning in circles.

The captain shouted at the top of his lungs, trying to be heard over the roar of the sea. "Where are the men? A thunderstorm's coming hold tight to the rudder and the mast!"

"Oh no! The boat's drifting back toward buoy zero, we're all dead meat!" someone cried out in panic.

Terror spread through the boat. Children screamed and sobbed; old women clasped their hands in prayer, chanting the Buddha's name. Everyone feared the same thing that the boat might capsize or be swept back into Vietnam's territorial waters, where they could be shot or imprisoned. Thuy held her daughter tightly, her whole body trembling. She looked for Binh and his cousins but couldn't find them in the chaos.

After nearly half an hour, as if by a miracle or divine mercy the sky cleared and the rain stopped. The rocking ceased. Calm returned to the vast, dark night. Only the soft slapping of waves against the hull could be heard.

"Don't worry, the storm has passed," the captain called out.

"Are you sure you know the way?" a woman's voice shouted back.

"Don't worry," a man replied confidently. "Strong winds and big waves are normal out here. Our boat's fine this month - it's next month, the stormy season, that you should fear."

His reassurance did little to ease the growing unease. People muttered in low voices.

"When they took our money, we thought the price was high, they said there'd be a motor! But this is just a rotten wooden boat with sails. It's like hanging a goat's head to sell dog meat!" someone cried out bitterly.

"The owner promised we'd have an experienced captain, a sturdy boat that we'd reach Hong Kong safely!" another shouted.

"You people from Quang Ninh are used to the sea," someone from the city replied. "Of course, you're not afraid. But we are. We don't belong out here."

The arguments went nowhere. One by one, people fell quiet and drifted off to sleep, though some lay awake, staring at the ceiling, worry pressing down on them like a weight.

Hien had long fallen asleep, but Thuy kept shifting, unable to find a comfortable position. Her legs rested on a bag, but her stomach felt tight and uneasy.

The boat was moving faster now, pushed by strong winds. All around was darkness endless shades of deep blue. Nothing could be seen except the faint outline of their small vessel, a speck lost in the vast ocean. No one knew where they were whether they had reached international waters or entered the South China Sea. The captain said nothing. He stood silently, eyes fixed on the compass laid on a nautical chart about a meter wide. He smoked constantly to stay awake, a cigarette always glowing near his lips. Three sailors stood nearby, keeping watch.

In the first few days, each family ate the dry food and drank the water they had brought with them. But before long, their supplies were gone. The boat owner provided two meals a day - one of rice, one of thin porridge with a bit of dried fish or pickled radish. Food was rationed carefully; the journey would be long and stores were limited.

The May heat was merciless in the middle of the ocean. The sun beat down on the small boat and the sea itself seemed to steam. Many of the women were seasick, dizzy and weak. They vomited until there was nothing left only bitter yellow and green bile.

The unbearable heat mixed with the stench of vomit, sweat and unwashed bodies. The cramped, airless cabin became almost impossible to endure.

Meanwhile, the men stayed on deck, breathing in the fresh sea air, unaware of the foul smell below. They used ladles to scoop seawater over themselves, washing their faces and bodies. At night, they gazed up at the endless blue-black sky, tracing the stars and constellations.

Everyone was hungry especially the children and the pregnant women. Thuy and her daughter were lucky not to get seasick, but the baby in her womb kicked constantly. She knew it was hunger. The captain and the boat owner's family, though, seemed well-fed. Even the sailor's wife from Quang Ninh was able to ask for extra food. Rumour had it she hadn't wanted to go at all two or three months pregnant, tricked by her husband's family into leaving Vietnam and now her husband was doing everything he could to keep her happy.

Little Hien complained of hunger constantly. Thuy was exhausted and weak herself. Her rations half a bowl of rice in the morning, a bowl of watery porridge in the afternoon were barely enough for her, let alone the baby growing inside her.

One night, Hien lay awake, listening. She heard the sound of someone chewing a crisp, juicy crunch. She sat up and followed the noise. The boat owner's son, a boy of about nine or ten, was holding a purple plum, a corner already bitten off.

Hien glanced at her mother, who immediately shook her head.

"I'm so hungry, Mum," Hien whispered.

Her eyes fixed on the plum. Each bite the boy took made her stomach ache even more.

"Big brother," she said softly, "can I have one bite?"

"No," he replied with a teasing grin. "Not unless you've got something to trade."

"I only have the baby in there," Hien said without thinking, pointing at her mother's belly.

The boy laughed. "The baby? I don't want that!"

"Just one bite, please," Hien begged.

He hesitated, then smiled and held out the half-eaten plum. "Okay, here you can have it all."

Hien took it, bit into it once a big, careful bite then handed it back.

"Why didn't you eat it all? You don't like it?" he asked, surprised.

"I just wanted one bite. Thank you," she said quickly, then turned and went back to sit beside her mother, head bowed.

The women sitting nearby had witnessed the exchange between the two children. Some smiled faintly; others shook their heads and clicked their tongues in sympathy. Thuy felt a wave of sadness and shame wash over her. Guilt tore at her heart, and tears began to roll down her cheeks.

Little Hien reached out with her small hand and gently wiped her mother's tears.

"Mum, why are you crying? Did the baby kick you and make your tummy hurt?"

Thuy stroked her daughter's hair, trying to steady her voice. "I'm sorry, my dear. You're so hungry. Today, I'll give you more of my porridge."

Hien shook her head firmly. "If you don't eat, Mum, then the baby will be hungry too. Then your stomach will hurt."

From that day on, Hien never asked anyone for food again.

The boat continued gliding through the waves, heading toward Hong Kong. Several passengers were still vomiting, too weak to move, some fainting from exhaustion. Thuy urged her daughter to lie down and rest, hoping sleep would ease her fatigue.

As they lay side by side, Thuy's thoughts drifted back to the life she had left behind.

She looked up at the curved ceiling of the boat at the bamboo and rattan slats woven together above her head. Some were cracked, others discoloured with age. Like human lives, she thought, nothing stays the same forever.

Would her little family make it safely to Hong Kong? She worried for her daughter and for the unborn baby she would soon have to care for. And where was Binh? Why hadn't he come to check on her and Hien?

Before they had left May Chai Wharf, Thuy had spoken frankly to her husband. "Binh," she said, "I'm very worried about this journey. I've had two difficult labours before and we lost our first child. I'm scared for this baby." She looked down at her stomach. "There's no doctor on this boat. If I go into labour and things go wrong, I don't want to cause trouble for anyone. So please, if it comes to that, throw me and the new born into the sea."

Her voice was calm but resolute. "You must take care of Hien. Raise her to be a good person. If she grows up safely with you, I'll be at peace. Promise me that, Binh."

"Why are you talking nonsense? What's wrong with you?" Binh snapped, his tone sharp.

"I've come to understand the kind of man you are," Thuy continued quietly. "I'm telling you this now, so if it happens, you'll know what to do. Promise me you'll do the right thing."

Binh looked at her without a word, his face expressionless. Thuy couldn't read what he was feeling but that wasn't unusual.

That conversation now felt like a lifetime ago. She hadn't seen him for days on the boat. All she could do was hope they would reach safety alive and together.

While she was lost in thought, a commotion broke out among the passengers. Several men rushed into the lower hold, shouting as they went.

"The boat's leaking! Water's coming in! Everyone stay where you are we'll bail it out and patch the cracks!"

Thuy could hear them clearly below, and so could everyone else. The men took turns bailing out water and plastering the gaps in the wooden hull.

The lonely boat drifted across the vast sea, unaware of the chaos within like an old man wandering aimlessly in a desert. Fear gripped everyone on board. Some clasped their hands and prayed to Buddha; others made the sign of the cross or whispered to the Sea Goddess for mercy.

They had only been at sea for two weeks and already the boat was leaking. It felt as if the owner had hidden the truth about the vessel's poor condition. This wasn't an iron ship with an engine as promised, but an old wooden fishing boat and yet, the passengers had paid dearly for their passage.

Sensing the danger, the boat owner finally announced that they would head toward Beihai, China, to make repairs.

Many boats were anchored along the Beihai coast, waiting for repairs. From afar, you could see people moving busily about on the shore. When Phuong's boat was finally tied up and lined up among the others, everyone was told to disembark. Carrying their bags and holding on to their children, the passengers clambered off the boat amid noise and confusion, stepping onto the sand at last.

Another hundred and forty-five people now joined the growing crowd of refugees stranded along the Beihai coast. Small tents had been built with poles stuck into the sand, covered with scraps of nylon, old blankets anything that could provide a bit of shelter from the rain or sun. Others lay completely exposed, with nothing to protect them at all.

Families with strong, able young men found better spots to rest. Thuy, burdened by her swollen belly and holding little Hien's hand, struggled to find a place. In the end, they managed to claim a patch of ground about a square meter wide relatively flat despite the small pebbles and sharp rocks. Fortunately, Thuy had brought a piece of green khaki cloth, which they spread out as a mat. A bag of clothes served as their pillow. On the boat, they had used a Vietnamese–English dictionary for that purpose, but it was now torn, discoloured and useless.

The families slept close together under the open sky, which stretched above them like an endless blue curtain. The scene was bleak people huddled on the sand, stripped of their homes and dignity but someone tried to lighten the mood by joking, "Everyone! We're staying at a thousand-star hotel tonight!"

Laughter rippled through the group soft, awkward, tinged with sorrow. They all knew it was true in the saddest way possible: once they had homes, now they slept on bare earth.

The boat owner told the passengers that the repairs would take a long time. Each person would be given a bowl of porridge with dried radish every day, but after that, they would have to fend for themselves.

-----

On this stretch of land, there were many Chinese and Vietnamese refugees from the damaged boats waiting for repairs. But there were also local Chinese farm workers who wanted to escape their own country, coming to Beihai to find a way to Hong Kong.

Even while the boat was being repaired, the owner's greed remained insatiable. He continued to take on more passengers, caring nothing for their safety, claiming the extra money was needed to cover repair costs.

There were too many people in Běihǎi and no one to maintain order. Trash piled up everywhere. Drinking water and washing water were scarce. Hunger and thirst led to frequent fights and shouting matches. The filth and desperation of the makeshift camp wore down everyone's patience; quarrels and chaos became part of daily life.

Amid it all, some people were reunited with relatives or friends. Almost every boat that had fled Vietnam had ended up here for repairs. The beach became a strange mix of joy and grief happiness at finding loved ones, sorrow at the shared misery surrounding them.

Some boat owners only provided uncooked rice, forcing passengers to find ways to cook their own food. On Phuong's boat, the owner gave out just one bowl of porridge per person each day barely enough to survive and so everyone was constantly hungry. The heat was relentless, the beach crowded and bare, without even a single tree for shade. The desperation grew by the hour.

Those who still had money went to the nearby market to buy rice. Here, food was sold freely there were no ration cards like back in Vietnam. But for those without money, it made no difference. Some of the women banded together and went into the nearby village to beg. They told each other to learn a few words of Mandarin, though one phrase was repeated most often:

"Qǐng gěi wǒ yīgè hóngshǔ." *(Please, give me a sweet potato.)*

Hunger and despair left them with no pride to protect. Begging became a way to survive.

The local people poor fishermen who lived by the sea were hardworking but kind. When they saw the women and children begging, they did not chase them away. Instead, they often invited them into their homes, offering boiled sweet potatoes, bowls of cold rice, or bits of burnt rice scraped from the pot whatever they could spare.

The refugees ate whatever they were given, never complaining. Hunger had stripped them of shame.

Their pride and dignity had withered away without them even realizing it.

Thuy thought about these women and then what she could sell to buy more food for her family. Then suddenly, her stomach hurt terribly. Her waters had broken. Her trousers were wet and she knew it was time to give birth. Luckily, she was on land, but where should she go to give birth?!

In a panic, she heard a voice tell her that there was an infirmary clinic on the other side of the river, but it cost money to take a boat there.

Thuy asked her friend from Hanoi to look after little Hien and together she and Binh stumbled over to the riverbank. Fortunately, there was a boatman waiting for his next customer when they arrived. She gave him 0.50 yuan to take her across the river. Her stomach ached in waves, sometimes dull then other times intense pain. The boatman could see what was happening to Thuy and rowed the two people as quickly as he could to the clinic.

At this moment in time, Binh's Cantonese was more helpful than it had ever been in Thuy's life. When they arrived at the clinic, two women hurriedly helped Thuy inside. The entire clinic room was bare, except for a bamboo bed with a thin mat, one table and a chair.

They told Thuy to lie down on the bed for the examination. Whatever they said, Binh translated for his wife. There was no need for any questions from Thuy, it was good to have someone to give instructions to her. Just like the previous two times, the pain was long and continuous. It hurt whether she stood or sat. She leaned against the wall with both hands, biting her lips until they bled, holding back from screaming.

The ladies at the clinic told Binh that Thuy wasn't thinking of herself anymore, her only fear was that the baby was suffocating because her water had broken.

No longer feeling pain, Thuy bit her lip, silently praying to the sacred Buddha to bless her and help her through this critical moment.

There was an ancient saying; *'Men cross the river with friends. Women give birth, alone.'*

Thuy was giving birth to a child, she didn't dare to cry out loud for fear of what had happened in the past. She prayed for its safety.

It was getting dark. The nurses would come in and out of the room to check on Thuy. Binh would follow them closely, listening in.

That night, with the time unknown, the stubborn son was born. Hearing the baby's cry, Thuy felt an overwhelming happiness and started crying herself.

Looking over at the nurse, she said "Fēicháng gǎnxiè." (Thank you very much). Her husband had taught her the words for thank you, in Mandarin. The nurse nodded and smiled back.

Binh happily told his wife, their son weighed eight pounds.

Thuy felt reassured and let her tears flow. It was indescribable joy. She silently thanked God and Buddha for blessing a mother and child. She fell into a deep sleep after a painful, tiring day.

The next morning, Thuy felt extremely hungry and thirsty. Binh had bought a piece of boiled green squash for her, which she greedily ate up.

Thuy asked Binh to find out how much they owed the clinic and was surprised when they wouldn't take any payment. She would never forget the kindness of these sisters. A small, simple infirmary clinic in a poor fishing village, but the people were full of humanity.

An hour later, Binh and his wife asked permission to return to the boat. Thuy welled up with tears again, when they were departing. She would forever be grateful. Holding her son, they took a boat across the river with overflowing joy and happiness.

-----

Hien had waited all day for her parents to return. When they still hadn't come home that evening, she was full of impatience.

"Aunty, why hasn't my mother come home yet?"

"Your mother went to pick up the baby, do you want a baby?" Kieu said, trying to console her.

"I want a baby to play with."

"Then you have to be good, tomorrow your mother will bring the baby home."

This seemed to settle Hien and she obediently listened to Kieu. When she woke up in the morning, Hien went out to wait for her mother. Around noon, Hien recognized her mother's figure from afar and shouted happily.

"Aunty Kieu! My mother, my mother is back!"

Kieu and other people heard Hien's loud cry, they looked in the direction Hien was pointing.

Binh walked beside Thuy, who was holding their son. He was tightly wrapped in a towel, sleeping. Hien quickly ran out to hug her mother's leg. She pulled Thuy's hand.

"Mum, let me see my baby, Mum?"

Everyone gathered around. There was a happy atmosphere in the camp. Congratulations were heard all around and relief that mother and child were both doing okay.

"I hope you ladies and sisters won't keep Thuy from going into their tent. It's too hot and sunny to be standing outside." Kieu announced.

The crowd dispersed to let the family pass. Kieu took the baby from Thuy's arms and Binh went inside, helping his wife sit down.

Outside, the voices continued talking and gossiping. Of course, Thuy and her new born baby were the topic of conversation for now.

Hien was very happy. She sat close to look at the baby, curiously touching the tiny fingers and the funny little nose.

"Mum, does the baby have a name? What do you call him?" Hien said, still looking at the baby.

Kieu also wanted to know. "Do you have a name for him? Did you sleep well last night?" Then more questions. "Have you eaten yet?"

"I don't know what time the baby was born. I only know that it was dark for a long time before he came out. Then I fell asleep, I was so tired." Thuy replied, still sounding exhausted, but continued. "After the baby was born, I was worried about how Hien was with you last night. Has the boat been repaired yet? How many more days will we have to wait here on the beach? What will happen to me and the baby?"

There were people who were on the same boat, sitting nearby. "Oh, you just gave birth, don't think too much, just take it as it comes, Binh will take care of you and the baby." Someone said, encouragingly.

"I heard the boat is not finished yet. No one knows when the boat will sail again. The boat owner is still feeding everyone porridge. You must eat so you have milk to breastfeed your baby, Thuy." Someone else said kindly. "Just tell me if you need anything, we will help you."

Thuy was touched by people's kind words. It meant even more, given the dramatic situation they were all forced to be in. There was no sign of Binh's relatives. This didn't surprise Thuy and she didn't want to ask.

A Vietnamese lady, Xoai, who had followed her husband here, spoke about wanting to have her own child soon. "Looking at him sleeping so soundly, my family is also hoping for a child, but with this chaos, the only option is to wait and see. What name will you give the baby?" Xoai asked.

Binh looked in from outside. "That's my gold bar. A souvenir from the sea, my baby was born here. Thuy wants to name him Bac Hai (Běihǎi) which also means North Sea."

The women laughed happily. "Then remember to take good care of the baby and nourish the gold bar and mother." Someone said directly to Binh. There was more teasing. "Binh, quickly cook some food for her!"

With the addition of a new life, the atmosphere of the surrounding tents became bustling and joyful. The women left the tent. Thuy put the baby in a small suitcase which had diapers and clothes in it. Hien lay down next to the baby.

Thuy took a tin of 'Ong Tho' sweetened condensed milk to make a cup of milk for herself and her child to drink. She brought ten tins from Hai Phong and had used up five tins already. Now it was even more precious to her, as they didn't know how long they would be stranded on this beach. She called out to Binh.

"I asked Kieu to cook for me and Hien today. We have a few provisions left, but tomorrow, you'll have to sell some of our things to buy more food. How do the boat owners think anyone can survive on one porridge bowl a day?"

Before they left their hometown, Thuy had packed clothes and nappies. Now they were in China, they had to let go of those things, she couldn't keep them any longer. There was a jacket made of nylon fabric that her father had sewn for her, a few sweaters, a watch and a khaki hammock. Those were just the first things to go. They needed money.

The next day, Binh left early to sell their possessions. Many boats leaving North Vietnam stopped at Běihăi to repair their boats. They were unsafe. The boat owners were greedy and bought the boats for as cheap as possible. They would also fix them as cheaply as possible and then paint them to look good. The foreign police officers knew but ignored it because the boat owners had bribed them.

Běihăi was where most boats from North Vietnam came. The space was overcrowded, at times there were more than a thousand people on the beach. The weather was unpredictable, there were spells of strong sunshine and then heavy rain. It was temporary living conditions, but it was difficult to keep clean, which meant people kept on getting sick.

After giving birth, the hardship continued. The tent was tiny and it was pitched on top of rocks and pebbles. During the day, the sun burned down on the land, making people itchy and uncomfortable. Some days were windy and dusty. Rubbish would fly everywhere and into tents. It wasn't ideal for someone who had just given birth.

The next day, Binh had collected fresh water for cooking. But Thuy, unable to bear the heat any longer, took the bucket to bathe. She poured the cool water over herself and as it ran down her body untouched by bathing for so long, she felt as though a great burden had lifted. She felt free at last.

However, the older women nearby saw what she had done.

"Oh my God! Why are you so reckless? You mustn't bathe in cold water right after giving birth! When you're old, your bones and joints will ache. Oh, Thuy!"

*What is there to abstain from when life is already this miserable?* Thuy thought. She would rather risk the pain later than remain hot, dirty and uncomfortable now. She laughed quietly, still savouring the simple pleasure of being clean.

A few days later, Binh came rushing into the tent, excited to share some good news. Not far from where they were, he had found an old wood workshop. Inside, wooden planks were stacked in piles, but the space was otherwise empty. The thatched roof looked sturdy and safe.

Binh brought Thuy and the children there to shelter from the wind and rain. Two neighbouring families also took down their tents and followed. Thuy carried the baby, while little Hien clung to her mother's shirt as they walked. Binh packed up their things and led the way. Each family hoped this new shelter might make life a little more bearable.

The workshop looked abandoned, but everyone's faces brightened with hope. Several men began unstacking planks and assembling makeshift beds. The building would keep them out of the sun, rain, and wind and at night, with a roof overhead, they would finally be warm.

Hien sat on one of the planks, bouncing happily. Baby Bac Hai slept soundly in the suitcase, so Thuy took the chance to lie down herself. It had been so long since she'd been able to stretch her legs. The days spent on the rocky, uneven beach had been torture. She closed her eyes, breathing in the salty sea breeze and the faint scent of wood.

But the joy didn't last. Suddenly, a bright flashlight shone in Thuy's face. The beam swept across the workshop, revealing armed men shouting in the local dialect. Everyone froze in fear. Binh and two young men who spoke Cantonese tried pleading with them to let the families stay for the night. But the guards refused, shaking their heads.

They ordered everyone to leave immediately, flashing lights into people's faces to intimidate them. The men kicked the wooden planks aside so no one could sit. With heavy hearts, everyone packed up again, leaving behind what had felt like a dream of safety.

Inside, Thuy's heart filled with sadness, anger and fear. When war breaks out, innocent people are left homeless. The Vietnamese had been forced out of their own country and now, in China, they weren't even allowed to rest in an abandoned workshop.

*Where could these lost birds fly?*
*Where could they land and where,*
*if anywhere, would they be safe?*

The families trudged back to their old spot. Thankfully, no one else had taken it. With weary hands and downcast eyes, they drove the stakes into the ground and rebuilt their tents once more.

"Is that Binh?" a voice called out.

The couple turned toward the sound. Thuy recognized the man at once. "Binh, it's your friend Vinh," she said with a smile.

"Oh, Vinh! I haven't seen you in ages! Which boat are you on?" Binh exclaimed, delighted to see his old school friend from the Chinese High School in Hanoi.

"Our boat's being repaired - it's been leaking for a week now. Did your wife just give birth?" Vinh asked.

"Hello, Vinh. Do you remember me? I gave birth just a few days ago," Thuy said.

"How could I forget you? I always told Binh he was lucky to have you," Vinh said kindly.

Binh laughed. "Still full of monkey talk, I see! Did your whole family come with you and your parents too?"

"Yes, we all came together. Thuy, why don't you go inside to rest? It's windy out here."

Then Vinh leaned in and whispered to Binh, "Tomorrow, I'll give you some Korean ginseng. Your wife looks very weak after childbirth. Buy her some chicken and tonic to help her recover." He waved goodbye and hurried off.

That night, the full moon hung bright in the vast sky. Another night of damp wind awaited them. Perhaps the Moon Lady would shine her pure light to help these suffering souls sleep beneath their makeshift blue blanket.

In the following days, the boat owner continued taking in more refugees from Chinese farms, even though the vessel still hadn't been fully repaired. People kept asking for updates until Phuong, the owner, finally made an announcement.

Ten days after baby Bac Hai was born, the boat was ready to sail again but Phuong refused to let Thuy and the newborn board.

"According to Vietnamese fishermen's customs, women who have just given birth aren't allowed on boats," she said. "It brings bad luck - danger to everyone on board."

Thuy didn't believe such superstitions, but what choice did she have? They planned to leave her behind. If her extended family had been there, maybe Phuong wouldn't dare abandon her, but the few men who'd travelled with them had disappeared after arriving in Běihǎi.

Thuy looked at her husband standing there helplessly. She shook her head, frustrated. Dizzy and weak, she was still bleeding heavily just ten days after giving birth. The heat was unbearable, the camp filthy and now this more humiliation. She had little milk for the baby and Phuong refused to refund even half of their money. Binh said nothing. Thuy felt utterly alone.

Soon, others in the camp began to speak up. Kieu and a few others shouted angrily at Phuong, calling her a greedy human trafficker who cared only for money and not for people's lives. They said she was robbing Thuy and her baby. But no amount of shouting could change Phuong's mind she wasn't afraid of words.

Thuy thought bitterly of the time she'd trusted her sister-in-law's connections and business partners. Now she saw the truth: they were all the same. Swindlers who would sell even their ancestors if it made them rich. She'd thought they were travelling on a solid, engine-powered boat safe and secure. But reality had stripped away that illusion. The closer the relationship, the deeper the pain.

There was nothing left to do but pray for mercy, for luck, for a miracle.

That evening, commotion spread through the camp near the boat owner's family tent. Thuy heard the rising voices.

"The baby's sleeping," she told her daughter. "Stay here with him. I'll go see what's happening."

Outside, four or five people were gathered, whispering. When Thuy approached, one woman called out, "Thuy, come quickly there's news!"

"I heard someone mention my name," Thuy said anxiously. "Is something wrong? Are people angry at me?"

"No, no," the woman replied. "We know the boat owner wouldn't let you and your baby on board but do you know? The boat can't leave yet."

Thuy frowned. "What? I thought they were about to sail. When I asked for my money back, they said we'd already been brought here to live in China. But we paid to go to Hong Kong."

"Yes, but you haven't heard the latest," another woman said. "Last night, the boat owner's mother died. They say she ate too much ginseng and deer antlers, and it killed her."

"Why are you all so happy about someone's death?" Thuy asked, puzzled.

"The boat hasn't sailed yet," a plump woman explained in broken Vietnamese. "Congratulations, you're lucky!"

"Lucky? Why?"

"It's compensation! If someone dies, another person can take their place. That means you and your baby can go now. See? Karma works fast!"

Thuy could hardly believe what she was hearing. What a strange superstition! But if it were true, it would mean salvation. She wanted to believe it.

T he women nodded, smiling. "Of course, it's true. How could they leave you here weak, with no money, no family? This must be fate. You're meant to continue your journey to Hong Kong."

Binh had gone to verify the rumour. When he returned, Thuy's heart raced.

"Any news, Binh?" she asked.

"I was going to confront Phuong today," Binh said, "but when I got there, I saw people going in and out of her tent. Her mother died last night."

"The women here have been talking about that," Thuy replied. "Did you find out anything else?"

"There's a lot of speculation about what'll happen next, but no one really knows."

"The boat can't leave yet," Thuy said thoughtfully. "Go over there tomorrow morning and see if you can learn more. I heard that if someone dies, they have to let a new born board the boat - it's part of the seafarers' code."

"Alright," Binh nodded. "I'll talk to them tomorrow. Let's leave them to mourn today."

There was still no news about Phuong's boat. Some boats that had arrived before Thuy's had already departed Běihǎi, while others kept arriving. People came and went constantly and life on the beach grew more chaotic by the day.

The boats that stopped there needed repairs and the owners used that as an excuse to take on extra passengers to cover the costs. Each boat stayed for at least two weeks, sometimes longer. The waiting made people restless and irritable.

Thuy's family was no different. Their makeshift camp was filthy and disorganized; no one took responsibility for anything. Their money was running low. The future looked uncertain only one thing was clear: they couldn't go on like this.

The next morning, Binh set out to demand a clear answer from the boat owner. But when he met Phuong, her tone was unexpectedly gentle.

"Mr Binh, please understand my situation," she said. "I'll allow your family to continue the journey but..." She paused for effect. "To ensure everyone's safety, you'll need to find a shaman to perform a ceremony to drive away evil spirits and remove bad luck from the boat."

"Why do we need a ceremony?" Binh asked, annoyed. "Where are these evil spirits you're talking about?"

Phuong smiled sweetly, her voice syrupy and practiced the voice of a seasoned merchant. "This is old wisdom, passed down by fishermen for generations. The journey ahead is long, Mr Binh. We all want the best, don't we?"

Binh sighed. He was a gentle man and her words softened him. It was impossible to stay angry. If this was what it took to reunite his family on the boat, he would do it.

"Where are we supposed to find a shaman?"

"I know someone," Phuong replied quickly, as if she'd anticipated the question. "There's a man on our boat who used to be a shaman back in Vietnam. If you agree, I'll call him. You can give him a small payment and everything will be taken care of."

*Money,* Binh thought bitterly. *It always comes down to money.* "I'll discuss it with my wife," he said aloud. "You find the shaman. When will the boat set sail?"

"Once the ceremony is completed for your wife and child, we'll depart. Go speak to your wife, we should do this quickly," Phuong replied calmly.

Binh hurried back toward the tent. People stopped him along the way, asking what Phuong had said. Vinh spotted him first.

"Binh! Why the rush?" he called out.

Binh stopped and explained.

Vinh chuckled darkly. "A bunch of vultures in human skin, taking advantage of your situation. I'd bet their 'shaman' is just another way to squeeze more money out of you."

Binh said nothing. He nodded briefly and went on. Near the tent, Kieu and a few other women were waiting.

"Sisters, is my wife inside?" he asked.

Everyone followed him as he entered. Thuy was sitting on the mat, breastfeeding, with little Hien beside her. She looked up anxiously.

"What's the situation?"

Binh sat down next to her, surrounded by curious faces.

"Phuong agreed to let you and the baby on the boat," he said slowly, "but she wants a shaman to perform a ceremony to exorcise evil spirits. She says it'll ward off bad luck."

The tent filled with murmurs.

"Where are we supposed to find a shaman?" Thuy asked, worried. "And how much will this cost?"

"Phuong says there's already one on the boat. She'll arrange it."

Thuy frowned. "Of course, she will. That shaman's one of her people. They won't give our money back and now they've found a way to take even more. They hold the knife we just have to follow orders."

Her head throbbed. The women around her kept talking, offering opinions and gossip, none of it helpful. *How much will this so-called shaman demand?* Thuy wondered. Binh sat in silence.

-----

In a corner of Phuong's boat stall, Thuy sat cross-legged with her son in her arms. She had her head bowed, while silently listening to the shaman mumble and pray. He wore a half grey and half-brown sacrificial robe crumpled as if it had been long forgotten and unused. His head was wrapped in a piece of faded black cloth and he wore a pair of sunglasses, with large frames, tied securely around his ears. He held onto a bowl of water.

His mumbles were indistinct and in between them, he would take a sip of water from the bowl and then spit the water over Thuy and the baby. Thuy felt disgusted.

Around the bottom of the boat, Binh and little Hien with many other people stood watching, following the shaman's spell to exorcise demons. Thuy bent down to shield her son from the sun, but also blocked the jets of water shooting from the shaman's mouth. She had no idea what he was saying and her legs were getting numb from sitting for so long. Her back was burning from the sun and Thuy's head felt like it was spinning.

Despite the discomfort, Thuy held her child tightly in arms, sitting still throughout the entire ceremony. It felt like it was going on forever, but then suddenly, as if raindrops were falling, the shaman used his hand to splash all the remaining water in the bowl all over Thuy and the baby. That was it! The evil spirit had flown away! The boat was safe and sound.

Thuy was so tired, she didn't understand what was going on, until Binh and a few women ran up to the boat stall to help her stand up. Thuy was allowed to step on to the boat. Everyone then took turns getting on themselves.

After the ceremony, Phuong's boat weighed anchor and left Běihǎi. Thuy was sitting next to Binh and little Hien, feeling more comfortable. She thought she could wait in peace for the departure time. Then someone came in and called for Binh. He was passing on a message from the boat owner's message.

"Thuy and her baby have to sit in the lower compartment. A woman who has just given birth cannot sit in the upper compartment, it is unacceptable."

How could she refuse? The boat is about to depart. Binh is forced to move Thuy and their son to the lower compartment, while he and little Hien sit on the upper deck with everyone else.

The lower compartment where Thuy sat was damp and gloomy, thick with the smell of dried fish. A musty scent of food mixed with the sour stench of human sweat drifting down from above. Every sound and smell was magnified: the heat from the sea, the hacking coughs, the spitting, the whining of children all closing in on Thuy and her baby.

A small bowl of porridge wasn't enough for anyone, least of all a mother who needed to breastfeed. Thuy was weak and hungry and she knew baby Bac Hai was suffering too.

She endured the misery as best she could. Her bleeding hadn't stopped. She was constantly exhausted, hungry, thirsty and forced to sit upright day and night, clutching her baby. She could see Bac

Hai growing thinner by the day, his tiny limbs like twigs, his skin wrinkled and loose. The sailors sometimes looked at her with pity, whispering to each other about how frail she and the baby looked. But no one did anything to help.

Day after day, the boat drifted across the open sea sometimes fast, sometimes slow, depending on the wind. Nothing happened for a long while. Then, without warning, the boat lurched sharply to one side, as if it had struck something.

Shouts rang out from above, in a dialect many on board didn't understand. The boat came to a complete stop. Then three large men climbed aboard, brandishing AK rifles. Their faces were red and coarse, their expressions cruel and wild. They pointed their guns directly at people's faces. The passengers froze, trembling in terror. Children hid behind their mothers. Old women clutched their prayer beads and whispered frantic prayers.

Thuy couldn't see what was happening, but she knew it was bad. She hugged her baby tightly and waited.

The boat owner and her crew went forward to speak with the armed men. After ten tense minutes, the owner returned and announced:

"Attention, everyone! After negotiating with the pirates, they have agreed to let us go, but only if we give them money, gold, or anything of value. If not... we will not survive."

No one protested. Everyone had heard of pirate attacks at sea. The crew began calling out the names of each family, listing what they were expected to hand over. People surrendered watches, rings, gold chains, earrings whatever they had.

Binh and Hien had nothing left to give. But one of the sailors, a young man, knew Thuy must still have something. He called her name loudly, ordering her to come up to the deck.

Slowly climbing the steps toward the voice that had called her, Thuy had to squint against the harsh light. Her head spun with dizziness. Binh gently took the baby from her arms and guided her to a seat. Before she could grasp what was happening, the young sailor pointed to her ear.

"Your family can pay with those earrings. That will be enough."

Unable to refuse, Thuy removed her earrings - two-tenths of real gold, her only remaining asset. She had kept them for an emergency and this was certainly one. Nearby, one of the pirates stood guard, gun in hand, watching each person closely to ensure no one resisted.

One by one, each passenger was checked off the list. The two young sailors collected everyone's valuables into two bags and handed them to the boat owner.

When the pirates were satisfied with their loot, they marched off the deck with heavy steps, as if none of it mattered. At the railing, they turned back for one last look at the people they had just robbed, then leapt onto their own boat.

Moments later, the deep rumble of their engine faded into the distance. Only then did the passengers release a collective sigh of relief.

Whispers began to spread who were they? Chinese fishermen? Coast guards? Whoever they were, they were still pirates. They had robbed the weak - the elderly, women and children - people already at their lowest.

After the raid, the boat carried on its course. Gradually, resentment gave way to exhaustion. People stopped talking. Most fell asleep, drained by heat, hunger and fear. What else could they do but sleep?

Thuy and her baby were sent back down to the lower deck. Looking at her frail, skeletal child, Thuy couldn't hold back her tears. The baby cried for milk, but there was none. Her breasts had shrivelled, the skin wrinkled, but little Bac Hai still suckled, searching for comfort. Thuy tried to give her child all the love left in her weary body, but she was too weak and her tears fell freely.

*Mother's tears fall,*
*Dripping onto the baby's lips.*
*He thinks it's milk*
*And smiles.*

Poor little boy, Thuy thought, her heart breaking.

----

The baby's diapers and clothes were running out. There was no clean water, no soap. Binh sat on the edge of the boat, rinsing their soiled clothes by dragging them through the seawater. Sometimes, he wasn't careful enough, and a piece would slip from his grasp lost forever to the waves. Each day, there were fewer nappies left for the baby.

Then, one day, water began seeping into the lower compartment, just a trickle at first, then more and more. Finally, Thuy cried out, panic in her voice:

"Everyone! Is the boat leaking? There's water coming in a lot of it!"

She heard movement and shouting above the captain being called, people rushing to help bail the water out. Only then did the boat owner agree to let Thuy and the baby come up to the top deck with Hien and Binh.

But how could this be happening? The boat had supposedly been repaired in Beihai and more money had been spent on ceremonies to ward off evil spirits and pray for good luck. Yet the water kept rising.

The men took turns bailing. The adults were anxious and silent; the children whined, hungry and frightened. Meanwhile, the captain's daughter-in-law had enough to eat and drink and her five-month-old daughter was plump and quiet. Not a single cry escaped the baby's lips, there was even so much milk that it soaked through her mother's shirt.

Once Thuy was on the top deck, the captain's daughter-in-law, Nghia, could see how thin and hungry baby Bac Hai was. As a mother and a kind-hearted woman, she felt she had to help. She held out her arms to take Bac Hai from Thuy, showing she wanted to breastfeed him. Thuy was so moved that she trembled as she handed her child over, filled with trust and deep gratitude.

The baby had been hungry for so long that he instinctively suckled at Nghia's breast. Thuy could clearly hear the steady gulping sounds he made. Bac Hai smiled innocently at his 'new mother' while he continued to feed. Everyone around them felt joy and relief for the baby and from that day onwards, Nghia would take the baby from Thuy's arms and breastfeed him as if he were her own. Thuy knew she would never forget such kindness.

-----

The boat drifted like a fragile leaf across the vast sea under the harsh summer sun. What fate awaited these lost souls?

"Look, there's a big ship approaching!" a voice cried out.

Everyone rushed to look. The loudspeaker blared first in Cantonese, then in English. Those who understood translated for the others.

"The boat is entering Macau territorial waters... request to stop..."

No one was afraid; instead, there was a sense of hope. Their boat was leaking and water kept seeping in. Would they rather die at sea or be detained by the Macau police?

The police ship drew closer, signalling them to head for shore. The small sailing boat complied, and the police followed closely behind until both reached the pier.

"The Macau police have asked us to get off and go ashore for inspection. Leave your belongings here," the boat owner announced.

Not everyone moved right away. There were murmurs among the passengers.

"This land is for gamblers, it's hard to find work. It's not suitable for refugees," someone argued.

"I'm not staying here! I have to go to Hong Kong," another said.

There were many opinions, but no one would know what awaited them until they disembarked. Slowly, one by one, young and old alike walked down a large wooden gangway onto the pier.

Below, the police stood watching each holding a gun, dressed in navy uniforms with matching hats, their faces solemn and stern. They ordered everyone to line up in two rows: one for women and young children, the other for men. A policeman with a stick tapped each person's shoulder as he counted. No one dared meet their gaze.

Thuy used the moment to look closely at the faces of those who had shared the journey with her. Everyone was exhausted, their hair matted from weeks without washing. The stench filled the air, coming both from others and from themselves. The men were unshaven, wearing little more than rags that barely covered them.

Little Hien was no different her face was dirty, and she huddled behind Binh. Her once-chubby cheeks had sunken, leaving a round face with wary eyes watching the policemen. The women were in no better state. The police looked at them with surprise, even unease, as if faced with something unfamiliar.

After counting everyone, the police led them into a building. Each person was given a bowl of white, cloudy liquid like lime water. No one knew what it was, but they drank anyway, too thirsty to care.

Accommodation was arranged. There was one row of houses for the men, another for the women and girls. Inside were bunk beds, with showers and toilets. For everyone, this was bliss to have a place to sleep and bathe felt like a miracle.

From the men's quarters came sounds of laughter. Each house had been given a packet of cigarettes. Disbelieving, they examined the packets carefully before sharing. They held the cigarettes to their noses, inhaling the scent before lighting up. The smoke filled their lungs and as they exhaled, they laughed together like children given sweets.

A woman from the next house passed by and saw this. She peeked into Thuy's room and said with a chuckle:

"Why doesn't Hien go next door to see her father smoking and laughing?"

"I can hear the laughter. What's going on?" Thuy asked.

"They haven't had a cigarette in weeks! This is pure happiness for them being given free cigarettes!

Just like savages from the forest coming to the city," she said, amused but not unkindly.

They had been close to starvation adrift, hungry, and thirsty for days. Now, they had beds, two meals a day with vegetables and meat and even discovered that the tap water was clean and safe to drink. To them, it was a wonder a true miracle.

Thuy ate well and her breasts filled with milk again. She could now feed Bac Hai herself, no longer relying on Nghia's generosity. The baby drank until he was full and fell asleep. Thuy felt immense relief knowing her child would no longer go hungry.

One day, the young men who had served as sailors on the boat confessed to Thuy,

"We're sorry. Back on the boat, we wondered whether the baby would survive… he looked like a withered leaf."

Thuy was heartbroken to hear this. She had spent sleepless nights weeping silently, watching her baby suckle at her dry breast, powerless to feed him. Now, hearing how others had noticed his frailty, she realised no one had been able to help.

Their week in Macau passed like a dream here one moment, gone the next. Then came the news: the refugees had to continue on to Hong Kong. The United Nations had set up a camp there to receive them. The group was divided women and children were to travel with the police on a large vessel, while the men and boys would remain on Phuong's boat.

No one understood why they were being separated. As the police led the women and girls away, the men were ordered to stay behind. Small girls cried, clinging to their fathers.

Binh was held back among the men. Hien grabbed her mother's shirt and turned to call, "Daddy! Daddy!" as she walked away in tears.

"Where are they taking them?" whispered some of the wives. "Why can't we go together?"

Fear spread many thought this was a final separation. Wives looked back at their husbands through tearful eyes as the police helped women and children aboard the large ship. Then they shouted orders at the men, forcing them back onto Phuong's boat. Soon, the two vessels were joined by a tow rope. The large Macau ship weighed anchor and pulled Phuong's boat behind it, heading for Hong Kong.

When the women saw the men's boat following, they sighed with relief. Sitting on the spacious ship, gliding smoothly over the waves, felt like a luxury Thuy could hardly imagine after being confined to the lower deck of Phuong's boat. Everyone relaxed, slept peacefully and ate proper meals twice a day.

As they neared Hong Kong, bright city lights shimmered ahead. The giant ship stopped, and the women and children were transferred back onto Phuong's boat. The tow rope was cut. The police ship turned back toward Macau, while the small boat sailed on towards Hong Kong. Hope filled the air once more.

"We're in Hong Kong! We're alive, we made it!" "Wake up, come and see! We're really here!" someone shouted.

There was no greater joy in that moment. Everyone rushed to the bow to look. In front of them stood tall buildings, glowing with dazzling lights. Many jumped up and down, laughing through tears of relief and happiness.

The Pearl of the Orient, right before their eyes. Thuy could hardly believe it, the name she had only ever read about in books. She hugged her baby tightly as Binh lifted Hien into his arms, smiling proudly. Thuy's family had survived and together with the others, they had finally reached Hong Kong peacefully with everyone.

# CHAPTER 7

# Hong Kong

*The King was only king in his land*
*Despite a four-hoes carriage,*
*In this place he was only a commoner.*

**Vietnamese folk song**

## Black Warehouse

More than a nautical mile from Hong Kong, the neon lights flashed and danced on the tall buildings, clearly visible from a distance. Everyone on the boat stared at the Pearl of the World, chatting noisily. After more than a month of drifting at sea and several weeks wandering aimlessly along the Běihǎi coast, with only a bowl of porridge to keep them alive, the mobile skeletons finally reached the horizon of freedom at dawn on the 1st July 1979.

While the passengers of the boat talked loudly, they were interrupted by the sound of a canoe and the headlights aimed at Phuong's boat. The loudspeaker spoke clearly and coherently in Cantonese and English. Firstly, asking the boat to stop, then to lower the sails and drop the anchor in place. The canoe came alongside and two police officers boarded the boat and asked to meet the boat owner.

Phuong stepped forward, along with the captain and sailors. After some talking, the police departed on the canoe, revving its engine and heading back to the mainland.

Phuong turned to the passengers and passed on the message. "Attention everyone, the Hong Kong police asked our boat to anchor here tonight. Tomorrow morning there will be a tugboat to take our boat to shore. There is still a lot of rice and food on the boat. Any family that requests a share, we will distribute fairly."

"Mr Binh, there is still a lot of rice. Take some for your wife, so she can feed your baby." The woman from Quang Ninh who was in charge of cooking on the boat called out.

"Thank you. The boat has given us enough to eat. My wife is content and not hungry anymore." Binh replied.

"Why don't you cook and give it to the people right now?" A woman's voice shouted over everyone's head.

"Oh my Gosh! We would be happy to no longer be hungry!" Some people burst out laughing. So happy that they don't know hunger!

How would they all cook the rice? There were no pots, no firewood! Would it be eaten raw? They are the swindlers and liars. Someone's voice was heard from behind.

There was hardly any sleep had by the boat people. There was restlessness and worrying about what tomorrow would bring. Hoping for good luck.

The next morning, around 7 o'clock, the police boat approached. A cable was thrown for the captain and crew to tie up and slowly Phuong's boat was pulled to the dock.

From afar, you could see many boats, big and small, anchored, haphazardly, in no particular order, just swaying in the waves. All of them were to be liquidated, as they were old and dilapidated. Boats that were once the possession of the fishing cooperatives of the Socialist Republic of Vietnam. sold to greedy boat owners.

On the shore, there were hundreds of old people, young men and women, all fighting over the water tap. People moving around, looking busy. Seeing this scene, Thuy imagined that life here would be many times more complicated than at Běihǎi beach, but she had taken the first steps to move forward in their lives, and now there were two small humans she had to think of first before herself. She was just one person amongst many people fleeing Vietnam, they had different reasons, but were all in the same place now.

After 30th April 1975, the government of the Republic of Vietnam collapsed and the Vietnamese people began to secretly cross the border by sea and by land. Then with the onslaught of the Sino - Vietnamese border war, which led to the expulsion and boycotting of the ethnic Chinese people of the communist government of Vietnam, the number of people who crossed the borders openly by sea increased rapidly.

Since 1979, thousands of people have crossed the seas from Vietnam making their way to welcoming countries, such as Hong Kong, Malaysia, Thailand, Indonesia and the Philippines. Although, Singapore had been hesitant in taking on Vietnamese refugees, only accepting boats that guaranteed resettlement to a third country within ninety days. According to incomplete statistics from the United Nations, thousands of people died at sea due to storms, accidents and pirates. In July 1979, more than sixty people died when their boat broke apart, having crashed into a reef, on the way to the Philippines.

Boats entering Hong Kong territory and anchoring near their shores, were given numbers, according to the order of entry. From today, Phuong's boat was named 769, like a prisoner's number. The loudspeaker would call out the numbers.

"Boat people 769, line up in the yard."

Everyone quickly lined up and sat quietly in front of the cement yard looking out to sea. A police officer would then read the camp's rules in Cantonese and English:

1. All dangerous items were to be handed in: knives, scissors, firearms, explosives and flammable substances, including matchboxes and lighters.

2. The use of fire was banned in all circumstances. (This made it very difficult for families with babies who needed to cook porridge and for smokers addicted to cigarettes and water pipe tobacco.)

3. Leaving the camp was strictly prohibited under any circumstances.

4. All detainees would receive two meals a day, from the camp's catering contractor, distributed according to the number assigned on arrival.

5. The camp authorities could check any detainee, at any time of the day or night.

6. Fighting and any other form of public disorder was forbidden and would be dealt with immediately.

After listening to the announcement of the regulations, everyone followed the police to a place called the Black Warehouse.

This was a big warehouse consisting of seven buildings located next to each other. They were all made of corrugated iron and were painted black. Each warehouse was about ten meters wide and twenty meters deep. The warehouse had been abandoned and was now assigned by the Hong Kong government to be used as temporary accommodation for the refugees that entered the country illegally.

Boat 769 was assigned to house 2 with a corrugated iron roof and walls and a cement floor. The camp distributed mats according to regulations. Two people were allocated one single mat and one plastic bucket to collect water in. So, Thuy's family of four received two mats and two buckets.

After their accommodation was assigned. Everyone gathered in the yard. They had to line up for the general sanitation procedures before going through to immigration.

There were two groups of medical staff, who were all covered in protective clothing from head to toe. Each family was called in front of the first group, which sprayed them with disinfectant, then the second group hosed them down to rinse the chemicals away.

Thuy's family were ordered to lower their heads and close their eyes. They sprayed a scalding, caustic chemical on their heads and were told to rub it into their hair. Thuy held onto her baby and bowed down to cover the baby. Little Hien stomped her feet and jumped up as if boiling water had been poured on her. Binh hugged her and rubbed her head to comfort her.

As they sprayed the disinfectant over them, the staff muttered spiteful words in Vietnamese; "You people have no hygiene. You Vietnamese are so filthy. Your hair and your clothes are full of lice."

After they hosed the medication from people's hair, they then sprayed their clothes with a reeking white disinfectant and hosed each person down again. Family after family, the 'cleaning' went on until noon.

When boat 769 had completed its sanitation procedure, all were allowed to go back to the warehouse to change their clothes and then have lunch.

For each boat's midday meal, there was one cask of cooked rice, one big pot of meat and one pot of vegetables. The pot of meat was cooked with tofu like a salty braised dish and the pot of vegetables were cooked until soft and juicy, half like a stir-fry and half like a soup. With hundreds of people on each boat, these quantities were not enough to share around.

Fortunately, boat 769 was regularly served by two young men who were responsible for distributing the rice. They were familiar with the task, so every family had enough to eat. However, when one of them was unable to assist in the even distribution of the rice, there were others who weren't so fair. These tended to dish out more rice to their families.

Hunger wasn't the only consequence of this uneven distribution. Fights would break out over a few grains of rice, which would then alert guards, who would use their cudgels to stop the squabbling.

Thuy's family lived on the far end of the warehouse, so when meals were distributed, they would be the last to receive anything and at this point there was very little left.

Little Hien would cry all night from hunger. One morning, when she woke up, she saw a nylon bag of cooked rice hanging on the wall. It was covered with flies.

“Mum, there is a bag of cooked rice hanging over there, can I eat it?” Hien pleaded.

“That rice belongs to someone else, it’s not mine.” Thuy whispered to her daughter.

“But I'm so hungry, please give me some?” Hien was now crying.

“Look, it's covered with flies and is dirty.”

“I don't care, I can eat flies too!” Hien said firmly.

Thuy looked at her child with pity. Then a woman lying on the mat next to her family said loudly.

“We should ask the men today to divide the meal from here first to be fair, otherwise our families will always go short.” Other people agreed with her.

A woman near them saw Hien crying with hunger and offered her a piece of apple she had just peeled. “Good girl, eat this piece of apple, there are flies on that rice, you can't eat it. If you cry, the baby will laugh.” The woman coaxed kindly.

Hien looked at her mother, reached out to take the piece of apple, but did not forget to say, thank you, aunty. Hien bit and chewed the apple with delight. It was delicious and helped her forget their hunger. She stopped crying and fell asleep. The children fell asleep easily, even in the hot weather.

There were hundreds of people in the warehouse, and because the walls and roof were made of corrugated iron, when the sun shone down on the building it was like being baked in an oven. The people in the warehouse felt like they were in a furnace, sweating non-stop. The men could go shirtless and wear only shorts, but the women could not. It was extremely stuffy and uncomfortable and they all wanted to take a bath.

The police let them out three times a day; morning, noon and evening. They were like prisoners. Everyone had to take advantage of this outdoor time. When they were allowed, Binh took Hien out and Thuy held the baby and stood near the warehouse door to get some fresh air. She would watch and observe the surroundings. There was a water tap in the yard for everyone to use and a bathing and laundry centre. The young people would laugh and joke, splashing everywhere. The old people could only watch.

Looking at that scene, Thuy smiled, suddenly remembering the time when she was still at home with her parents and siblings. They bathed at the pretty well in the corner of the yard and played games of splashing water, chasing each other, laughing and talking happily under the moonlight.

Suddenly there was a voice calling from outside the gate. "Is Mr Lan home?"

"Oh! Hurry up and run into the house, you guys!" The older brother shouted. Everyone ran into the house.

Thinking of this made Thuy miss home. She felt a sharp pain in her heart, not knowing how to let her father know that she had arrived safely in Hong Kong.

The young men were so happy being outside. Thuy looked at the women with small children who were grumbling and trying to scrub their children clean. They could not stand still and it looked like hard work. Everyone was soaked. Then at a distance, she could see a woman dragging her children towards the toilets. Nearer to her, Thuy watched a daughter helping her old mother walk slowly step by step, getting wet before they even reached the faucet.

Surrounding the faucet, people were arguing and fighting. Some were bathing topless, some were washing clothes. The police stood guard with batons in their hands, their faces sullen and annoyed, their mouths cursing. Thuy felt ashamed for the thoughtless people in the yard who had created a bad impression of the refugees.

The camp guard's whistle blared loudly, signalling the end of the hour. They used their whips to strike the cement floor, threatening and shouting.

For those unfortunate souls who were too slow to listen, the whip would hit their legs and body, causing excruciating pain. Some people were pulling up their pants while running, making them trip and fall. Some people didn't have time to put on their pants and were still running naked. Seeing all this was comical, but also sad and humiliating.

Families with old and weak parents had the hardest time. Hearing the whistle, they wanted to walk quickly but their legs were too weak and slow. If they accidentally slipped, the person helping them would fall too. The police didn't care or sympathize with individual difficulties. They were cruel and ruthless. They would turn on the water tap as fast as it would flow and point the hose straight at people. It didn't matter whether they had clothes on or not or whether they were old or young. They shouted abuse at them and threatened to cut their food rations.

In the veins of these policemen and refugees were the same Chinese blood. This didn't help them to empathise with their situation though. They didn't understand this was their last resort and were able to treat them so inhumanly without blinking twice. Rumour went around that these policemen were originally notorious brutal prison guards, but because of the need for more police in this area, they were assigned here.

There was one policeman, who was the most brutal of them all. He was known as the Fat lieutenant. No one knew his real name, but they saw him as being very fat, who cursed profanely and who always held a baton in his hand, ready to beat anyone. Everyone hated and resented him, but most of all feared him.

With the influx of thousands of refugees into the country and all being locked up in the Black Warehouse, there was one major problem. Not enough toilets. The police had to create facilities for the new residents. They used the abandoned boats as public toilets.

The 'toilet boat' swayed with the waves. People with bare feet would step on the floor of the boat, immediately getting their feet soaked with urine. 'Snakes' lay coiled horizontally and vertically, not in any order, giving off a horrendous stench.

Occasionally when a motorboat passed by, the boat would sway up and down with the waves and if there were unsteady feet, it was easy to fall down and crush the snakes on the floor of the boat or fall into the sea.

Little Hien was so scared every time she went to the 'toilet boat', that she stopped going. However, when the need was too much, she had to just close her eyes and hold her breath.

Back in the warehouse, this topic created a heated discussion. "Before arriving at Hong Kong, I was so foolish as to throw my sandals into the sea."

"Me too, but I heard that Chinese objects with Chinese characters had to be thrown away. If we had them on us, they would just take them away. Going barefoot to the toilet is scary and disgusting."

"Do you know, today I almost got whipped because I was slow to come out of the toilet!"

Hearing all this, Thuy was cautious when taking her child to the toilet. She brought with them a basin, which she placed near the entrance of the boat. Hien could then sit on it and she could immediately scoop up the sea water and wash the contents away. It made it all less stressful for mother and child.

When little Hien goes out into the yard and sees the fat policeman, she stands still frozen with fright. She's seen him beat people without mercy several times.

"Mum, I hate that fatty man so much. Why is he so cruel?" Hien whispers to her mother, but watching the policeman.

-----

The daily routine is chaotic and into the night there is no respite. In the summer of July, the Black

Warehouse is not shaded by any trees. The sun relentlessly shines down on the metal building. The heat is scorching, adding to the frustration and stress of a refugee's life. At night the heat is torturous and there is little chance of sleep, slowly suffocating as in an oven.

Outside, people took advantage of these desperate times. They would whisper into the buildings and tempt those inside with goods they were selling. However, the only goods they were selling into the Black Warehouse were packets of instant noodles. They sold packets of ten for 0.1oz of 24 carat gold. It was very expensive, but there was always high demand from the many families with children. Greed was stirred up, some tried to sneak out to trade, causing chaos that affected the rest of the group.

On numerous nights the police would suddenly blow their whistles, waking up the whole warehouse. They made everyone line up in the yard to take roll calls. It was difficult enough to fall asleep, but when this happened, there was no way of falling back asleep. There were nights though, that nothing happened, just the air of sleeplessness that had to be endured.

On rare occasions, the sea breeze blew into the warehouse. The women would then gather together and sit near the entrance, combing their hair, picking lice and chatting. Even though they had been sprayed with insecticide to kill lice, there was no getting away from them, living in cramped, close conditions. The lice still clung to them constantly laying more eggs.

To avoid the lice from infecting her child, Thuy gritted her teeth and cut off her long, silky black hair, which had been the beauty of her girlhood.

Once when she was breastfeeding Bac Hai, she watched him suckle and then pause for a moment. He looked at his mother and smiled, happy with the abundance of milk he was able to drink. Thuy lovingly nodded and talked to her child, he was only two months old, with sparse hair, but the lice did not spare him.

Thuy noticed the lice slowly crawling on his head and into his hair. "Sisters, my little boy also has lice." She shouted to the women sitting nearby.

"Your lice jumped onto his head. Thuy is so dirty!" Everyone burst out laughing at Thuy's worried face. The baby was so small, why did she only see it today? How much blood had already been taken? Thuy blamed herself and spent the rest of the day looking and killing each of lice on Bac Hai's head.

-----

The days living in this place were a series of heavy and stressful times. The police treated the refugees like criminals in a detention camp. No one wanted to continue living like that, so when they heard that they were called for an interview, everyone was hoping for change. In fact, they were going to declare their personal history, full name, date of birth, hometown and previous occupation.

In a small room about four square meters, there was a rectangular table. Sitting at the table were three white people, along with a young girl who would interpret for them. Opposite them, there was a long chair, where each family would sit, while being questioned.

Hearing their family name being called, Binh leads his daughter inside, while Thuy carries her son into the room. They were all nervous. The three white men smiled at the family as they entered. This was slightly reassuring, but still they were on edge.

"Please sit down. Let me introduce these three people. They are members of the United Nations delegation. Today's meeting is mainly to check the completeness and accuracy of the documents declared upon entry." The interpreter happily explained.

The gentleman sitting in the middle asked each person questions. Firstly, Binh the head of the household then Thuy about their relation to one another. The questions were like a CV declaration form including; full name, date of birth, place of birth, ethnicity, reason for leaving and where they had come from. Thuy and her husband answered honestly. The cheerful and gentle approach of the three people and the quick interpreter, created a pleasant atmosphere. They were no longer as nervous as they first were.

Hien hid behind her mother, but gradually peered around to look at the people asking the questions.

"After a period of time in the Hong Kong refugee camp, which country does your family want to settle in? You can register in three countries." The girl asked the two refugees.

"Please tell us, are we allowed to register as we wish? Or are we forced to follow your arrangements?" Binh asked.

"Please rest assured, you can register in three countries of your choice, then depending on the number of registrations, depending on the requirements and standards of the country accepting asylum seekers. We will consider all applications and notify you later. This is just the first step, there will be many more meetings." The man smiled looking at them, but directing the interpreter to translate.

The couple looked at each other. They were surprised by this question, that they hadn't at all thought of where they might want to go after Hong Kong. There were three places that caught their attention as they looked down the list.

"We have a choice. Which three countries do you want to go to?" Binh asked his wife.

"We have two small children, my health is not good, the very cold climates of these countries are not suitable." Thuy turned to the interpreter and asked. "Can you tell me which countries we can register for?"

"Countries that accept refugees include; the United Kingdom, the Federal Republic of Germany, the United States, Australia, Canada, Switzerland, Sweden, Spain, France, Belgium, Portugal, Israel."

"There will be more meetings, so for now, let's give them the names of three countries we like the sound of. We can think about it some more after" Binh said, looking at his wife.

The three men did not understand what the couple were talking about, they just looked at each other and smiled.

After a while, Binh let the interpreter know their decision. "These are the three countries we'd like to register for. First one being the United Kingdom, second the Federal Republic of Germany and then Australia."

Family after family were seen and interviewed. The process lasted for several days and it seemed like the only subject people wanted to talk about. Thuy didn't really participate in all the gossip and speculations, she liked to keep to herself.

The next day, Binh told her that his cousins did not register for the UK. Even though they were confined to the same building, since leaving Vietnam, there was no interaction between Thuy and Binh's relatives. It was as though they didn't exist to one another. Now they were planning to go in completely different directions, without discussion or consultation with their uncle. As for Binh, he didn't say when he spoke to them and Thuy didn't ask. They didn't take any interest in meeting their new baby cousin or even playing with Hien. It was hurtful and confusing and Thuy felt a pang of loneliness for herself and her children, but really she shouldn't have been surprised. Since living in the same small room together in Hai Phong, there was no interest or care from them. Is blood really thicker than water?

Linh and her younger brother Tuat registered to go to the U.S.A. They had dreams that America was the richest country in the world and that it would be easy for them to earn a lot of money there.

"Did Linh and Tuat speak to you before registering?" Thuy asked her husband.

Binh shook his head. "They registered before telling me."

"So which country has Hoa and her younger brother Thinh decided to go to?"

"Hoa and her daughter have registered to go to Germany and her younger brother has not decided where to go yet." Binh slowly said.

Day after day, people living in the Black Warehouse talked and asked each other which countries they wished to go to. There was excitement in the air and something to keep everyone distracted from the mundane of living in a box.

-----

A few days later, the United Nations delegation called Thuy's family to the office for the second time. The officials spoke without wasting any time.

"The standards for accepting refugees in the UK, Germany and Australia are as follows; Germany and Australia will not accept families with young children, so these countries are not an option for you. However, the UK is accepting refugees in large numbers. So it looks like the UK is your only option from your three choices. How do you feel about that?"

They had discussed it previously and were ready to explain their situation and decision. "We have been thinking about this carefully. We didn't know where we would go after we left Vietnam. The war threw us out of the country of our birth. We need a place to call our home and are happy to go to the UK."

Since that day of the decision, the delegation hadn't called Thuy's family again. Some families who were on the same boat were still undecided and hesitant. It was a life changing choice.

However, Thuy was determined. She knew neither of them were used to manual labour and the two children were too young to not be cared for constantly. She never thought of settling in America, having just gone through so many years of war with them. Would the United States even be a peaceful for them to live in?

Although England was only known through books and newspapers. This island was covered in fog all year round, but it was still a rich and powerful country. Thuy had read that during the two world wars, people often mentioned England, France and America together, meaning these were the three great powers.

A few weeks later, Thuy's family and some others of boat 769 were notified to transfer to a different camp. That was all they were told, so they didn't know what that meant and if it would be better than being where they were. What they did know was it was a miserable life staying at the Black warehouse. This place wasn't a prison, yet it wasn't a refugee camp either. The police treated them like international criminals. The news of being transferred to another camp was a ray of hope for everyone.

**Tuen Mun Camp**

At around 7 am, one morning, a police officer blew his whistle and ordered everyone in Warehouse Two to line up in the yard. A second officer stood guard with a baton, while a third held a list of names. Not everyone from Boat 769 was called to move to another camp only about a dozen families. Binh's family was one of them.

After reading out the list, the families who weren't called were told to return to Warehouse Two. Thuy recognised some of the families from the boat. There were so many people in the warehouse that, with no room to move, you could go days without seeing the same faces twice.

The families whose names were called lined up obediently. At the gates of the Black Warehouse, several black trucks were waiting. The tarpaulins were rolled back to reveal two rows of long benches along either side of the truck beds.

When the sirens blared again, the police guided everyone onto the trucks. Those who got on first found seats, while those at the end had to stand wherever there was space, shuffling around their bags and suitcases.

Once everyone was on board, the officer blew his whistle again to signal departure. The trucks rumbled slowly away, leaving the Black Warehouse behind.

As they travelled, they passed rows of high-rise buildings taller than any they had ever seen in Vietnam. People bustled along the streets, moving quickly, intent on their business. On both sides of the road, shops with flashing neon signs sold all kinds of goods. Fruit stalls displayed oranges, apples and pears piled high like mountains, dazzling to the eye. Everyone watched the streets in wonder as they drove past these new sights. Children gaped wide-eyed, swallowing their saliva in longing. No one cared where the trucks were taking them, all eyes were fixed on Hong Kong, the Pearl of the Far East.

They were like a flock of birds lost in a forest of bright, unfamiliar flowers.

The trucks stopped in front of a half-built building. Confused, everyone looked at each other anxiously. The police officer ordered the refugees to disembark.

"From today onwards, everyone will live here. Follow me to the 21 storey house," he said, marching into the building.

People carried their belongings as best they could some bags, some children all following silently up the stairs.

Thuy's family, along with a few others, was sent to the 11th floor. They were shown an empty floor with large windows airy and bright. The families from Boat 769 were all housed together and Thuy felt comforted to be among familiar faces. They spread out the mats that had been handed out at the Black Warehouse, using them to sleep on, as there were no beds, tables or chairs. At one end of the floor were toilets and separate showers for men and women surprisingly clean compared to the iron huts they had just left.

As the building was still under construction, there were no separate rooms. To create boundaries between families, people built makeshift walls out of whatever they could find mostly cardboard sheets.

While Thuy sat down to breastfeed baby Bac Hai, Hien sat beside her and Binh arranged the cardboard into a "fence" around their space. As she nursed her son, Thuy watched the others. They all looked happy and excited such a contrast to life in the Black Warehouse.

A woman unpacking her things nearby looked over at Thuy. "Are you and your children well?" she asked kindly.

Thuy smiled back. "Thank you, we're fine."

"We were on the same boat from Hai Phong but never had a chance to talk."

"Now that we're neighbours, we can. What's your name?

"Sorry, I haven't introduced myself. I'm Thu. My husband and I are from Quang Ninh. We don't have children. The boat was so crowded that it was hard to speak to anyone properly, but I remember you that day in Běihǎi, when the shaman performed a ceremony before you and your baby were allowed on the boat."

"I didn't have a choice," Thuy replied softly. "I had to go through with it. But now that we're in Hong Kong, I feel lucky."

Tuen Mun Camp was funded by the United Nations. It supported refugees with three meals a day rice, instant noodles, canned fish, meat and bread, depending on family size. Even though Bac Hai wasn't on solid food yet, he still received a full ration, so there was always plenty to eat. In fact, compared with what they had endured in recent months, they sometimes couldn't even finish all the food.

-----

There was no privacy, when you lived in a space with walls that were made of cardboard. There was a lot of whispering that could be heard across the floors. Thu and Thuy were neighbours so the two talked happily, like everyone else did.

After a week, the person in charge announced that everyone living in the building was free to move around the floors. This was exciting news for everyone. At last, some freedom.

People took this opportunity to look for and ask for news about their relatives that were on the other floors. Thuy had no relatives to speak of, but was curious to move about to the other floors.

There was an air of excitement as people were reunited. Mrs Hung came home that afternoon smiling happily, telling Thuy that she spoke to her cousin's family on the 7th floor.

Mr Tan from Hanoi, who was usually a quiet man, excitedly told everyone around him that he met someone who told him that his younger brother's family had escaped from Lao Cai. They were now in Hai Phong and were waiting for the boat to set sail.

The atmosphere on the 11th floor was filled with joy, not at all like the gloomy days in the Black Warehouse. Some people received hand-delivered letters, some learned about their brothers and family members who were living safely in the Chinese farm. Those who were lucky enough to be reunited with their relatives in the same building were even happier.

Thu and her husband, like Thuy, were not looking for anyone but were still happy to share in the joyous atmosphere of the building.

On Thuy's left side, there was a family of four from Lao Cai. A mother, who was about forty years old with her three sons. The oldest who was about twenty and the youngest who was probably twelve or thirteen years old. The mother was a gentle woman and the three sons were quiet and constantly obedient to their mother's wishes.

These four people lived quietly, rarely talking. Occasionally, she caught her eyes looking at Thuy and the baby. Thuy wondered if she should get to know her. After the announcement that they were free to move around, the mother remained calm and stayed where she was, but her three sons often left early in the morning and returned late in the evening. Whispering to one another as they returned to their mother.

They had a chance to speak, when one day Thuy thought she could quickly go to the bathroom on her own. When she returned the mother was holding Bac Hai, with little Hien sitting next to them. Seeing her holding the baby and rocking him to sleep, Thuy understood that this woman was a kind person. Thuy was touched by this act of kindness.

"Thank you very much, I have troubled you enough." She said quickly, as she sat down and took her son back into her arms.

"Mum, when you left, the baby started to cry. He was very naughty, he cried so loudly that this grandma couldn't sleep." Hien explained.

"I'm sorry, I had fed my baby." Thuy began. "I thought I had time to go to the bathroom, but still I don't have peace."

"There's nothing to be sorry for. I wasn't sleeping." Her voice was gentle. "My last name is Le, but do use Le, it's easier. Seeing you and your child reminded me of my life, so I understand and sympathize with what you're going through. If you need anything then please, don't be shy. We're neighbours and my children are always off somewhere. I'm happy to help you."

Thuy felt like it was fate that brought Mrs Le to Thuy, from then she considered her as a relative.

"That is fate! We have the same surname!" Mrs Le smiled happily.

It had been a long time since Thuy had felt comfortable with anyone as she did with Mrs Le. Leaving Vietnam and being on the run was lonely, and meeting good people was a rarity.

Being free to travel, Mrs Le's three sons were able to find jobs. "Ms Thuy, my children have jobs!" She shared the good news with her new friend.

"Really? Congratulations!" Thuy smiled with genuine joy.

"I and my children escaped from a farm in China and ran to the Běihǎi. We used all our savings to get on a boat that would take us away to a better life." Mrs Le continued. "Now we are here and they give us enough food, but can our children live like this forever?"

"I don't know which country will let us settle there, but I really want to go to work. I want to provide for my children." Thuy felt safe confiding in Mrs Le.

"You just take good care of the two children, your husband is working, what do you have to worry about?"

Thuy was silent, not knowing what to say to outsiders. Currently Thuy was busy, taking care of her children wholeheartedly. She would listen to people talking, if they didn't have their children to look after, finding a job would be easy.

She heard that there were people who collected leftover canned food or instant noodles from families on all floors and then sold them at the day market. Thuy wanted to be free, wanted to go out to work, but with a baby, she had to give up that idea for now.

Thuy hoped that Binh, who could read and speak Cantonese and Mandarin, would find a job and take care of his family. Linh, Binh's niece, boasted to her that she was working in a factory making dolls. She said she was earning 50 HK dollars a day and that they were only accepting women and girls so it was easy to get a job there.

This was enticing for Thuy and she wanted to earn some money to buy things for her children. When Thuy suggested the idea to Binh, he immediately dismissed it.

"If you go to work, who will take care of the children, who will breastfeed the baby? And Hien is only three years old." He said to his wife, annoyed at the idea.

"Since they said we were free to look for work, every single person around here has been looking for one. You know the language, can read and write in Chinese, it is easier for you to find a job than most people here. I don't understand why you won't try to find work? One of us must go to work. We can't stay at home and wait for people to give us food. Linh says the place she works at is still looking for more women. I could earn 50 Hong Kong dollars a day!" Thuy reminded her husband.

Even after long, heated discussions, Binh refused to let her go to work. She even learnt to sign some words in Chinese. Day after day, she would watch the people around her go out to work and come home late in the evening from work. They were doing what Thuy wished she could.

Mrs Le's three children were busy working too. During the day the floor was very deserted, only the elderly, children and people who were breastfeeding babies stayed behind.

Thuy spent her days busy taking care of her children's food and doing laundry. She had to hurry and do chores quickly, when the baby was fast asleep.

-----

Hong Kong was an international trading port. It was constantly bustling with trade. There were many factories producing consumer goods and they were all in need of unskilled labourers. Early each morning, on the ground floor of the building, the owners of electronics, watch, doll and clothing factories would send their foremen to recruit workers. There were many young and dynamic people, who were hired immediately. They would then introduce their relatives and friends to the work, even if they didn't speak Cantonese, they were hired. Unskilled labourers, no qualifications or skills were required, just those that were willing to work hard.

Binh's niece, Linh, went to work from the very first week they were all allowed to go to work. She asked Thuy to cook and wash her clothes and in return gave Thuy a 5kg bag of rice. Linh had invited Thuy to work, but Binh didn't let her go, so they relied on the daily food distribution. Tuen Mun camp only provided tinned food and when they couldn't finish it all, Thuy sold the leftovers, so she had some money to buy vegetables and meat for the children.

A month later, Binh applied for a job in a tobacco factory, but it was far from the camp, so he always ate and slept at the factory, only coming home on Sundays. According to Binh, everything was expensive, so he only occasionally bought new clothes for Bac Hai and dresses for Hien. Thuy had no idea how much his salary was, he didn't tell her. She knew he had been addicted to cigarettes since he was a child and now he was working in a tobacco factory. He knew his wife and children had been provided with food so didn't think they needed anything else.

Every family had a member that went out to work. Thuy could see the benefits they were all getting from the extra money. They had nice clothes and shoes and when they weren't working, they went to restaurants, watched movies and were able to freely move around the city without a care. These were things Thuy and her children didn't even dare to dream of doing.

Tuen Mun camp was a very special camp. It gave out food every day whether people worked or not. Many families used all their surplus tins of fish and ham and sold them. With the money they could buy radios, jeans and anything else that would be of value when they sent them back to their families in Vietnam.

Children are thought to be innocent and carefree, without the same worries and sorrows as adults, but if you pay close enough attention, you will see they are the same.

In the evening, when people were back from work, there would be light-hearted talk and laughter, with fresh apples and pears being shared or new clothes being tried on. Hien sat there with her eyes wide open staring longingly, swallowing her saliva, but saying nothing. She would lean down pretending to talk to Bac Hai. Thuy never heard what Hien said.

Watching everything that was happening around her, Thuy saw her daughter looking at what everyone else had but pretended to see nothing. Thuy wanted to cry for her daughter, but was also grateful Hien didn't need consoling.

Thuy felt useless for not being able to give her child enough happiness, but who could she blame to be angry with now? She had to remind herself that they were in a building that kept them dry, away from the wind and the rain. They weren't outside in a tent like when they were in Běihǎi by the sea, surviving on just one bowl of porridge. They had escaped death at sea and had clothes to change into and had three full meals a day.

Thuy loved her child, more so because she never whined or demanded anything. She did feel that her child had changed somewhat from when she was in Vietnam though. She was less talkative, more obedient, acting more like an older sister, since the arrival of the baby. Perhaps their circumstances and the events they had been through these past few months has made Hien more mature, knowing that she had to accept her reality.

-----

Another family close to Thuy was the Kieu family. All five members were working. The mother, who was over fifty years old, was lucky enough to get a job as a babysitter for a wealthy family, eating and sleeping at the owner's house. Her employers bought her nice clothes and gave her a salary of 30 HK dollars a day. Every two weeks, she went back to the camp to visit her children. She would bring a big bag full of old clothes for adults and children. The old clothes the owner gave her were still in good condition and quite beautiful. Little Hien watched as she would hold these clothes up to show everyone. She liked the look of them very much but didn't dare to say anything.

Once, Binh came home and bought a floral dress made of stockinette fabric. Hien would wear it and show off to the families next door.

"Daddy when you get your next salary, can you take me and mum to the movies?" Hien asked her dad. Binh nodded in agreement.

From that day on, Hien would wish for her dad to come home soon, so she could go to the movies.

Poor little thing, she waited and waited for what seemed to her the longest time. Then a few weeks later, on a Sunday, when the sun was shining and there was no rain, Binh came home. Hien jumped up happily.

"Ah-ha! Daddy is coming home. Today we can go out, mum!"

"Hurry up, I'll take you and the kids to the movies. I promised Hien." Binh urged his wife.

Thuy was also happy and nervous, no less than Hien. She had been in the camp for several months and had not been able to leave the building. She stayed on her floor and had no idea what the outside city looked like. Le was also happy for Thuy and her child.

"Ms Thuy, have a good time, don't worry, I'll look after your things."

At nearly 10 am, for the first time since arriving at the camp, Thuy and her children left the 21 storey building. Hien ran around in front, asking all sorts of questions. Thuy carried her baby on her chest (luckily, Thuy still had the brocade sling from Vietnam). They were like wild birds lost in the crowded city full of people and cars.

Looking up at the towering buildings and the stores with flashing red and green neon lights, displaying so many clothes and shoes, her eyes couldn't focus on one spot for too long. She couldn't get enough of all these new sights. The city was noisy. The sunlight reflected on the concrete floors made the space even more stuffy and uncomfortable. The baby refused to sleep in the sling and kept on moving around the whole time. Thuy grew tired.

As they approached the cinema, they could see many people gathered around the movie theatre door. It was a holiday and the place was overcrowded. There were street vendors selling soft drinks and snacks. People gathered around to look at the posters for new movies, adult movies, movies for children or just stare at the beautiful actors. Hien looked attentively.

Binh bought the tickets. Inside the cinema there were only a few people, about half of the seats were empty. Thuy didn't care what movie it was, it was just fun to have a change of scenery. After they found their seats, Hien wouldn't sit still, she stood looking around, observing everything, she was just too excited.

"It's almost time for the movie, you have to sit down and be quiet." Binh reminded her.

The lights in the theatre went off. It was completely dark and the movie was about to start. Hien sat obediently next to Binh and Thuy took the opportunity to take off the baby carrier to breastfeed. However, after watching for less than fifteen minutes, Bac Hai released a big poop, which was clearly audible to the whole theatre.

"Binh, I have to change the baby's nappy." Thuy whispered. Binh pulled Hien along and the movie time was ruined.

On the way home, Hien didn't say anything. She was obviously disappointed. Seeing how upset his daughter was, Binh bought her an ice cream, comforting her as they walked. Before returning to the camp building, Thuy took this opportunity to shop for some oranges, apples, pears and other food items they could save for later. This was the first time she had bought anything in a store in Hong Kong and it was a small taste of freedom.

That Sunday was the last time they went out as a family. The next morning Binh went to work as usual. The three of them continued their daily routine like a machine. They weren't hungry like the long days on the boat and there was plenty of milk for Bac Hai, who grew bigger and stronger each day. Hien, although only three years old, was obedient and loved her younger brother. She looked after him while her mother did the laundry and cooked. Mrs Le, the kind and gentle neighbour, also helped look after the children for Thuy.

Thuy didn't dare to ask for anything fancy or any sort of luxury. She felt fortunate to have escaped death, after a long journey full of hardship and deprivation. She silently thanked God and Buddha for protecting her family and providing a safe passage to Hong Kong. She knew life in the refugee camp was only going to be temporary, but she was still unsure what the future would hold for them in another place. Each day there is hope that they are closer to moving to their final destination, England.

Four months later, Thuy's family and several other families received notice to move to another camp. The Kãi Dé Tóng camp.

**Kãi Dé Tóng camp**

Kãi Dé Tóng camp is located next to the Kăi Dé Airport. From afar you can clearly see planes taking off and landing and if you are close enough you could hear the rumbling of engines.

Kai De Airport, Hong Kong's only airport, was located in Kowloon and was established in 1925. It closed in 1998 and was replaced by Hong Kong International Airport. It officially started operating on the 6th July 1998 on the reclaimed island of Chek Lap Kok. During the aftermath of the recent wars in Vietnam, the Hong Kong government gave up part of the airport to set up a camp to receive refugees who crossed the sea from Vietnam.

Thuy's family and many others were transferred to Kăi Dé camp after nearly four months in Tuen Mun camp. Binh's cousins were transported to a separate camp and Mrs Le and her children weren't on the same transfer as Thuy's.

The camp had many rows of units numbered A1 to A30. They were large and spacious with corrugated iron roofs and walls. There were fans on the ceiling and two doors to the entrance. Unlike previous camp sites, there were actual beds to sleep on. Two rows of bunk beds lined either side of a path way down the middle of the space.

One row of bunk beds were three bunks high and the other only two. The bunk beds were mostly for families with small children. Thuy's family of four set up beds in the two bunk rows, but as Hien was too small to be climbing up to the top bunk, the three of them all slept in the lower bed.

The row of three bunks were mostly occupied by men, young people and newlyweds. Unmarried girls housed themselves on the top bunks, trying to find ways of creating a cover for their own privacy, away from prying eyes. Those that got the middle bunks were the luckiest, as they were the most private and safest beds.

Kăi Dé camp had separate bathrooms and toilets for men and women. The camp had a medical room to examine patients, hand out medicine for colds, fevers, stomach-aches and common illnesses. There was also an area that allows the refugees to cook freely.

Thuy's family settled on in the bottom bunks, near the entrance of house A1. It was the noisiest part of the building with people constantly coming and going. All day long, you could hear people arguing, shouting, and fighting over the cooking area. The loudest voices could be heard scolding their children or husbands and wives quarrelling, angrily hurling vulgar words that Thuy has never heard before.

Little Hien and the other innocent children have all these words pouring into their ears. On top of that, they have to witness with their own eyes the savage fights and abusive husbands.

Theft is also commonplace. Some people complain about losing newly bought clothes, others complain about losing pots and pans that they left in the cooking area.

-----

Kăi Dé camp only provided the refugees with two weeks of subsidy. After that they were expected to find a job and make their own money. The only ones that were exempt from this were the elderly and those with small children. They were given an entry card.

There was a member in each family who would go to work. The morning rituals would be a buzz of people rushing around to get breakfast before making their way to work. There were women who had jobs selling snacks in Vietnam, which they then carried on doing in the camps, earning money the way they had always done.

In the early mornings, they would set up their stalls with rows of snacks. There would be green bean sticky rice balls, peanut sticky rice balls, all kinds of fried cakes coated with sugar, cakes filled with green beans, minced pork porridge, chicken porridge, sweet desserts and soft drinks. These were all very popular and sold out quickly. The snacks were well suited to the Hong Kong summer climate and the stalls were convenient places to find food for those who didn't want to cook for themselves.

-----

Binh found a job at a fish sauce factory which was far from the camp. Again, he had to stay there overnight for most of the week and would only come back to his family on Sundays.

Little Hien looked forward to Sunday when her father would come back. She would be given enough money to buy fried cakes or sticky rice, otherwise each morning she only ate cold rice or instant noodles.

Thuy was constantly busy with her two young children and had to rely on her husband for some extra cash. The small amount of money he gave her was just enough for her to buy rice and food to cook two meals a day for her and the children. Although they were not as well-off as other families, there was always milk for Bac Hai to feel full.

Little Hien played happily with her baby brother, and he slept well without crying. Sometimes Thuy would let Hien wander around the camp with the other children. There were always fights and thefts and lots of unpredictability. Children would run around carefree, but to Thuy, this meant they could be taken advantage of. She would always remind Hien not to go too far, or she might get lost or even kidnapped by bad people! This was more Thuy's fear than Hien's, but Hien would always listen to her mother and never went far out of sight.

One incident that Thuy will never forget was when they were sitting on their bed. Thuy was changing the baby's nappy and Hien was sitting next to them, when suddenly a young man rushed in the door and collapsed on her neighbour's bed. There was blood on his back, which had soaked through his shirt. Thuy could see that it was a knife wound, about 10 cm long. Fortunately, Mr Zin, whose bed the young man had collapsed on, was not at work that day. He quickly took a bottle of Chinese powder medicine and sprinkled it on the wound. He then gave the person a red pill the size of a soybean to swallow. Miraculously, after ten minutes the bleeding stopped and the injured man lay motionless.

"Do you know this person? What if the person who has a grudge against this man gets into a fight with you?" Thuy asked worriedly.

"Sister, look at me. I'm not afraid of anyone. I don't know this person, but I can see he needed help, so I had to act quickly." Zin smiled calmly.

After witnessing the incident with her own eyes, Thuy was no longer afraid of her neighbour. Previously, not having spoken to Zin, but only seeing all the tattoos of snakes and dragons on his arms, she thought he was a very different person from her. On their first day at the camp, she was too afraid to even look at his face, or draw any attention to herself and her family.

Zin and his wife had two sons; the youngest one was four years old and the oldest seven years. They were on the same boat but only found this out when they arrived at this camp.

Every day, the couple would go to work and leave their two sons at the camp. Thuy kept an eye on them. It was good for little Hien, who now had two boys who played with her. They looked after her, like she was their little sister. Sometimes Zin's wife bought vegetables, meat and food for Thuy. The two families became closer over time.

After the incident, Thuy thought that judging people by their appearance was not necessarily correct. However, as Binh was away so much, it made her feel safer to be Zin's neighbour. He was so tall and fierce looking, who wouldn't be afraid of him!

The quietness of any day was always short-lived at the camp, whether there was gossip about a man being wounded by a knife or not, by evening there were all sorts of sounds pervading the camp. There were the voices of people talking loudly, machines being operated, music being played as well as loud singing.

The harsh weather meant that the bathrooms and toilets were overcrowded. It was a place where people rushed to, to get rid of all the dirt and fatigue after a day of work. Although there were separate bathrooms for men and women, people went in and out wherever they could find the space.

The large number of people in the height of summer made the corrugated iron camp even hotter and people more irritable. The camp was noisy during the day and at night. Combined with the sound of airplane engines taking off and landing, it was a barrage of sounds, not unlike a night market.

The police of Kăi Dé camp were friendly and cheerful, they did not scold or beat the refugees like back at the Black Warehouse, so there was a more relaxed atmosphere.

-----

Near the camp, there were many markets selling all kinds of goods. Someone said there was even a Ladies Market at Tung Choi Street! Thuy was curious and wanted to go see what it was like, so on Sunday, when Binh returned home, Thuy left the children at home with him. She went with a woman named Lao and her four children, who were from Hanoi. Her husband's last name was Lao, but everyone called him and her Lao. Her younger brother, Cuong, went to the same school as Binh in Hanoi and had attended Thuy's wedding. Cuong worked as an interpreter for the Ministry of Agriculture and had planned to get married in 1979 to his girlfriend. However, when the Sino - Vietnamese war broke out, his girlfriend's family broke off the engagement. As Cuong was Chinese they feared it would affect his job and life. His girlfriend then left him and he lost his job. Cuong became depressed and fell sick. He couldn't escape the country with his sister's family and now there was no news from him.

On Sunday when Thuy was able to go to the Ladies Market with Lao, she felt happier than she had done in a long time. After walking for half an hour and almost reaching the market, where they could see the many stalls displaying many colourful goods. The smell of all the dishes were wafting their way, enticing them even more. Thuy knew little Hien would have loved to have come along, how happy her daughter would be to taste everything!

Then while being absorbed by all the sights and delicious smells, Thuy suddenly felt something cold and wet down her front. Her milk was flowing down and wetting her shirt. Lao saw this and knew Thuy was embarrassed, so she told her daughters. "You guys keep going, I'll take Ms Thuy back to the camp right away. We can't leave her like this, the baby is hungry and crying, her milk is leaking. She's wet and will easily catch a cold."

The shopping trip was over. The second time out was also not successful! After that, Thuy never went out again.

-----

Thuy's life stayed the same as it had done for months, while other people around her were changing their lives. Some left the camp, rented their own houses, some let their daughters marry Hong Kong citizens, hoping to settle down in Hong Kong.

Thuy and her family kept on waiting for their call to resettle in the United Kingdom. Occasionally, representatives of the United Nations High Commissioner for Refugees visited the Kăi Dé camp to check on the situation. They would listen to the refugees' feedback. This gave Lao and Thuy hope that their move would be soon.

When the day came, the people in charge of running the camp, announced the list of people and the date to gather for a health check before their departure. Binh came home from work with his wife and children. They all anxiously prepared.

Lao's family of six adults had been working for several months, so they had bought a lot of things. Thuy's family was the poorest, Binh had a low salary, just enough to cover his own expenses. Thuy did not work and never even had one day out in Hong Kong. The three of them were like prisoners on this island for several months, but now they were almost free, there was just one last hurdle to jump.

Thuy had spent the past few months of surviving, concentrating on her children and their well-being that she didn't pay much attention to her own health. On the day the whole family went for a health check, the doctor suspected that Thuy had a problem with her lungs. If that was the case, then she wouldn't be able to make the trip to the UK.

Thuy worried and was tense for days wondering whether she would get better in time. Everyone advised Binh to buy good food to nourish his wife, but how could he nourish her in a few days, when her health and spirit had been worn out for so many months?

Thuy prayed to God and Buddha to help her and her children overcome another obstacle. She hoped and wished for a good future for her two children. Thuy had to live, had to be healthy to go with her children to the place she wanted to settle in. Everything that they had gone through, couldn't be in vain.

During the last check-up, Thuy no longer had her cough and she felt comfortable and full of hope. After taking an X-ray and a heart and lung examination, the doctor concluded that she was healthy enough to go to England. That was the happiest day for the family!

They got on the bus to Hěnjiǔ yǐqián camp, the last gathering place before boarding the plane.

On January 30, 1980, Thuy's family got on a plane for the first time. They walked up the stairs to the plane's entrance. Thuy suddenly felt sad and remembered the wooden bridge at May Chai wharf in Hai Phong. The bridge that shook, as though it was encouraging her to get on the boat quickly.

The stairs to the plane were big, wide and sturdy. With one hand she held her child and with the other, she held the handrail. She was walking happily, confident in her steps and the path she had chosen.

# CHAPTER 8

# The United Kingdom
# Thorney Island Refugee Camp

*Good land attracts bird*

**Vietnamese idiom**

*When in Rome do as the Romans do.*

**English idiom**

There were two flight attendants on the plane to the United Kingdom. They wore blue and black uniforms. The left side of their vests had the words British Airways and the flight attendant's name on a patch. Their shirts were white with a red and black scarf around their neck and a blue and black beret on their head. They were young, beautiful and charming, with cheerful smiles on their faces.

They greeted everyone by the door of the plane, checking tickets and pointing towards the seats inside. Inside, there were other flight attendants showing each passenger their rows and seat numbers and helping them put their luggage in the overhead compartments.

Thuy stepped inside, she couldn't believe what she was seeing. The plane's cabin was as big as a building. There were three rows of seats; the middle row had sets of four seats and the two side rows had three. This sequence of rows ran all the way down the length of the plane.

Thuy's family followed the flight attendants to the 10th row. They sat in the right row with three seats next to each other. After putting the luggage in the above compartment, Binh sat outside near the aisle and little Hien was happy she was able to sit next to the window, where she could look out of the window and stand up on the seat.

More than twenty minutes later, after settling into their seats, two flight attendants stood in the middle of the aisle. One attendant held a microphone and spoke in English. The other attendant demonstrated safety procedures with seat belts and life jackets. Fortunately, there was an interpreter for the fifty-four Vietnamese refugees. Mai Anh stood up to translate what the flight attendant instructed to the new passengers. Thuy and everyone looked at each other, nodding and smiling.

Binh turned to fasten Hien's seat belt. "Good girl, sit still and don't look around or you'll fall."

"Yes, yes father." Hien obediently nodded and sat down.

Next, the pilot's voice on the loudspeaker introduced the flight crew responsible for taking the passengers from Hong Kong to London. After asking everyone to settle down and fasten their seat belts, the lights in the cabin dimmed and the loud rumble of the plane engine started up.

On the right was her husband, on the left was little Hien. Thuy still couldn't believe that this was real, she was sitting on a plane headed to England. She felt an indescribable feeling of joy and relief. Hien held on to the seat with both hands, her eyes intently looking out of the window. The plane slowly rolled onto the runway. A few minutes later the engine roared, accelerated and the whole plane shook, then took off the ground and soared into the blue sky. Hien's face was both surprised and delighted, looking over at her mother and smiling.

Thuy and Binh looked at each other with trembling lips and tears in their eyes. They were filled with joy and happiness. Unable to fully comprehend that they were actually sitting on a plane. This was the moment they never dared to dream of. The refugee life had begun a new chapter, with an uncertain future. It was surely going to be better than the past few months.

Thuy looked at all the faces on the flight. These had been the same people who shared the same boat experience as she did, but now everybody was dressed smartly and looked clean. Their faces still showed signs of fatigue and thinness, but there was a hope in their eyes now. The fifty-four refugees on the flight looked almost like a group of tourists sitting close together in the six rows of seats.

While immersed in happy thoughts, Thuy was startled by the lights turning on. The flight attendants were preparing to hand out breakfast to the passengers. There were trolleys carrying food and drinks from the rear of the plane along the two aisles. Menus were handed out to passengers, where they could choose their food and drinks. The menu was written in English but there were pictures of each dish. Thuy was surprised that the British plane had Vietnamese food. There was rice, fried fish with a tomato sauce and stir-fried beans. Thuy's family received three of these dishes. This was the first meal she had ever had on a plane and it was delicious. She would never forget it.

After clearing up all the finished meal trays, the flight attendants took turns serving drinks; black coffee, coffee with milk and other soft drinks. Thuy and Binh drank brown coffee and Hien had a coke.

An hour later, the lights in the cabin dimmed, only the sound of the plane's engine could be heard above everything else. The dim light was cool, lulling some passengers to sleep while other people read books and sipped on their coffees. Little Hien slept well. Thuy's arms were tired from holding Bac Hai for so long. She passed him to Binh to hold, while she leant her head back and closed her eyes. She fell quietly to sleep.

Thuy was unsure of how many hours had passed, but when the lights were turned on and an announcement was made that the plane was preparing to land, all the passengers sat up to attention. Seat belts were fastened as everyone waited anxiously for the plane to land on the runway.

The plane shook violently when the wheels touched the ground, first running fast then gradually slowing down. The British Airways Boeing 747 landed safely at London Heathrow Airport at 6 am London time on the 31st January 31, 1980.

Everyone got off and followed Mai Anh who completed the immigration process for the whole group quickly. After all the luggage was pulled out of the compartments, everyone went down the steps onto the concourse. There was a female refugee camp staff standing in the lobby. Mai Anh and the camp staff shook hands and introduced themselves.

"It is a great honour. I am Ann, an office staff member on behalf of the Thorney Island Refugee

Camp. Welcome to you all." She smiled at the bewildered group.

"I am Mai Anh, the passenger's interpreter. I'm responsible for taking this group of fifty-four people from Hong Kong to the camp."

From this moment on, the group followed the new staff member. Arriving in a foreign country, yet meeting someone who spoke Vietnamese, made everyone at ease. Their fears subsided and there was excitement in the air.

There was only the sound of footsteps and suitcase wheels rolling steadily on the hallway, while everyone quietly followed the two ladies.

The hallways through the airport were long, from one section to another, they continued walking, headed towards the parking lot. The airport was so big and clean, the lights were bright all along the corridors. Children happily ran, chasing after the silhouettes of people on the road.

Hien was happy to run at first, but after a while, she asked her father to carry her. Too tired to carry on, Binh picked his child up and carried her with one hand while pulling the suitcase with the other hand. This caused a wave of children to ask their parents to carry them.

It was about fifteen minutes' walk to get to the parking area. The coach driver quickly got out when he saw the group of people approaching. He opened the luggage compartment underneath the coach and started helping them store their luggage. One by one everyone got on the coach. Before the coach started moving, Ann stood next to the driver holding the microphone.

"Dear fellow countrymen, Thorney Island camp where we are staying is located on the south coast of England. It takes five hours to get to the camp. I know you are very tired after the long flight, but we will try to get back to the camp before it gets dark. There will be stops so everyone can eat, stretch their legs and go to the restroom. Does anyone have any questions?"

There were no questions, just silence, so the journey continued without further hesitation. "Please fasten your seat belts for your own safety. We'll be traveling on the motorways with many other cars driving at high speed."

The coach slowly rolled out of the parking area, through the gate with the toll machine, the coach turned around to face south.

The flow of traffic on the motorways run in both directions, with three lanes on both routes. Those that sat at the front of the coach could watch their journey through the window straight ahead of them. Those without a front row view stared out of their side windows, glued at every passing scene. It was a foggy day, with the coach driving through patches of mist, sometimes visible, then other times hidden.

In the morning, the roads were full of cars with people going to work. The coach was traveling at the busiest time of day.

The weather in January was imprinted with the cold winter. The sun occasionally appeared but it couldn't disperse the layer of fog that lingered on the roads. On both sides of the road, the white frost covered everything. There were huge bundles of hay sitting across the fields. Flocks of sheep leisurely grazed on the grass.

Everyone attentively admired the scenery of this foreign country, knowing it would be their home from now on. The coach slowed down and turned into a petrol station. Once in a parking bay, it stopped completely.

"Ladies and gentlemen, the coach will stop here for one hour break. Please take the opportunity to use the restroom and then gather in front of the entrance to the cafe. I will take you inside for lunch, then we will continue our journey afterwards." Ann announced to the group.

"Can I say, we don't have any money!" A woman raised her voice to speak.

"Please rest assured, the meal is covered by the camp fund, I am responsible for paying." Ann immediately replied.

Ann's words erased all the worries of the people. They all knew an hour wasn't much time, so told each other to hurry up. They followed Ann and Mai Anh through the parking lot towards the restrooms. The group of refugees seemed lost in a world they had never seen before.

The rest stop was as wide as a bustling shopping centre. There were people coming and going and there were many shops selling all sorts of things. The flashing coloured lights attracted the eye and enticed the shopper. There were coffee shops with cakes on display, fast food for eating in or taking away, souvenir shops, clothes of all kinds, for all ages and books and newspapers. It sold convenience for those traveling on the motorway.

It was not just the refugee children who were bewildered, adults also stood in groups, glued to the shop windows. The smell of coffee and cake wafting through the air was so enticing.

Thuy could see how differently the people of England behaved compared to the Vietnamese. People lined up calmly and patiently here, there was no pushing and jostling and everyone politely spoke with one another.

Thuy's family along with the whole group gathered around the dining area waiting for Mai Anh and Ann. They had to find a space that was big enough to seat them all. Ann gave each table a menu to choose from. As they had to be quick, they had to choose a sandwich, cake, a drink, either coffee or fruit juice and then everyone was given a bottle of mineral water.

Once the waiter had taken the orders, it wasn't long before he returned with drinks and sweet cakes and pastries. There was a curved cake Thuy had never seen before, later she would come to know it as a croissant. Everyone smiled and happily ate what was in front of them.

"Make yourself comfortable. I have settled the payment with the store. In forty-five minutes, we will need to get back on the coach to continue the journey to the camp as planned."

A light lunch in true western style, so very different from the common Vietnamese food. There was the smell of butter and milk, which was strange to the refugees' palettes, but they were all hungry. The children were polite and considerate, sitting obediently and eating up without demanding anything. The adults also ate and drank in silence, heads filled with thoughts of what lay ahead.

After eating and drinking, they continued their journey with peace of mind. Back on the coach, Hien rested her head on Binh's lap and slept soundly. Once Thuy had fed Bac Hai, he dozed off and slept the whole way without a single cry.

The atmosphere on the bus was quiet. A bit of weak sunlight shone through the windows, blinding the people sitting nearest and then the fog cleared away, revealing the vast, straight fields.

At around 3 pm, the coach turned onto the small road leading to the Thorney Island camp. In 1979, the British government's Prime minister, Margaret Thatcher, who was the head of the Conservative Party, officially accepted 19,000 Vietnamese refugees from camps in Hong Kong, Macau, the Philippines and Malaysia into the United Kingdom.

Thorney Island was formerly a military station. In August 1979, the camp was established, sponsored and managed by the British Refugee Council. In 1980, it developed into one of the three largest refugee camps in the UK. The purpose, before resettlement, was to help its new residents to learn English, give them health checks, find them permanent accommodation and jobs for resettlement, mainly preparing them for integration into British society.

From afar, the four storey, red-brown brick building could be seen clearly. It stood tall on a large piece of land. The coach stopped in front of the camp's yard. Above the main door of the building was a 60 cm wide by 2 metres long cloth with the words 'Welcome Vietnamese friends to Thorney Island camp' stretched horizontally across the building.

A group of five or six people were standing at the entrance, holding bouquets of flowers. This warm welcome moved everyone. The sign was written in Vietnamese, white writing on a red background, so the whole coach understood it immediately. It felt like they were returning to their homeland after all those months away. Eyes started welling with tears at the welcome.

Everyone got out of the coach one by one. The driver opened the door to reveal their suitcases and bags for people to retrieve. People were shivering, which might have been because of the cold weather, or from excitement or both. The group of people at the front of the building held out the flowers to Mai Anh and some of the elderly people.

A tall British gentleman enthusiastically shook Mai Anh's hand and the group of people pulling suitcases and carrying bags went inside the building following instructions to store their belongings in one room before walking over to the reception area.

There were several rows of tables in the middle, and two rows of chairs on both sides of the reception room. On the table were vases of colourful fresh flowers.

The British gentleman, who was a member of the camp's management board, spoke, while Ann stood next to him. Then a few other people spoke. The reception procedure took place quickly in a friendly and jovial atmosphere.

"Now you will be given keys to your room. Each family has a room, fully equipped with facilities. If you could get settled and return to the communal dining room on the first floor for 6 pm today. Dinner will be served." Ann continued. "Camp staff and floor leaders will now guide you to check-in. Today and tomorrow, everyone gets to rest and arrange their rooms, then you will be informed of the time for the health check."

Hearing voices starting to rise, Ann clapped her hands to signal for quiet. "The camp provides three meals a day: breakfast at 7.30 am, lunch at 12 pm and dinner at 5.30 pm, all served in the communal dining room." Everyone was tired and eager to check-in so they didn't really pay much attention. Each family received a piece of paper with the room and floor number written on it, as well as two keys.

Binh pulled their suitcase in one hand, carried the travel bag in the other. He followed the head of the group, Tien. Hien held hands with her mother and they both followed behind.

Thuy's family and two other families were allocated rooms on the second floor. Mr Tien was the team leader for the second floor, where there were already twenty households and today he welcomed three more families.

When the door opened, in front of them was a square room with white painted walls. On the left were two bunk beds, on the right was a pretty dining table and four chairs and directly opposite them was a standing cabinet.

"Inside, there is a cooking area, bathroom and toilet. Although the camp has a communal dining room that serves three meals, the camp management board does not prohibit people from cooking their own meals. They understand new residents won't be used to the food here." The team leader pointed out.

"Can I ask you, does the dining room usually serve Vietnamese or western food?" Thuy asked Mr Tien.

"We are living in England now, we have to adapt to all aspects of society here. It will be strange at first, but familiar later. I have to go to another family, you can find out more later." Mr Tien answered indirectly.

Binh put their suitcase in the standing cabinet, and went with Thuy to take a look at the bathroom. The two of them stopped in front of a neat little room with a sink, a bathtub and a shower head. The toilet was clean and there was a pretty mirror attached to the wall.

Their small room had all the amenities they needed and after months of hardship the couple looked at each other not knowing what to say. Then Hien started tugging on her mother's shirt.

"Mum and Dad! Can our whole family stay here forever? It's so beautiful, I love it, we don't have to suffer like in Hong Kong anymore." The little girl pleaded with delight.

Hien's words brought Thuy back to reality. Yes, this was reality and not a dream. Thuy walked over to the bunk beds where her son, Bac Hai was still sleeping soundly. He didn't need to know where he was, he just needed milk and sleep.

Thuy took the opportunity to arrange their clothes in the drawer. "You watch our son. Hien and I are going to take a bath before we have to meet everyone again at 6 o'clock." Thuy took clothes and towels and together with her child they started their wash in their very own bathroom. It was a luxury.

Binh looked around the room, his son was still sleeping soundly, so he lay down on the bed next to him. It was so comfortable and so easy to fall asleep after almost 24hrs of not being able to lie down.

After Thuy and her daughter had finished bathing, Hien wore a floral dress and a long-sleeved sweater over it. She looked very different from when she first came in, much prettier. She then spotted a doll in a red dress sitting on the small table in their room. Hien hugged it close to her chest. She took it with her and sat next to her baby brother. When Thuy came out of the bathroom, she encouraged Binh to have one too. They were all going to look refreshed for dinner.

After bathing, Thuy felt relaxed and comfortable, the fatigue of the long flight drifting away. Now she could take in the room. From today onwards it would be the family's small house and there would be no more days of lying on a hard cement floor. Thuy and her children's lives had finally reached a new chapter in their lives.

When leaving Vietnam, Thuy did not dare to think that she would arrive safely in another country, where people looked different and spoke a different language to her. This was a country that she had only read about in books and hadn't imagined what it would truly be like to live in. This afternoon, however, after witnessing the warmth of the welcome committee, life seemed to be going in a positive direction now.

*The place where I was born,*
*I had to leave.*
*The place I feared,*
*Welcomed us warmly.*

Thuy was lost in her thoughts, when Hien woke her. "Mum! The baby is awake!"

Thuy was startled and gently picked up Bac Hai. "Oh, you're awake now, son? You slept so well. Now, mum will check to see if you did a pee-pee. If you have, Hien will laugh at you." She teased.

The boy kicked his feet and laughed loudly, just as Binh finished bathing and came back into the room. "Is my dear boy awake?"

Thuy carried her son into the bathroom to wash him. She asked Binh what time it was, but it was still 20 minutes to 6 o'clock, yet already dark outside. They couldn't see anything.

"We are clean and smell good. Now only the little boy is dirty, right, my daughter?" Binh said while drying Hien's hair.

Hien smiled and pointed for her father to look. "Mum is also washing the baby and he's being a good boy. He's not crying and mum is praising him."

"Yes, our whole family is good." Binh nodded.

After washing her son, Thuy sat on the chair to breastfeed him. In her head, she made a mental check-list of things that needed doing. There was only a small basin in the bathroom, but she had brought with them a kettle, a rice cooker and tea set from Hong Kong. They still needed to get some bowls, chopsticks, spoons, salt and more.

She would buy the essentials for now, when she figured out where they could get them from. She said to Binh that they should take a walk around the grounds after dinner to find out what there was.

"Let's all go together." Hien said enthusiastically.

"Yes, that would be a good idea." Binh nodded in agreement.

They could hear the squeaky dragging of feet on the hallway outside their room. Thuy thought this was a very annoying habit of Chinese and Vietnamese people, refusing to lift their feet when they walked. She knew everyone was headed to dinner. Binh looked at his watch, urging Thuy to hurry up, so they wouldn't be the last to arrive.

It was only about twenty steps down the stairs to the ground floor. The camp's communal dining hall ran across half the ground floor. The kitchen was separated by a long row of tables. The seating was more long rows of tables with chairs either side.

People lined up near the kitchen, picked up a wooden tray and a large plate each, waiting for their food to be served. The kitchen staff brought food out and handed them out by the room's number. Binh and Thuy stood in line and followed suit.

When they got their meals, they went to a long table with chairs to sit down to eat.

That night was the first meal Thuy's family had at Thorney Island Refugee Camp. The kitchen staff gave chips and crispy fried fish with some steamed green beans. The plate was full of food. The children's food portions were smaller than the adults. Thuy's family had two adult portions and one child. As Bac Hai was still being breast fed, they gave him fresh milk and two small jars of nutritious food to eat which was the standard meal for children under 12 months.

This traditional English meal of fish and chips would be one that the Vietnamese people would know very well over next few weeks and gratefully received.

Many people after finishing their meal, went straight back up to their rooms. Thuy was confused with the jar of baby food. When the woman next to her saw the look on her face, she spoke up.

"It's not necessarily for you to feed him right now. Take it to your room, when the baby is hungry, you can give him some of the food in the jar." She continued. "Your family must have just arrived at the camp?"

"Yes, we got here this afternoon." Thuy said shyly. "Should I just give him the food just like this?" She said looking at the jar.

"Some children can eat it cold, or you could let the jar stand in hot water to warm it up. It's very good for the baby, full of nutrients."

"Thank you. Everything is strange and confusing right now."

"Don't worry, you will gradually get used to it. I've finished eating and my kids are already in our room." The woman said getting up to leave.

"Yes, thank you, see you later."

Binh and Hien finish their meals, so Binh holds Bac Hai, letting Thuy finish her meal in more comfort.

"Mum, eat it all so you have more milk for the baby. The fish and fried potatoes are so tasty. I have never eaten such delicious food." Hien said with a happy look on her face.

Thuy thought about everything they had gone through and how much her little daughter has had to endure. Being homeless, hungry, dirty and scared. It was a lot for a three-years old to go through and then hearing her say how delicious the food was, broke her heart.

There was another group of people waiting to have their dinner. The dining room was open until 7.30 pm.

Thuy took Bac Hai's food jar back to their room. Outside in the hallway, people were leisurely walking. Hien was watching and walked ahead of them, while her baby brother raised his hands to follow his big sister.

On the other side of the ground floor, there were lots of people milling around. There was a room which had the words 'Mini shop' written above the door.

Thuy was so happy to see this place and went straight inside, with Hien following after her. "I'll take the baby to the room next door. You and Hien buy what we need" Binh said contently.

The small shop sold mostly household essentials; soaps, sewing needles, thread. Thuy looked around to see if they sold pots, when she heard a soft call from behind.

"Is that you, Thuy?"

Thuy turned around and recognized Minh, who was from the same hometown as Binh. She was so happy to see a familiar face.

"Oh, is that Minh? When did your family get here? Where is your husband?"

Minh was also delighted to see Thuy and patted Hien's shoulder when the little girl looked up at her.

"I've been here for two weeks. Since we last saw each other in Tuen Mun, I've not heard any news about you. Where is Binh and the little boy?" She smiled and then turned to Hien. "Hien looks so pretty today."

"Binh and Bac Hai are just waiting outside. I just wanted to get a few things here."

"Only buy what you really need. Each week there's a coach that takes people to the centre of town. There are bigger stores there, with more things and it's cheaper than here." Minh advised. "Don't worry, you can buy things gradually. I'll show you my room. Do you have any British pounds yet?"

Thuy suddenly remembered, she didn't. "I only have some Hong Kong dollars."

"I'll buy a big basin and bar of soap for you. Then we can go to my room, we can talk more there."

After they bought what Thuy needed, they went out of the shop and saw Binh and the boy waiting. Binh was also really pleased to see Minh and they started speaking in their ethnic language, but remembered Thuy couldn't understand and returned to Vietnamese.

"My husband will be very happy to see you. Thuy and I will have lots to talk about too!" Minh motioned for them to start walking.

They all climbed the stairs together. "My room is on the second floor, the last room down the corridor." Minh explains.

"Our room is on this floor as well. That means we'll be close to each other!" Thuy said with a smile.

Thuy remembered what she was carrying and turned to Binh. "Can you take the basin and the soap to our room? I'll go to Minh's room with the children first."

It was a lucky chance that the two rooms were close to each other. Minh has three children, the oldest son is over ten years old, with one daughter being seven and the other only a few months younger than Hien.

Minh opens the door. Inside her husband is sitting on a chair, attentively looking at the papers.

As soon as Minh is inside the room, she calls to her husband.

"Hung, do you recognize who this is?"

Confused and surprised, Hung looks up. He's never met Thuy before.

"I am Thuy, Binh's wife, who was from the same hometown as you." Thuy introduces herself, then encourages Hien.

"Did you forget something?"

"Hello big uncle Hung!" Hien greeted.

"You are such a good girl!" Minh says. "Sister Thuy, Hung is younger than Binh."

Hung invites Thuy to sit down and asks Minh to make some tea.

"My family have been in this camp for two weeks now, but we haven't met any old acquaintances. We're happy your family is here, now we have a shared background of the same hometown. We understand each other."

Thuy sat down on the chair, while Bac Hai tried standing up and starts jumping up and down on his mother's lap, laughing loudly.

"I think so too." Thuy nodded in agreement with Hung.

There was a knock at the door, Hung stood up and opened it. He saw Binh and smiled happily, shaking his hand.

"Oh my God! Binh, come in."

They both laughed out loud and competed to talk. Bac Hai didn't understand anything, but jumped even harder to show he was part of this reunion too. Hien stood next to her brother and held his hand. The room echoed with the laughter of the two men. Thuy held her child and stood up to give the chair to Binh.

Hung and Binh sit down. Taking turns to talk and ask questions. There was so much to say and find out.

It was the first time Thuy had seen her husband smile and talk so much. They were speaking in their local language, where they were both born and raised. Thuy looked around the room, which also had two bunk beds and a standing wardrobe. The kitchen and bathroom were in another room, where Minh was making tea.

"Where are your children?" Thuy asked.

"Every evening after dinner, they ask permission to go out to play. They get bored staying in this room. There's nothing really for them to do. When there is a movie, they watch it, then come back to do some homework." Minh replied. "The two older children are in a different class to the youngest. How old is Hien?"

Thuy said. "She turned four a couple of weeks ago. Where do the children go to school, Minh?"

"So, as Hien is a few months older than Xuan, she will also go to kindergarten. In the morning there is a coach to pick her up at the front of the camp, then at noon the coach will bring her back here." Minh paused. "My two older children study two and a half hours in the morning and two and a half hours in the afternoon. Maybe Hien will be in the same class as Xuan."

Thuy wanted to ask more but was shy, Minh took the initiative. "Is there anything else you want to know, just ask and I can help. No need to be shy." Minh said kindly.

"Are there classes for the adults to go to?" This was Thuy's first question, which led straight onto another. "The team leader said we could cook at home, but where do we buy utensils and food from? And we don't have money. There are so many things we don't know yet."

"Don't worry, at first I worried like you. Now I know what is going on. There will be a gathering to go over the camp's rules." Minh explained. "Men and young people have separate classes. Because you and I have small children, we only attend for half a day either in the morning or the afternoon. At weekends, there's a coach that goes into the town centre for anyone who wants to visit the bigger shops. We could go together one day."

"But I must get some English currency and pay you back."

"I can let you owe me and then I'll charge you a high interest." Minh teased, then smiled. "Don't worry, each person gets five dollars a week, sorry, the money here is pounds. There are five people in my family, so we get twenty-five pounds a week, your family of four will receive twenty pounds."

This eased Thuy's mind and she felt more relaxed. Then whispered. "You know, I still don't believe we're here. Is it completely different from the refugee camp in Hong Kong? Do the Westerners yell at us?"

"No. They don't look like us. They're tall, have different skin colours and don't have black hair, but they are friendly. At first, I was afraid and didn't dare stand near them, but now I'm used to seeing them around."

Outside, Binh and Hung were chatting non-stop as old friends do. There was a knock on the door, their children came back, saw Binh and Thuy, they bowed their heads and said hello.

"Those are my children. They've been playing outside the building." Hung said to Binh.

The eldest boy quietly went to the bed and sat down and the two daughters ran inside to their mother. Xuan was about Hien's age. The two girls glanced at each other. Minh waved to Hien and put her hand on Thu and Xuan's shoulder.

"Hien, you get to know Thu and Xuan. They are my daughters. Hien is Thuy's daughter, a little older than Xuan. From now on our two families will live closely together, so the three girls must love each other, help each other and listen to Thu, OK?"

The three girls said yes, then looked at each other and smiled. Children are so innocent and carefree. They might be shy at first, but then start playing with one another as if they had known each other for a long time.

Bac Hai was no longer smiling like before. No one was playing with him so he started to frown. Thuy could sense her son's change of mood and said to Binh that it was time to go home.

Binh stood up and shook hands with Hung. "Thank you Hung and Minh very much. I am so happy to meet my fellow countrymen, see you two tomorrow."

Thuy called Hien and thanked Minh and Hung. "Thank you to you both. It's late now, the little boy is crying for food. Tomorrow we'll see you at breakfast."

Minh, Hung and the three children said goodbye. There was homework the children had to do before they went to bed.

Even though they were from the same hometown, Hung and Binh both worked far away, rarely seeing each other. Now that they are reacquainted in this strange land, how could they not be happy to see each other again?

Back in the room, Thuy urged Hien to brush her teeth before going to bed. She then put the kettle on to heat the jar of food for Bac Hai. Binh searched the cupboard for some blankets. He placed one on each bed.

"It's cold outside, but inside the building it's warm. I think we might still need blankets." Binh said half talking to himself. "Hong Kong was very hot, but it's cold here in winter. I wonder what the summer will be like."

Thuy took a large bowl and placed the jar of baby food in it. Then poured the hot water from the kettle into the bowl.

"You and Hung haven't seen each other for a long time, so you must have been very happy to see him today?"

"Yes, I was. Hung was a driver in Vietnam and was away from home quite often. I rarely saw him. People love this couple. They're kind and gentle."

Thuy fed Bac Hai while talking. She reminded Hien again to brush her teeth carefully and wash her hands and face. Binh went into the bathroom to check and watched Hien washing her face.

"You go out and wait for me to clean up, then I'll help you get into bed."

Bac Hai opened his mouth continuously, not refusing the western food, until he was completely full.

As Binh came out of the bathroom, Thuy handed Bac Hai to him. "Can you take the baby, so I can brush my teeth and wash my face. Then I'll get him ready for bed." She paused in thought. "Tomorrow after breakfast, we can have a look around the camp, what do you think?"

"We can do that and also ask Hung if there is anything we can find out for ourselves."

Thuy came out of the bathroom and could see Bac Hai sleeping happily in Binh's arms. Hien lay still on the bed and started to doze off.

"I think tonight we'll all get a good night's sleep in these beds. I thought maybe the children could sleep with us on the two bottom beds, even though there's a wooden bar on the top bed, I'm worried Hien might falling out. Could she sleep with you on the lower bed tonight?"

"I'm also worried that Hien will roll out, we'll try tonight, if it's not comfortable, tomorrow night Hien can go on the top bunk."Binh nodded.

Everything was done and it was almost 9 pm. Binh turned off the lights. The room had a large window, where the light from outside shone in, which made it easier to see if they needed to get up at night.

Bac Hai lay soundly asleep. Thuy felt grateful to be able to close her eyes. Those days lying curled up on the boat or the rough and rocky ground on Běihǎi beach were past. She could no longer see the dark blue sky above them, with the hundreds of twinkling stars teasing them below.

Her back must have been calloused and hardened to suit the burning cement floor in the Hong Kong camps. Her mind was always tense. The weather changed constantly but was always beating down on them, whether it was sunny or rainy or windy. There was so much hardship, deprivation and hunger.

Again, Thuy silently thanked God and Buddha for their mercy and blessing on her family. Surely it was them who helped them get through this arduous journey without sickness and injury. Many others were not so fortunate.

Their first night in England, lying on a soft, warm mattress, her back relaxed, stretching out comfortably. This was bliss. Looking up at the pure white ceiling, the scenes slowly replayed in her head. Thuy still couldn't quite believe this was real, the ceiling swayed and tilted as if she was lying on a boat in the middle of a turbulent ocean. Tears of happiness fell onto her pillow and then she gradually fell into a deep sleep.

-----

Last night, everyone slept soundly. Bac Hai did not wake up once. Then Thuy woke up with a start and looked through the window. It was still dark outside. Binh's snoring was screeching, rumbling like a train whistle. Hien was still sleeping peacefully beside her.

Thuy looked at the clock beside her. It was almost 6 am. She didn't want to wake everyone up, so went to the toilet as quietly as she could. She knew they needed the extra sleep.

After washing her face and brushing her teeth, Thuy walked out of the bathroom and saw Binh already awake. He got up, almost hitting his head on the top bunk and stretched.

"I'll probably get a swollen head sleeping on the lower bunk. Did you and the children sleep well last night?" Binh continued. "I slept soundly, like there was nothing to know! It's been a long time since we've had such a good night's sleep."

"We slept straight through, none of us woke up once in the night."

Bac Hai stirred and kicked his feet. Hien sat up in the bed next to him, rubbed her eyes and called to her mother. "Mum, the baby is awake!"

The two children now awake created a homely atmosphere to the room with their childish voices. Thuy heated another food jar for the baby. Binh finished making the bed and went into the bathroom.

"Hien, go wash your face and brush your teeth."

Hien listened to her father and went to the bathroom. Binh sat on the chair near Thuy who was feeding Bac Hai. They had no idea what was in the jar, just that Bac Hai couldn't get enough of it.

"Today are you planning to get more of those or change to something else?" Binh asked.

"I don't know yet, maybe if they have others, we could try something different. I'm curious about what the ingredients are that make it smell so good."

Binh didn't need to think too hard about it. "The food must be nutritious, that's why most westerners are so tall and strong."

They both laughed.

"My little baby has suffered a lot, right? Only now can he enjoy western food, to make up for all those days on the boat when there was no milk, sucking on the dry skin of nipples." Thuy teased, patting her son's cheeks that were filling out now.

The boy smiled innocently, not understanding anything. "You think mum is praising you, so you smiled, but don't you know you were naughty, hurting mummy like that." Hien giggled, giving her brother a hug.

Thuy pulled Hien towards her, enveloping them in her arms. "Mummy apologises to both of you, making you suffer, it's all over now. Hopefully, from now on our lives will be different."

Binh looked at his watch, it was almost 7.30 am. The sun had risen and a few rays of sunlight were shining through the window onto the floor, making the space warmer. He urged his wife and children to go to breakfast. They all got up and out of the door, while Binh locked it behind them.

At the same time, Hung and Minh's family were walking along the corridor. "Good morning, I was just about to knock on your door, so we could have breakfast together." Hung said.

Going down the stairs to the ground floor, they met Mr Tien, the group leader. "That is lucky I've bumped into you. I was going to let you know at 10 am, your family is invited to the meeting room to hear the camp's schedule of activities." Mr Tien said.

"Thank you. Let's go have breakfast together?"

"I must call my wife and children to breakfast first." Mr Tien said apologetically.

Everyone laughed happily.

In the dining room, many people had arrived early and there was already a long queue. Thuy looked at the far corner of the dining area and saw food products being handed out. She discovered from Minh that they were distributing products to mothers with children under two years old. Minh encouraged Thuy to get something for Bac Hai. Binh and Hien stayed where they were for the hot breakfast.

Thuy went and stood in the queue for the baby food. The kitchen staff brought out many different types of jars of food, as well as paper milk boxes and bowls of soup. Mothers could choose food for their children.

When it was Thuy's turn, she looked up at the young man in the kitchen.

"Sir, can I ask you, do all these jars have different ingredients?"

"The flavours are a little different. There is a chicken jar, beef, carrot, potato. Which would you like? Each meal consists of two jars and one box of fresh milk." He replied.

"Can my four years old child get some fresh milk too?"

"Under five years old can get two milk cartons a day. Let me know your room number, floor number and I'll record it on my list."

Thuy chooses two different jars from last night's handout for Bac Hai. She wants him to get used to all sorts of flavours. An average meal for Bac Hai would be two jars or one bowl of thick soup along with one carton of fresh milk. Thuy collects two milk cartons for Hien and rejoins her family.

Binh and Hien were taking their trays of food to a table. Hung and Minh's family with their children were already eating. The two families sat close together, chatting about life back in Vietnam, only remembering the good days.

Thuy remembered the clothes they had changed out of yesterday. "Where does your family wash and dry your clothes?" She asked Minh.

"There is a building, only twenty metres from this one. There are two laundry houses, each one has about five or six very large washing machines. All you do is put the soap powder in the compartment, put the clothes in the machine, turn it on and the machine washes, rinses and dries all your clothes.

That's it, clean and dry and smells nice. Then take it out and bring it home." Minh said wanting to impress Thuy.

"Really? That sounds so good! I've been worrying about where to wash and dry clothes."

Hung smiled, looked at Binh and joked. "You see, Binh, women tend to worry about far away things, unlike us men."

"It's true that women have to worry, I hope you two will worry about important matters for men, where we women will benefit." Thuy jested back.

Everyone burst out laughing but Binh blushed and was silent from then on, not saying a single word.

After breakfast, Thuy and Binh asked what was happening next.

"My wife and I have to go to English class. The children also have classes that start at 8.30 am. The coach will pick Xuan up at the front of the camp. So, we've all got to get ready back in our room, but we'll see you later." Hung said.

Thuy's family decided to take a walk along the other side of the ground floor, where they discovered the grocery store.

There was a room with two ping pong tables, next to a large room with many long chairs with backs close together. Thuy thought it might be the room the English gentleman spoke to them in. Maybe the 10 am meeting was here. On the other side of the room there were many chairs arranged in rows in front of a large television that sat on a table.

"Yesterday I was here with Bac Hai. There were quite a few people watching something on that television, maybe it was a film. Not sure what is in the other rooms, all those doors were closed." Binh said, looking around.

Binh held Hien's hand and walked ahead. There were lots of people milling along the hallway.

Almost everyone had finished breakfast and the dining room was looking depleted. Adults holding books and notebooks went down the stairs from the upper floors one by one. The younger ones went with their parents. Adults and children were all walking towards a site more than 100 meters away from the camp. They must all be going to their classes, Thuy thought.

A coach parked in the middle of the camp yard to pick up children for kindergarten. They would have lunch at school and be dropped back at 3 o'clock in the afternoon.

Around the building, the land was vast and there were many large, leafless trees. A few hundred meters further away, a few houses were scattered around. This was the peaceful countryside, far from the city. If it wasn't for the presence of a few hundred refugees, it would probably be deserted.

After wandering around the camp area until it was time for their 10 o'clock meeting, the whole family went inside. There were already a few people sitting in the large room. They all sat down on chairs and waited.

At exactly 10 o'clock, the British gentleman and Ms Ann entered. Ann introduced him as a member of the leadership team to talk about the camp's activities.

The English man would speak and then Ms Ann would translate into Vietnamese for the refugees. This gave the dozens of newcomers a better understanding of the organization and activities there were in the camp. What everyone was most interested in were related to their day to day lives at the camp.

"The camp is a centre for solving resettlement issues for Vietnamese refugees from other countries." Ann translated. "For now, it is providing you all with accommodation and all the living necessities you need."

"You all know there are three free meals a day served in the communal dining hall. Children under five years old have an additional allocation of fresh milk."

"There is an Education program for adults and children to learn English. A second language to integrate into the community."

"The camp has a medical room for health care and sports facilities such as soccer, table tennis and badminton."

"We respect freedom of religion and belief." Ann continued.

"Any disorderly behaviour, fighting is absolutely prohibited and you must all maintain good public hygiene."

Many issues were raised and explained to everyone. It relieved the anxiety and questions of most newcomers. However, arriving from a poor country, with completely different lifestyles, customs and practices, it was not easy to integrate right away. They had also experienced a lot of trauma before and during their time in the Hong Kong refugee camps. "There were many difficulties and confusing issues for the refugees and not all of them were easy for the camp staff and management team to sort out."

At the end of the meeting, they reminded everyone not to leave the camp for the first two weeks due to the required health check-ups that needed to be done. They would notify each family of their appointment for examination, blood collection, stool and urine testing etc.

On the first day of arriving at the Thorney Island camp, everyone looked bewildered. It was a strange place they had to call their home, but with time people adapted and adjusted to their new lives.

-----

Thuy gradually takes on the essential activities in the camp. Binh goes to the adult English classes every day. Hien goes to kindergarten with Xuan. Hung and Minh's older children go to their classes not far from the main building.

The class that Thuy attends is for mothers with young children and babies, so Thuy takes Bac Hai with her. Occasionally in the classroom, while she is enthusiastically listening to the teacher, Bac Hai cries loudly and Thuy has to take the child out.

The class is always filled with laughter; a mother holds her child and tries to write, but can't see clearly what is written on the board; a child breaks something; a hand gets kicked; a person breastfeeds her child and reads along, but doesn't really take anything in. They are supposed to be learning but when they leave the class, they can't recall a single word from the lesson.

The cold weather doesn't suit Thuy's health. Her body is weak and still recovering. One day she's got a cold, then another day Bac Hai has a fever or stomach-ache or diarrhoea. Sometimes Hien is sick and can't go to school. When these things happen to the children, Thuy has to stay home to look after them.

Occasionally the camp organises talks for breastfeeding mothers. They would explain and instruct on how to care for, dress and even how to wrap cloth nappies on babies.

In the afternoons, Thuy would take her children on walks along the hallways. One day on their walk, Thuy comes across a couple who knew Binh. The husband was Thien and the wife was Mai. They had been at this camp for two months but had only just come across one another on this day. They realised that Thien and Mai lived in the Gulet building across the road. They were a young couple without children, so they weren't busy outside of their English lessons.

"Are you and your husband well? When did you arrive at the camp?" Thien asked Thuy.

"Fine, our family is fine. You've been here longer than us, are you used to everything now?"

Before he answered Thuy's question, Thien jumped into asking another one to Thuy. "Have you received any news from your family in Vietnam?

Now that we are in England and are free, have you written a letter to let your family know?"

"Write a letter?" Thuy was confused.

"So you still haven't contacted your family in Vietnam?" Thien smiled kindly.

"Not yet." Thuy confessed. "I'm just taking my children for a walk around. They get bored if they're in that room for too long."

Thien and Mai said goodbye to Thuy then went back to their house across the road. Thuy and her children went to the entertainment room. There were people watching TV. Thuy took Hien inside and they sat down to watch along with the others. Mostly the news was on, but they have been there when there have been films showing. There was a film about cowboys who were horse riding and shooting. They were fascinating to watch, but they didn't understand a word that was being said. Everyone loved them though. The children's mouths would drop open, as they watched the horses galloping across the screen. They watched attentively until they saw the words 'The End', then there would be a lot of Oh nos!

-----

The next day, at lunch, Thuy's family saw Thien and Mai lining up to eat. They agreed they would all go over to Thuy's room after they had finished eating.

As they had just met, Thuy and Mai didn't really have much to talk about. They asked each other a few polite questions, then it was a bit awkward. However, Binh and Thien were very chatty. They talked about boating and their time in Hong Kong, then they would return to the present. Binh asked Thien if there was any news from his uncle? Thien's uncle is Duc's husband, Binh's young brother-in-law.

"I heard you said you haven't written a letter to your family in Vietnam yet. Why don't you write one? I sent one to my family in China." Thien said enthusiastically.

"I wonder if the situation has changed much? Before we left it was very stressful." Binh said, worriedly.

"It's different now, we're in a Western country, there's nothing to be afraid of." Then Thien changed the subject slightly. "You know, here we don't need to use cooked rice to stick stamps and envelopes down. I stick my tongue out to lick the envelope and the stamps and it stays stuck like that. It's fast and convenient, but isn't that strange?"

Binh and Thuy were surprised. "Really? We haven't bought any envelopes or stamps yet."

"Tomorrow I'll give you the stamp and envelope, you can send a letter home to reassure your family." Thien said.

Thuy found it unusual to hear Mai calling her and Binh 'sister' and 'brother', yet Thien would call Binh uncle and Thuy aunty. Thuy didn't really care, they weren't related to her, whatever they called her.

Since Thien had told them he had sent a letter back to his family in China, Thuy thought a lot about doing the same for her family in Vietnam. She was worried about her father in Vietnam, but knew she had to send a letter to reassure her family.

That night, Thuy had trouble sleeping. She was afraid that the letter wouldn't reach her family or that writing to them would implicate them in some way and make their lives more difficult. However, hearing that Thien had done it, gave Thuy the confidence to do the same.

Two weeks later, Thuy's family received their subsidy after deductions were made. There were expenses for the housing, food and books for school. Each person receives five pounds a week. That meant for Thuy's family of four, after two weeks, they received £40. With this money Thuy was able to pay back the money she borrowed from Minh when they first arrived at the camp.

"This Saturday there is a coach to take people to the town centre, do you want to go with me?" Minh asked.

"Of course, but I might wait until I have more money to buy things. What do you usually buy there, Minh?"

"When you get there, you'll see, they only sell Western things. I usually go to buy packets of long white noodles, some tomatoes and a bit of lard to cook in my room. It makes a nice change from eating the same meal every day in the dining hall. Eating potatoes and bread all the time gets boring."

Thuy was looking forward to Saturday when she could go into town to see what there was.

The two women went to the market, while Hung and Binh took care of the children. In Hong Kong she never really got to go out, but now they were in England, the country they would settle in, Thuy made sure she could do and go to all the places on offer.

Thuy thought about her father and siblings in Vietnam. She had finally written and sent letters, but didn't know when or if they received any of them. She thought of her father being so worried about her, but hopefully if he got the letters, he would know she was safe. She wondered if her two younger brothers had returned safely from war.

-----

Thuy left her home and her family before she was even sixteen. She thought all those years not being with her family would have hardened her to not missing them. So, why did she feel so lost now? She was now living in a country thousands of miles away from her birth home and she didn't want to feel like this. She was a mother in a time of war and had the responsibility of protecting her children. There wasn't a choice not to leave, so here she is now.

Thuy looked forward to tomorrow where she could take the coach into town. Binh didn't pay any attention to his wife's feelings. He didn't understand why she was excited about going to town? His adult classes consisted of several hours a day studying in a classroom, along with visits to external places. They could practice their English in appropriate settings, such as stores selling electronics, household appliances, clothes, post offices and job search centres. They would also listen to lectures on law, public order and social insurance. Thuy's class was not like that, mothers with young children had little time in class, it was never a full day and there were definitely no practicing their English outside of the camp.

The next morning, at 9 o'clock Thuy and Minh gathered to wait for the coach to pick them up. Those who had been in the camp for a long time were used to this routine, but Thuy and the other newcomers were very excited. Sitting inside the coach, they attentively looked out of the window all the way there. Some women talked endlessly without seeming to get tired or bored. Thuy had hoped for some quiet, so she could just watch the world go by. It was difficult to relax though with the constant distraction of the chattering voices. Minh sat next to her, dozing off, so Thuy let her sleep and waited till she was awake to ask her questions.

Thuy was one year younger than Minh, but because Binh was older than her, Thuy took on the title of 'older sister.'

Minh spoke of her family living in a province near the border to China. When the Sino -Vietnamese war broke out, Minh's older brother was shot dead by local militiamen. She said the orders hadn't come from above, which meant the whole family was at risk. They decided to all flee together.

The coach stopped at its designated place. Everyone got out and the driver said they had two hours before they should meet him back here. People went their separate ways. Thuy followed Minh wherever she went. Today the coach had taken them to Emsworth town, in the Havant district, which was in the county of Hampshire in the South of England. The population was about ten thousand people.

Emsworth's streets were narrow, with two rows of houses on either side. The houses all looked the same, built with the same brown bricks. There were small roads that were spread out in different directions. The shopping area wasn't crowded. It was a quiet and peaceful part of the country.

In the centre of the town there were many shops. Those selling household items as well as books and newspapers. There were pharmacies, hairdressers and even a museum. However, the places where people were seen going in and out the most were cafes. They sold cafe staples, such as sandwiches, pies and cakes, as well as the popular fried fish and chips, which was what the camp served daily.

Right in the heart of the town there is a flower garden, which usually displays beautiful blooms. However, over winter most have died down for the season. There are a few yellow buds trying to break through, reminding people there was still vitality in the garden. In the north of the town, there used to be a fishing village, with a boat building and repair shop in a small harbour.

Thuy followed Minh to the vegetable and fruit store. There were many kinds of green vegetables like the winter vegetables in Vietnam; heads of cabbage, cauliflower, broccoli, carrots, potatoes and tomatoes. There were lots of fruits too; oranges, apples, bananas, green grapes, red grapes, neatly arranged in beautiful shelves.

The shelves didn't store any Vietnamese foods, but had rows of milk bottles and canned milk. The sausages looked like Vietnamese sausages and there were many kinds of bread, noodles and flour.

Minh bought some long thin noodles, a kilo of tomatoes, a bunch of spring onions and a rectangular paper package of lard. Minh explained this was pork fat used for cooking. Thuy bought the same as Minh but in a smaller quantity. She also made sure she got some apples and a bunch of grapes to help improve their diet. There were no chopsticks or bowls to purchase, although the store did sell beautiful ceramic bowls and plates. These were just too expensive for her to buy.

When she got back to the camp, Minh gave her some pairs of chopsticks that she had brought in Hong Kong, Thuy could borrow them until she found her own. The day's trip to the town centre was a little disappointing, but she should have realised they wouldn't sell Vietnamese essentials, they were in England.

-----

Thuy started cooking noodles with tomatoes in the morning, to add variety to the family's diet. Almost every day the kitchen served them fried fish. It was a plain diet if you ate too much and they were all getting bored of it, even Hien!

Occasionally Thuy brought the fish back to their room to make fish floss. Everyone said it was delicious and Minh started making it too.

When Hien and her father were at their lessons. Thuy carried Bac Hai along with a bag of clothes to the laundry building. While waiting for the wash to finish, Bac Hai would sleep.

Thuy would take this chance to study Binh's class notebook. She focused on learning and day by day she also picked up a few words.

In the camp there was a charity storage room. Each week the locals and the church brought clothes and donated items to be distributed amongst the refugees in the camp. Although the items were used, they were still in good, clean condition. People were generous with their donations, so much more than any other camp they had been at.

Thuy often looked in this room. She would find toys for Bac Hai, dresses and sweaters for Hien. To her, they looked new and beautiful and she was grateful to have them.

When she found some knitting needles and blue wool, she knitted two pairs of overalls for Bac Hai. They were cute and didn't cost anything. People had also donated children's shoes that were brand new, sometimes still in their boxes. When Hien was there with her, she saw a pair of reddish-brown shoes she wanted to wear, but she also chose a pair of soft shoes for Bac Hai. She said he was learning to walk so needed something comfortable on his feet.

When the two children had shoes, Hien showed them off to her father as soon as she could. Thuy looked at them and thought the standard of living of the British people was truly comfortable and abundant. To Thuy, even though it was just a dress and a pair of shoes, it showed her that English people were kind and tolerant and wanted to share what they had and help however they could.

There were people in the camp that refused to take old things, but Thuy thought, if the items met her needs then they were a treasure. None of them should turn their noses up at this generosity. There was an ancient saying, 'A piece when hungry is worth a package when full.'

In the charity room, people had donated large bowls, beautiful enamel plates, brightly decorated and of good quality. Thuy found two plates and two large bowls she liked. They were definitely not inferior to those in the town shops. Thuy would never forget these items and the people who would have thought kindly to hand them to those in much more need than themselves.

-----

The camp continued to welcome new people from Hong Kong and at the same time found housing for many families to settle in. The time-scale that the camp was going by to resettle refugees into permanent homes was usually six months, but in many cases it was longer.

Time passed and in what felt like a moment, Bac Hai was already walking. When Hien held his hand, she looked just like a proud older sister. This gave Thuy the break she needed from carrying him all the time. She gathered her strength back and felt less tired, her arms were especially thankful!

Winter passed, then spring and during the summer, it was fortunate that the camp was near the sea. The climate was cool, the air was fresh.

It seemed like the camp was having difficulty finding a home for Thuy's family. They offered them a house in Devon with three bedrooms, but the family had to live and work on a horse farm owned by a Chinese person. Binh and Thuy immediately refused. So, the search continued.

Christmas arrived and it was the first Christmas in the United Kingdom for Thuy's family. Vietnamese people value the Lunar New Year. In the West, Christmas and New Year are the most solemn and joyful holidays. Offices, factories, agencies and organizations all stop working and everyone prepares for Christmas celebrations and welcoming in the New Year.

The camp had a Christmas tree that was decorated. The colourful gold paper and coloured lights were there to celebrate Jesus by flashing day and night. There was excitement in the air, with everyone happy to join in, with whatever that involves.

On Christmas Eve, the kitchen cooked a traditional Christmas meal; a roast turkey, baked potatoes, small round cabbage balls Thuy's family had never come across before, carrots, bacon and many different types of flour cakes.

Chưng cake is normally made at Vietnamese Tết, here there is Christmas pudding. Thuy took a little to try, but the flavours were too unusual for her. Binh and many others ate it and found it delicious though.

Christmas and New Year passed and then came the traditional Vietnamese Tết. The camp organized a celebration on New Year's Eve according to the lunar calendar. There was candy, art performances where young men and women were able to participate. The atmosphere of the Tết celebrations was a happy time. It was kind of the camp organisers to hold these celebrations, but it did make the refugees miss their relatives back in Vietnam. When the colourful fireworks exploded in the sky, Thuy could not hold back her tears, the longing for her family in Vietnam tore at her heart.

-----

After those first happy holidays, Thuy's family was assigned a three bedroom flat in London. After eleven months living in a refugee camp, Minh's family had also been allocated a home, but it was thirty-two miles northeast of Thuy's. The two families reluctantly said goodbye after months of sharing a life together in Thorney Island. On the morning of the 5th January 1981, Thuy's family resettled to their permanent home in London.

# CHAPTER 9

## Resettlement

*Only people capable of loving strongly can also suffer great sorrow - but this same necessity of love serves to counteract their grief and heals them.*

**Les Tolstoy**

At 7.00 am, on 5 January 1981, a loudspeaker announced the names of three families who were to gather at the front of the building. Thuy's family was among them. They had all known the night before that they would be leaving, so everyone was packed and ready to go.

Ms Ann checked all the families in thirteen people in total. Once that was done, the van started its engine and, by 7.30 am, slowly rolled away.

Everyone inside the van looked out through the windows at the small crowd waving goodbye. They waved back to their friends, and to the place that had been their home. Most of them would probably never return. It was moving to hear the shouts of well wishes.

"Good luck to all of you!"

"Wish you all the best! Remember to write to us..."

This was the very spot where they had first arrived and where they were now departing. It was a scene that repeated every week. Minh's family, and Thien and Mai, the couple, had left a couple of months earlier.

Thuy looked at the people standing in the yard. Some faces were familiar; others she didn't recognise at all. The four-storey building where she had lived for eleven months stirred up mixed feelings of sadness and joy. This was goodbye to her first home Thorney Island camp.

The van drove along narrow country roads before turning onto the motorway and heading towards London. At first, the adults sat in silence, lost in thought. The children, however, began chatting as soon as the van started moving. They glanced at each other, assessing the situation, but soon were talking and laughing together carefree and innocent. It helped them bond. *Perhaps we'll all end up in the same town and go to the same school,* Thuy thought.

Some people in the van seemed to know what would happen once they arrived - they must have spoken to those who had gone before. Each family had brought food for the journey; rice, sandwiches, whatever they could manage. The kitchen staff had served them breakfast early that morning, their last meal in the refugee camp.

On the way, the van stopped at a service station for forty minutes so everyone could use the toilets. Over three hours later, the van began to approach East London.

"In ten minutes, we'll arrive at your new homes," Ms Ann announced. "There will be someone there to welcome you and take you inside. They'll be your guardians, helping you with everything. The list of families will be given to the guardian in charge."

People exchanged nervous looks and waited. The van stopped in the car park of a five-storey, U shaped block of white-painted flats. The buildings looked new and solid, with flat roofs, windows and small balconies.

Two British people - one man and one woman - were waiting in the car park. Hoang's family got out first. Ms Ann shook hands with the two guardians and introduced them.

"This is Mr Ray," she said. "He'll be your family's guardian and will take you to your new home. Anything you need from now on, you can ask Mr Ray."

She turned to him and spoke in English. "This is Mr Hoang and his family of four. Their details are in this file." She handed it over.

Mr Ray, a tall man with a friendly beard and a warm laugh, greeted Hoang's family. They didn't have many belongings, so they said their goodbyes and followed him towards the left side of the building.

Ms Ann then introduced Thuy's and Phan's families to the British woman, a large and cheerful figure.

"Ms Hill will be the guardian for both families," Ms Ann said. "She'll help you with anything you need."

Pointing to each group in turn, she continued in English: "Mr Phan's family has five people; Mr Truong's family has four."

Ms Hill shook everyone's hands warmly, repeating, "Welcome! Welcome!" with a wide smile.

Ms Ann turned to them all. "Now please follow Ms Hill. She'll take you to your new homes. I'll be returning to Thorney Island with the van. I wish you all the best in your new lives. Goodbye!"

She waved for the last time and climbed back into the van.

Ms Hill walked between the children, talking to them in slow, careful English. They didn't understand much, but her kindness quickly won them over.

Hien held her younger brother's hand as they followed behind the adults, who were carrying suitcases and bags.

The building had lifts, but each could only fit one family at a time. Thuy's family went up first with Ms Hill.

"We're going to the fifth floor," she said, pressing the button. After a few seconds, the lift stopped with a cheerful *ding*.

"We're here." She held the door open with her suitcase. "Please, step out."

Hien took Ms Hill's hand and led the way, with Binh and Thuy following behind. They walked only a short distance along the concrete corridor before stopping in front of a brown door marked *156*.

"This is your new home," Ms Hill said with a smile. She unlocked the door, switched on the light and gestured for them to go inside. "Please, please come in!"

She bent down and held out her hands to welcome Bac Hai and Hien. Thuy and Binh carried their bags inside. Behind the door was a small hallway, followed by a short flight of ten steps leading down to another level.

Although the front door was on the fifth floor, the rooms were on the fourth. As they followed Ms Hill down the stairs, Thuy was amazed at how spacious the flat was.

In the middle room, Ms Hill handed the keys to Binh. "Have a look around," she said. "I need to go and collect Mr Phan's family now they're also on the fifth floor but in another block."

Binh walked her back to the door and thanked her. Then he began carrying their suitcases down to the lower level. The children followed, exploring every room in awe.

"Mum, there are so many rooms! Are these all for us?" Hien said, wide-eyed.

Thuy could hardly believe it herself. There were two small bedrooms, each with a single bed and a small chest of drawers and a larger bedroom with a mattress slightly bigger than a single. The floors were carpeted in brown. Built into the wall was an old wooden wardrobe with a drawer and a rail for hanging clothes.

Next to the bedrooms was a small bathroom with a bath, sink and toilet. On the other side of the kitchen was a balcony.

"I still can't believe this is our new home," Binh called out.

"How do you feel?" he asked his daughter.

"Mum! Dad! I like this house the best!" Hien said happily.

Thuy looked at her daughter, her heart full. "I like it too," she said softly. "They treat us so kindly here, it's not like in Vietnam. Thinking about the past still frightens me."

The kitchen was spacious big enough for four or five people to cook together. The fridge, though not new, was clean and stocked with two boxes of eggs, a bottle of milk and some bottles of water. On the table sat a kettle, a toaster and an electric cooker. There were pots, pans, plates and bowls neatly arranged in the cupboards. In the drawers were knives, forks and spoons, everything they might need. Thuy felt a wave of gratitude; she had only hoped for a roof over their heads.

The middle room had a long sofa and a matching armchair covered in grey fabric. *This must be the living room,* Thuy thought - a space she had only read about in English lessons. The carpet underfoot felt soft and warm. Thuy and Binh sat on the sofa.

"Sister Hien, come sit here, it's so soft!" Bac Hai said, climbing onto the armchair.

While they were still taking everything in, there was a knock at the door. Binh hurried upstairs and found Ms Hill standing there, smiling. He invited her in and as soon as Hien heard her voice, she ran to take her hand and led her to the living room.

Ms Hill spoke slowly, using gestures to help them understand. Thuy caught a few words but looked to Binh, whose expression was blank.

"Do you understand what she's saying?" she whispered.

"Only a little," he admitted shyly.

"Didn't you go to those English classes every day? You still can't understand anything?" Thuy said, half-teasing.

The couple were murmuring to each other when Hien piped up. "She said she thinks we all want to rest now, so she'll come back tomorrow. We can ask her questions then."

"Yes, yes, thank you! Tomorrow," Thuy said to Ms Hill, smiling.

Ms Hill nodded. "Goodbye for now."

Feeling braver, Thuy followed her to the door and said, "Thank you very much. See you tomorrow."

Ms Hill smiled, put her arms around Thuy and then bent to hug and kiss Hien - a warm, open gesture that felt unfamiliar but comforting.

"Bye-bye, my dear!" she said.

Thuy and Hien watched her walk towards the lift.

"Bye-bye!" Hien called out.

Thuy began tidying up straight away, unpacking and arranging their things. Her hands were busy, but her mind was still floating she could hardly believe this home was theirs.

Hien was delighted, wandering from room to room without tiring. The two men in the family were calmer. Little Bac Hai didn't really understand what was happening and as for Binh, Thuy couldn't quite tell what he was thinking.

After so many years together, she was used to that. She focused on getting the home in order and didn't press him. People often said that was a woman's work anyway.

Binh and the children went out onto the balcony, pointing and talking excitedly about everything they could see.

As night fell, the children grew hungry. They still had some rice and bread from the camp. Sitting in the square kitchen the children on chairs, Thuy and Binh standing, they shared a simple first meal in their new home. It was cosy, full of laughter and chatter. Thuy looked at her children and thought that from today, their lives were truly turning a new page.

-----

That night, all four of them slept in the large bedroom. Bac Hai had never slept apart from his mother and Hien said the house felt strange too big, and full of ghosts, she claimed but really, she just didn't want to sleep alone. For the first night, it was easier for them all to stay together. Thuy knew it would take time to change that habit.

This new country still felt strange. Everywhere they looked, there were white English faces. But slowly, thanks to Ms Hill's help, life in London began to feel a little less foreign.

The spoken English of the three men from the three Vietnamese families were all very poor. The two guardians would visit them all often, talking and trying to understand what was needed. Thuy understood some of the sentences and communicated through gestures, slowly and calmly explaining herself to the guardian, Ms Hill.

Back on Thorney Island, Binh and Hien attended their classes every day, but Binh was slow and quiet, with very limited communication skills. He wasn't very helpful in translating or understanding what the guardians were saying. Hien could understand and speak better than her father. Thuy thought to herself that she must ask Ms Hill to find a school for Hien as soon as possible.

Thuy and her family gradually adapted to their new environment with the support from Ms Hill and Mr Ray. They would bring all sorts of essentials to the families. Items such as pots, bottles of washing up liquid, clothes, blankets and even chairs, a table and a vacuum cleaner, all donated by members of the church and the local community. Thuy was forever grateful and continually surprised by these strangers' generosity.

-----

When Ms Hill and Mr Ray found out there would be three refugee families arriving from Vietnam to settle in the area, Mr Ray stood up in church and asked members to donate what they could.

In the first few months, every Sunday the guardians came to pick them up to go to church. All three families had no idea what was being said, but they followed them dutifully. In Vietnam, they never went to church and they didn't understand anything about the Christian religion and Jesus.

During the first few mornings, the families would try their best to follow what everyone else was doing. When everyone in church stood up, they also stood up. When people were holding the bible to read, they didn't know what they were reading or singing, but they held the bible up too. They would murmur along, not really saying the words or singing the hymns. When everyone was given a cup of water, later revealed to be holy, Bac Hai tipped it back and drank it in one gulp. They laughed about that moment many times afterwards.

Slowly though, it was obvious that the families didn't want to attend church anymore. They didn't really understand what was being said and didn't follow the conversations that were had at the end of the morning's worship. They felt silly and thought they might seem like pitiful fools in front of everyone else. The two guardians empathised with their situation and never forced them to attend and stopped picking them up on Sunday mornings. Although, they all felt a bit of guilt for giving up on the church.

"It feels wrong for our families to stop going to church. It is really hard to think about that." Hoang said to Thuy.

"We're embarrassed about that too, especially when they come and visit us and are always so helpful." Binh added.

"But when we're there, we don't understand anything and our children don't sit still, they want to run and jump around." Phan said, making excuses.

After two weeks of getting used to their new home, the guardians helped them with some paperwork. They took them to the job centre to sign up for social benefits and then registered the children for school and the whole family registered at a local GP surgery. Hien and the older children were placed in classes according to their age, but Bac Hai stayed at home with Thuy as he was just nineteen months old.

The three men had difficulty finding work, because they didn't understand English, they couldn't apply for any jobs. Everyone looked skinny and weak and no employer wanted to hire them, so they had to go to English classes. They found a class for foreigners and from then on Binh, Hoang and Phan attended free English classes for adults, three mornings a week, two hours each session. The women would stay at home and do the housework and look after their children that weren't at school.

-----

There were no Asian shops near where they all lived. Thuy was finding it hard eating bread and potatoes every day, so along with the two other Vietnamese women, they decided to search for somewhere that might sell other types of foods.

The church members had given each family a baby stroller, so they all pushed their little ones along the streets searching. They had walked over a kilometre without anything to hold their attention, until a sign with squiggly words appeared a little way ahead. All three women walked quickly towards it. Oh my God! It was an Indian shop! They were delighted, inside they found bags of long grain rice. Everyone bought one 5kg bag of rice, plus a few small packets of dried shrimp. It was a successful trip for them all and Thuy felt secure knowing she could get rice from here when she wanted.

Thuy had to drop Hien off and pick her up from school four times a day. Bac Hai would sit in his stroller during all these transitions, he was happy observing as they walked. Hien's school was about two hundred meters from their home. It was good exercise for Thuy!

Then Ms Hill introduced Thuy to an English class. She was so happy going to school and making new friends.

Phan's wife was Yen. They lived on the same floor in the same block of flats as Thuy's family. They were only ten doors away from them. Yen's youngest daughter was almost three years old. She was registered for the same class as Hien, but for some reason, after two or three sessions they stopped taking her, saying she was busy and couldn't study.

Thuy didn't ask questions. She knew that back in Vietnam, Yen only finished the second year of primary school herself. Her parents thought girls didn't need to study and that they would just grow up and get married and then their husbands would take care of them. Yen is Vietnamese and followed her husband who is from the Chinese ethnic group called Hoa, to the UK.

Thuy attended an English class for foreign women. Zenh, Hoang's wife, refused to attend right from the start. Thuy understood why she didn't want to go. Zenh was two years younger than Thuy, but came from a family that pampered her. She didn't have to do anything, she didn't even have to learn to write Vietnamese or Chinese and it seemed like leaving the country still didn't make her want to learn anything. She had had a completely different life to Thuy in Vietnam. There, Zenh was living off of her parents, she didn't study anything and was illiterate, she then got married and now depends on her husband for everything. They were too different to be good friends. After taking Hien to school, Thuy went to her English class alone, which was two mornings a week.

The place where Thuy studied was a local leisure centre, which had a swimming pool, a gymnastics room, table tennis facilities and held English classes. There was also a canteen for the elderly to meet with one another and a playroom for children under three years old to roam freely and safely. There were lots of toys, so Bac Hai played happily in that room, while Thuy took her class next door.

The class never really had that many attendees. At the most, there would be eleven or twelve people. These students were over twenty years old and from many different countries; India, Pakistan, Japan, Thailand.

The children created opportunities for their mothers to get to know each other. On the first day in the class, the women would use gestures and a few polite words to try and communicate with each other, but it was still difficult for Thuy to understand what her classmates were saying. With the help of the teacher and her motivation to learn, Thuy's English gradually increased and she was gaining more confidence with each lesson. It was only four hours of class a week but it helped Thuy communicate in the community. She became less anxious and stressed.

Ms Hill would visit Thuy's family every Sunday after church. She was not married and lived with her younger sister and elderly mother. With time, there grew a bond between Thuy and Ms Hill. She could see what a kind person Ms Hill was and how she understood that the families must find living in a foreign country unsettling and perhaps frightening. The guardians were also what connected the families to each other too, but one day, Yen confided with Thuy.

"How do you feel about the guardians? I feel embarrassed, every time Ms Hill comes to our home, my husband does not want to see her."

"She is a good person, who wants to help us, not just because she has been appointed to this job." Thuy said defending Ms Hill.

"At first we didn't know anything, but now we don't need them anymore." Yen went on.

Thuy was surprised to hear them say these things. It was heartless and ungrateful of them. Thuy started to process this and thought of all the other things that had happened between them. She thought that being far from their homeland, she would find a fellow neighbour to be close to, that they would confide and encourage each other. There is a Vietnamese saying, 'Disease comes through the mouth. Disaster from the words.' After hearing Yen and Phan's true feelings, she knew she had to be careful with what she shared with them. They weren't the type of people she could now trust.

In London Thuy had still not received any news from her father and family in Vietnam. She kept on hoping they were okay and that she would hear something soon. It was almost a year later before a letter arrived. The envelope had red and white lines around it, a typical Vietnamese envelope.

Her hands trembled as she opened it. There were two pages torn from a note book, full of writing. She recognised her father's handwriting, as beautiful as before. There were a few lines blurred out and Thuy thought her dad must have been crying when he wrote this. She started reading, 'To Thuy, my dear daughter…' and then choked up and couldn't continue. She handed the letter to Binh.

The two pages briefly summarised all the news of her siblings. Thuy had been away from Vietnam for more than two years, the days and months passed without any news, but everyone was still hopeful. Her two younger brothers were still in the army. Her younger sister was married. All of them were safe and healthy. Thuy understood implicitly that there were things her father could not say in full. One sentence began, 'After you left, they took me to a concentration camp… but don't worry' was all that part read. This was her father's way of indirectly informing Thuy that there were strict controls.

The letters that were sent and received took a long time to travel, but human feelings have no borders and have to be told. Thuy believed that and she hoped that the relationship between Vietnam and the UK would continue to develop positively with time.

-----

Hoang and Phan's family relationship with the guardians started fading. They had their reasons, but Thuy did not feel the same. She was happy to stay in contact with both guardians and Hien was attached to Ms Hill. If two weeks went by without seeing her, Hien would be wondering why.

Thuy had heard many people say that unmarried older women were difficult and grumpy, but she found this wasn't true of Ms Hill. She always felt she was sincere, warm and friendly. She could tell from the honesty in her eyes that she enjoyed seeing them too. She always kept her promises and was always enthusiastic and thoughtful to anyone who needed her help.

-----

On Hien and Bac Hai's birthdays, Thuy invited the guardians to share the celebrations with the family. They would have cake and there would be some Vietnamese food. It was a time of joy and the children loved seeing them both.

Sometimes, the family would be invited to Ms Hill's house. The three women lived together in a spacious house with four or five large bedrooms. The living room was the same size as the flat Thuy lived in.

Hien and Bac Hai loved to run and play in the garden, surrounded by many flowers. At the back of the garden were apple and pear trees. In spring, white flowers would bloom on them and when the wind blew the flowers would fall like snowflakes. They would sit together in the garden on a piece of cloth under the sunlight. There would be the laughter of the two children that would pervade the air and create a cozy family atmosphere. They would drink tea and eat butter biscuits, it was very special.

Ms Hill's frail mother and sick younger sister, who sat in a wheelchair, would watch the children playing and laughing. Thuy could see these were special memories being made and she felt that a bond was building between the two families that would grow stronger with time. There were emotions that had been buried for so long and were coming to the surface and she cherished it.

-----

Thuy really wanted to work, she didn't want to be stuck just looking after her children and doing housework. Then one day, the couple went to visit a family from the same hometown as Binh.

Bao and Be lived in south London and on their visit to see them, they unexpectedly met Minh, Thuy's old friend from Thorney Island was also there. The three women sat and talked, telling each other about their new home.

"Our English isn't very good yet and we're all busy with our children, but I want to earn some money. Winter is cold here and we don't have enough warm clothes. Does anyone have any ideas on how we can make money?" Be asked the other two.

They looked at each other, not really having any ideas to speak of. Every mother's wish is the same, Be is the oldest, agile and strong like a man, so Thuy and Minh looked at her and waited to see what she might say.

"I can ask to work in a shop, leaving early in the morning and coming back late at night, but who will I look after my children?" Be paused before suggesting. "Someone told me about sewing machine work. It can be done at home, which means we can still be there to look after our children and all the other housework we have to do. I know none of us know how to sew, but I can learn first and then show you both after?"

Thuy wondered how they could work together when they didn't live near one another.

After that day, Be followed up on her idea. She was told about a place that taught how to use a sewing machine. A few weeks later, she invited Thuy and Minh to her home. They saw that Be had already learnt how to sew shirts. This encouraged Thuy and Minh to do the same. They both had lessons at Be's house. There was only one sewing machine, so they all took it in turns sitting and practicing at the machine.

They first practised making easy things, then onto more trickier skills, like connecting the body shirt to the curves in the armpits and collars. All day long the three ladies were happy to learn a new skill and encouraged each other. A week later, everyone was able to finish a product by themselves and joked that they had graduated from the 'college of home'.

The achievement was so satisfying. Now that they could sew, they now needed a sewing machine and to find a garment factory that would supply them with work. It was important for Thuy to earn some money, she had always worked from a young age and it was depressing that she wasn't working right now.

Minh's husband worked part-time so they had some income to support the family. Be's mother-in-law heard that the three women were learning to sew.

"Don't worry, I have a few gold rings that I can sell. I will lend you the money to buy the machines, just pay me back when you're earning." Be's mother-in-law said, generously. Thuy was overjoyed, but she did have some worries that she wouldn't be able to pay her back. She thought about what it meant for her children if they had a bit more money and this made her determined to make a success of this sewing work.

Thuy borrowed the money from Be's mother-in-law to buy a sewing machine. With the machine, she then had to think about where she was going to find the work. She wasn't a skilled worker, yet, so what manager would risk handing over their goods to someone who would keep it for a week before returning it. She had to convince them it was worth taking the risk.

They were introduced to a manager of a clothes factory. He was from Hong Kong and he felt sorry for Minh and Be, because they were from the ethnic group, Hoa. They spoke Cantonese together and he agreed to give the three women a trial. Thuy was given a small bundle to try first. He said he hadn't checked the contents this time, but would do next time before she took them. She didn't want to argue back that she was trustworthy, at least she was given the chance.

At home, Thuy worked quickly and as carefully as she could. She was able to finish it all before the deadline. Thuy brought the goods back, where the manager checked over the clothes inch by inch, as if he wanted to find mistakes in the garments. Finally, he nodded his approval and laughed. "Hǎo, hǎo. Fēicháng xìngyùn!" (Good, very good. You did it very beautifully.)

"You won't find any mistakes, old man!" Thuy said in her head.

He handed over two more bundles to Thuy and held up his two fingers, which meant they wanted them finished in two weeks. When she got home, she told the story to Minh and Be, who both laughed.

Time flew by so quickly. Thuy was so busy that she didn't have time to think anymore. She still took Hien to school in the mornings and still went to her English classes twice a week. In between all that she would pick up clothes to work on and always return them on time. Her debt to Be's mother-in-law was paid off and she was able to use the extra money to buy winter clothes for her and the children.

-----

The easy times did not last that long. One day on the way to get more work, she slipped and fell. That winter was very cold, there was a lot of snow. At night the snow froze into ice and that caused Thuy to slip and land on her bottom. She was in excruciating pain and couldn't stand up. Luckily Be and Minh were with her and helped her get home.

After the accident, Thuy had to stay rested and limit her movements. She had gone to the GP for a check-up and was given drugs to relieve the pain. It felt like a long time, but two weeks later she felt much better and returned to her routine. She thought how much quicker she would have recovered if she was younger. The fall would affect her health of her pelvic area and lower back for years to come.

-----

In the winter of 1983, snow fell continuously for two days and two nights. It covered the whole city in white, leaving only faint tracks of car wheels on the road. The school had to close and people going to work found they encountered many delays on public transport.

Sitting inside the flat and looking out at the white world, the snowflakes were like flowers dancing in the wind. The snow gathered on the branches creating a snowflake tree. When one flower fell off another one would form. Thuy remembered watching Soviet movies in Vietnam. In the winter scenes, the young men and women threw snow at each other, laughing and joking happily. It looked so romantic and beautiful. It made everyone hope for snow and that maybe they would enjoy it as much as the actors did.

Now though, she hoped the snow would stop falling. She wanted the warm sun to melt the piles of snow and for everything to return to normal. People's hearts were difficult to please and to understand.

The children loved the snow. They wanted to catch it, slide on it and build snowmen with it.

Carrots were used for the nose. Adults felt cold and shivered, but the children didn't feel the cold, they were too busy having fun and refused to go home.

-----

On one cold winter's evening, Mr Ray visited Thuy's family with a gift. Binh opened the door to Mr Ray, who was covered in snow and was holding a TV set.

"Hello! May I come in?" He said with kind smile.

"Good evening, Mr Ray, come in, come in, please!" Binh said, helping him inside.

Binh closed the door on the cold night and took the TV from Mr Ray's hands. Mr Ray hung his coat on the hanger and gently wiped his shoes on the small mat. The two of them carefully went downstairs, where Thuy and the children were waiting.

"Pastor, the pastor is here, mum!" Bac Hai's voice chirped.

"Hello! Hello!" Mr Ray said and bent down to pat the two children on their heads.

Hien and Bac Hai held his hands and walked into the living room with him. He sat down on the single chair, blowing into his hands to warm them up.

"Would you like a cup of tea or coffee?" Thuy said, looking at Mr Ray.

"Yes, may I have white tea, one sugar, please!"

Binh put the TV down and looked at Mr Ray in confusion. "Someone from church donated this TV. I picked it up tonight and brought it straight over for your family to have." Mr Ray explained.

"It's our TV, mum!" Hien shouted, jumping up and down in excitement.

Thuy brought out a cup of tea. "Be careful you two, stay still, there's hot water. Let him drink tea first."

Thuy placed the cup of tea and butter biscuits on the small table next to Mr Ray's chair. Bac Hai was sitting on his lap, brushing away the snowflakes on his beard. Looking at the two of them smiling at each other, being intimate like a grandfather and grandson. Her father had not even met his grandson yet and she wondered if he ever would.

The television was placed on the small but sturdy wooden table. Hien and Bac Hai couldn't take their eyes off the TV set. Thuy asked Binh to plug it in and Mr Ray attached the antenna, switched the set on while everyone waited anxiously.

The screen lit up and sound came out. All eyes were on the black and white picture, it was similar to the one in Thorney Island.

"There's a picture!" Hien and Bac Hai cheered.

Mr Ray took a sip of tea. "Good! That's good!" He laughed out loud.

It was going to be a beautiful memory of that winter that Thuy would never forget.

-----

The cold season continued with more snow. The air was freezing cold and all the flats were deadly silent. Only the sound of the wind blowing through the cracks in the window could be heard. Thuy began to fear the winter and the cold, which aggravated her back pain, since she had that fall.

Lunar New Year celebrations in Vietnam would usually follow with a burst of spring. The climate in the UK however was still cold. Even into March and April, there was still lots of rain and cold winds. Glimmers of spring approaching were in sight. Green buds were sprouting on the bushes. When the cold winter finally moved on, everyone felt relieved and began to look forward to warmer months.

-----

On Sundays, there was an open-air market not too far from where they lived. All sorts of things, old and new were sold there. It was a nice change of scenery and a family outing they all enjoyed.

Many years passed without Thuy coming across any old friends. She thought she might, at these types of places, but all the Vietnamese faces she saw at the market or anywhere else she didn't recognise.

She often felt lost and lonely amongst all the crowds of the city.

The two children loved going to the Sunday market. They were like birds that had flown out of their cages, moving around freely and being fascinated by everything they saw. Hien and Bac Hai were polite children, they never asked to buy anything. Thuy would always remind them before they got there, that she was only going to buy things they needed for school. They couldn't afford to buy just anything.

They would take a bus to the market and the children would count the ten stops it takes to get there. They didn't go every week, but when they did, it was more as a treat for Hien and Bac Hai.

-----

When Bac Hai turned five years old, Thuy registered him to go to the same school as his big sister. In September, both of them went to school from 8.45 am to 3.30 pm.

Thuy started applying for jobs in many places. Everywhere the answer was short; 'we need someone with experience and with a degree.' She had heard many people say that applying for jobs here was the age of 'unfinished spring'. Without a UK degree and without previous experience, Asians with yellow skins would find it hard to get a good job.

It wasn't just finding a job that made life harder, but some adults and children also made them feel unwelcome. Shouting out at them, 'Go back to your country!' Even when they were children, it still got Thuy down and made her feel bitter. They didn't know, she didn't want to leave her country and go far away from all she knew to live in a completely foreign land to what she knew.

The number of unemployed people in the UK increased every year, so finding a job was difficult. Many refugees applied for any job they could get with the established Hong Kong businesses. These people had started working in the UK many years ago. They mostly ran Chinese supermarkets and restaurants, which although was very hard work, it was also the fastest way to earn money.

Some people had different jobs depending on the profession they had previously. Phan, her neighbour, was a carpenter in Vietnam. He was able to make tables, chairs and most wooden furniture. His customers would just phone him and he would get work that way.

Thuy had not gone to get sewing supplies with Be since the accident. The manager at the factory introduced her to some sewing workshops near her house, so she didn't have to travel that far. Her two children were still young and she was their main carer.

-----

For over a year now, Binh's health had declined. He had been to see a doctor regularly. The GP surgery tested his blood, stool, urine and had also taken X-rays, but they hadn't figured out what the issue was. He was getting weaker though, so everything that needed to be done for the family fell on to Thuy. Binh had always been a slow man, an inactive scholar, but now with such ill health, everyone thought he was nearly sixty not fifty.

Thuy didn't really have anyone she could call on to help. She was worried about her husband's health, but she also had to take care of the children and keep on earning some money for the household. Although her husband's relatives were in the same city and not very near to where they lived, none of them called to see how he was doing or what help she might need. Thuy knew what they were like and didn't expect anything from them. It was because of her husband and his family that Thuy had to run from her country of birth. Thuy kept on telling herself to be strong, so she could take care of the children and they would grow up to be good citizens of this new land.

-----

The UK was a free country. It wasn't an oppressive regime like Vietnam, so Thuy had hope that her children's future would not be hindered by politics. People often said, 'women rely on their husbands' but Thuy was never like that. She did feel like God was always challenging her, forcing her to think, worry and work harder than other women. Those other women with hardworking husbands were the lucky ones.

One day after her English class, her classmate Emmy, a Japanese lady, asked if she would like to go with her to a Japanese store that opened last month. She said it wasn't far, only six bus stop rides away.

It was a small store, near the train station and sold Japanese food and Japanese style utensils. Thuy was fascinated by it all, as she had never seen products from Japan before. In the store that day she came across a woman who was on the same boat as they were from Hai Phong. It was a long time since she had seen Lien. On the boat they were like strangers, but here seeing someone from your birth country, they were both extremely happy to see each other.

"Is that you, Thuy? It's been such a long time since I've seen you. Do you recognize me? It's me, Lien!"

"Yes! Yes! We were on the same boat. How is your family doing?"

There were so many questions they wanted to ask each other, but there wasn't enough time. Lien had also married a Chinese man, so her reasons for being in the UK were the same as Thuy's. Thuy learnt that she now has a third child, but along with her husband's brothers, they had jointly opened a fast food takeaway as well as a clothing factory. The two exchanged phone numbers and promised to contact each other. Lien's life was so much easier than Thuy's, but she was happy for her, hopefully they would become friends and support one another.

After that meeting, the two talked on the phone often. Lien's family had a car so they were able to drive to Thuy's house to visit. Lien and her husband were young, cheerful and easy to get along with. Her husband and father-in-law were in the leadership of the local Party and Youth Union in Vietnam. The reason for leaving was similar to Thuy's.

Lien's eldest child was about the same age as Hien. The moment they got in the flat, they would stick together like glue, as if they had known each other all their lives!

Lien's husband's business was doing well. Many refugees were employed by them, probably due to shared experiences.

Lien had suggested many times to Thuy to work at her husband's factory. They understood her situation. Binh was still very sick and couldn't earn any money. Lien's husband, Nguyen, persuaded Thuy that the best way forward was to work at his sewing factory. The two families knew each other and the work and time would be arranged to suit Thuy's needs.

"I can see you're struggling to make money. You followed your husband here, just as I did. You've not had an easy time, let us help you."

Thuy knew Lien and Nguyen were right and that they cared and were trying to help. She agreed to work at Nguyen's factory while her children were at school. It was only a few bus-stops from their home, so she was able to take her children to school in the morning and then be back in time to pick them up in the afternoon.

In return for Nguyen and Lien's thoughtfulness, Thuy worked diligently and sewed beautifully and carefully. When the head of the company came down to inspect the work, he was so impressed he then trusted her to sew samples. These would be the prototypes for new designs and outfits.

The working environment was friendly and everyone seemed happy to be there. Thuy enjoyed her time at the factory and the conversations that were thrown around. Her mind was at ease for the first time in a long time.

It wasn't all easy though, there were times when the weather was so bad she couldn't get to school on time to pick the children up, so Binh had to do that.

Thuy was juggling her time between housework and factory work, as well as taking care of her husband and children. God seemed to understand her situation and kept her in good health. Sewing the samples meant better pay and that encouraged Thuy to work more. She would bring the samples home to sew in the evening while Binh helped the children to do their homework. As Thuy was busy with lots of things, she had less time with the children. Luckily, Hien and Bac Hai were healthy, so they didn't require a lot of her attention.

At the end of the academic year, Hien's school work was graded as good. Her teachers loved her and the school sent home a certificate of merit for overall achievement.

-----

Before her work at the factory, Thuy was the one who spent the most time with her children, but since she started to work, Bac Hai would follow his father everywhere and he would listen to Hien. After school, they were in harmony with each other, Hien acted like an older sister, looking after her younger brother and Binh watched over them both while Thuy worked.

Every day after work, Thuy would ask the children the same question. "Were you two good today? Did you play well so that your father could rest?"

"I'm a good boy, mum. Today my teacher praised me." Bac Hai quickly boasted. "Tonight, when Hien finishes her homework, can we watch cartoons before going to bed?"

"Mum, next week is the half term holiday. Uncle Phan is taking their family to the beach." Hien informed Thuy.

Thuy hugged Bac Hai. "You are a good boy, who loves his dad and mum a lot, right? You and Hien are doing really well at school, which means I can go to work without worrying about you both." Thuy was sad she had to say this. "Your dad is not well and can't really take you out to play with your friends, so we can't go out without him either. When he gets better, our family can go out and have fun together."

Hien came over and sat next to her. "Don't worry, mum, I'm grown up now. Starting from tomorrow, I'll help you to cook." She comforted her mum.

Thuy smiled as she hugged her two children. "Oh, you two are amazing! You both help me so much every day and now my daughter will be by my side in the kitchen - she's really growing up!"

"You must keep on taking your medicine Dad. You'll be better soon and then we can be a happy family again." Hien looked at her Dad. "Promise you'll get better Dad?"

"Yes, I promise..." Binh nodded.

Looking at Binh and the two children together, helped her forget about the strains of the day. It was really heart-warming for her to see them care for each other. This was her family, the only relatives they could rely on. It was a simple set up but a happy one.

There was a saying, 'When you are sick, you must pray in all directions.' Thuy took on advice from anyone who was kind enough to offer it. She was going to follow up on the idea of treating Binh with Chinese herbal remedies. She would take Binh into China Town tomorrow, where she was told about a famous Chinese doctor from Hong Kong. Anything was worth a try.

oOo

Returning home after picking up the children from school, Thuy checked on Binh the moment they got home.

"Did you remember to take the medicine I boiled in the pot today?" Thuy asked tentatively. "How are you feeling? Do you think it's making a difference?" Binh looked at Thuy, his face seemed optimistic. "I think I am feeling better."

"I know the medicine is bitter, but let's keep trying." Thuy said, hopeful.

Thuy asked Hien and Bac Hai to play nicely in the living room. "Please tidy up when you're finished playing with your toys, that would really help me." She looked at them both. They were good children. "I'm going to make more of Dad's medicine now, and then afterwards Hien can help me cook the dinner?"

"Yes, mum!" Hien said, happily.

Like clockwork when she got in for work, Thuy would clean up, vacuum, put the clothes in the washing machine and then go into the kitchen to set up a pot of Chinese medicine. This would last the whole day for Binh the following day. After a few weeks of taking the herbal concoction, Binh's face was bright and he felt less pain. This gave Thuy hope.

-----

Working at the factory, there were many different stories and experiences from that were talked about. Each person had something to share and most people liked to listen. Usually Loan was cheerful at work. She liked to talk a lot about herself, but today she was quiet, sewing silently looking down at her work. She had often bragged that her husband worked at the Chinese restaurant in the centre and earned a lot of money. With this money she bought nice clothes and wore gold jewellery. She acted as though it made her better than everyone else.

Thuy didn't pay too much attention to the way Loan acted. Today though, some of the women could see something wasn't the same with Loan.

At lunch, it all came out. "I was bored at home and caught up with work. He left around noon and didn't come back until nearly morning. I thought the restaurant was busy and he had to work overtime."

"That's why you're the richest woman in this workshop!" Someone said, teasingly, which only made her cry more.

"For the past few months, he hasn't given me a single penny. He lost everything gambling and then borrowed money from a gang."

Loan sobbed some more. There were some women who took pity on her, while others continued teasing. Thuy didn't want to be part of this, so sat down to eat quietly on her own.

Thuy thought about life back in Vietnam, they were poor, but they were happy. Now, in this new country, with new things, there were also bad habits to tempt them. Husbands and wives fighting and cursing each other. Some become addicted to gambling, forgetting their responsibilities and love for their children. The rich have their own sufferings, the poor live in hardship, but who is happier?

-----

Binh's health improved with the Chinese remedies. He started putting on weight and his complexion grew rosier. Thuy became happier and felt more at ease. In the evenings, their small flat was always filled with laughter and conversation.

Thuy wanted to learn to drive. She felt it would give them more freedom as a family. She studied for the theory test, her English was now quite good and after passing, she was determined to pass the practical. When she did, she felt a great achievement, she wouldn't have had this chance back in Vietnam.

Binh was now in charge of taking the children to school, so she didn't have to rush home early. Hien now knew how to cook a few simple dishes. After eating, she washed the dishes, not letting her parents do it. This allowed Thuy to have a break from working and doing all the chores in the house.

The school had organized an overnight camping trip, which Thuy said was a great idea for Hien to go on. She thought it would be good for Hien to be exposed to nature and wild surroundings. She couldn't learn everything from being indoors.

With a driver's license, Thuy bought a second-hand car from someone at work. They sold it to her for a relatively good price, otherwise they wouldn't have been able to buy one at all. Hien and Bac Hai were very excited at the idea of a family car. They jumped up and down when they saw their mother driving the car home from work. Thuy drove them all around the block a few times. The two siblings held hands and sat still, looking out on both sides of the road with awe. Thuy looked at her children and could not hold back her tears of happiness.

Other families that they knew all had cars, but Hien and Bac Hai never asked their parents to buy one. They never really asked for anything, they understood what their parents were going through. Thuy knew her daughter's character well. They were both growing into kind and considerate little adults, which made Thuy love and cherish them even more.

At dinner, she promised to drive the whole family to the beach on Sunday, which made the children so excited. It would be their first visit to a seaside. This made them want to please their mother even more, so they helped with the chores in the flat without having to be asked.

"You see, Binh, since I promised to take them to the beach, they have been in a really good mood." She said to her husband. "They are still children, so we need to give them treats sometimes." They both smiled, looking at their children proudly.

Thuy kept constant communication with her father and family in Vietnam. Although the correspondence was very slow, they were both happy to hear from each other. Thuy's father learnt about his grandchildren through letters and he would talk to anyone who would listen about them.

-----

The years after Thuy had left Vietnam were the most difficult and deprived period for the country. The government also controlled what information went in and out of the country. Letters arriving from abroad were all opened and checked before being delivered to the recipient. Thuy could only write about the family's health and the children's education, she didn't dare to talk about politics or the economic state of Vietnam.

Thuy had asked her father what the best way to send packages was to him. She was earning some money now and wanted to share that with her family in Vietnam. People in Hanoi and the big city could receive them more easily and faster. Thuy's father lived in the small provinces, letters checked and delayed, let alone boxes. She sent three boxes, but one was 'lost'. She sent some beautiful silk clothes and other fabrics, but they still took several months to arrive. Not only that, her father had to bribe, give gifts and pay 100% taxes to receive them.

It was becoming very costly and complicated to receive these packages and her father persuaded Thuy not to send any more things. Instead, in the following years, Thuy sent money via acquaintances who were visiting Vietnam. This was the best option and Thuy felt assured it would arrive safely to her father.

-----

Thuy and Lien's families still visited each other and the five children became good friends. In the summer, along with Be's family, they would all go to the seaside together. Be had two children and all seven of them played happily together. There was always a funfair at the seaside, which kept the children entertained for hours.

The adults went fishing, picked clams and oysters to have on the BBQ on the beach. The summer days were fun and the families' bond grew.

With the passing of the years, they all got used to English life and integrated themselves as best they could. However, the yearning for their birth country didn't disappear. Thuy and her friends, who had all married ethnic Hoa men, were desperate to see their parents and relatives in Vietnam.

-----

Life is not always peaceful and calm like a river without ripples. Over the past two weeks, Binh has started to feel pain again and fatigue all over. Although his appetite was still good, he had lost a lot of weight and the doctors couldn't find any reason for it. Binh's actions and gestures were also changing. He would remember some things and then forget the same things the following day. Sometimes he would sit silently for hours, not answering when he was spoken to. Thuy had a feeling that something bad was about to happen.

One day, after coming home from work, Hien told her mum about the strange thing that Binh had done. "Mum, this afternoon Dad said he was sleepy and wanted to go to the bedroom, but he went to the kitchen and sat on the chair to sleep instead. Then he went to Bac Hai's room to sleep."

Thuy took Binh to the GP surgery. After two weeks of losing weight very quickly, she knew something was very wrong. She wasn't satisfied with the uncertainty of the GP, so she suggested sending him to the hospital.

The first few days in hospital, Binh went through numerous tests. At this point he looked like a skeleton with many tangled leads going into his body. The hospital asked Thuy to sign a consent form to let them drain his bone marrow. She didn't really understand what that was for, but she signed the form. Almost a month later, the test results came back, Binh had bone cancer!

The three of them heard the news like a thunderclap of lightning. Thuy was silent, it felt like her heart had stopped beating. She couldn't believe what she was hearing. Why? Why? What do they do now? Confused and full of worry. How many people have survived cancer? All they could do was wait for a hopeful solution from the hospital.

At first, Binh could eat a little soup, understand and answer a few short sentences. Then he stopped talking. He would lie in bed grimacing from the excruciating pain. The doctor said the treatment was no longer effective for Binh, the cancer had spread to other parts of his body.

Every day Thuy visited. She would wash Binh while he was still lying on the hospital bed. She could feel just skin and bones on his body. He didn't recognize his wife and children, he didn't know anything around him. His friends and acquaintances from far away came to visit, to talk to the body lying motionless, without emotion.

Thuy was heartbroken and felt so much love for her dying husband. She was sure Binh could hear the voices of his wife and children, but just couldn't answer. When she saw tears rolling down from the corners of his eyes, she was so excited, but the doctor explained what was going on.

"That is the final sign, there is no hope. The cancer has spread to the brain, lungs and other internal organs. We cannot say exactly when, but the family should prepare and inform relatives to come and see him one last time."

The doctors had done all they could, there was no more to be done. Thuy hugged her two children, choking with pain. She swallowed her tears deep down and looked at her husband feeling helpless.

Binh was still lying there, eyes open, staring into space. He wasn't gone, but his soul had left them the moment he contracted the disease.

They were warned and they would have to accept the inevitable. Thuy's endurance level was being tested again. She was only human and could only take so much heartache in her life. It was a journey of struggle, physical and mental pain.

Two weeks later, Binh passed away, in a foreign land, leaving his wife and not yet fully-grown children behind. The person who goes first is at peace, while the person left behind holds all the heavy responsibilities.

Binh's death was a huge shock to Thuy and her children. Ms Hill supported her as best she could, visiting often and helping her plan the funeral. When her friends came to visit they could see how much weight she had lost herself. They brought food and she was never alone.

Binh's funeral was on a beautiful sunny, but cold day. It was rare to see the sunshine at this time of year and everyone welcomed the warmth. It was a different feeling for Thuy that day. The sun shining on her face could not dispel the storm in her heart. Her tears fell, as she felt absent-minded, with a soulless body, slowly walking in the procession of people seeing Binh off to his final resting place that day.

-----

The days that followed passed painfully slowly. For Thuy and her children, each one seemed to stretch on without end. The warm, lively evenings they once shared filled with voices and laughter had slipped away. Hien and her brother became quiet and sombre, each trying in their own way to grasp the reality of losing their dad. They tried making light conversation to distract them from their sadness, but it was hard not to mention Binh's name.

Thuy thought a lot about her children's present life and what the future might hold for them. She had to stay strong for them. Hien had reached adulthood, she was no longer a child, but not yet a true adult. Thuy still had to take care of them both. She now had to be a mother and father to them. She missed her husband every second of the day, but had to hide it in her heart. Every night when Hien and Bac Hai were sleeping soundly, Thuy would say to herself and to Binh;

*I can't follow you like ten years ago,*
*If I follow you,*
*What will happen to the two children?*
*I have to come to you in my dreams,*
*And when I wake up,*
*tears have fallen on my pillow.*

-----

Time is the best medicine that helps people heal emotional wounds in their hearts. They cannot be immersed in the past forever, they have to return to the present. Thuy's father, brothers and friends in Vietnam sent many letters of support. With their encouragement, she continued to go to work.

Thuy became closer to Ms Hill. She confided in her, shared with her, her sad and happy thoughts.

She was like a sister to Thuy giving advice and spiritual support.

For many years to come they would celebrate the joyous events together and console one another during the more difficult moments in their lives.

Hien gradually took on more responsibilities at home, helping her mother and looking out for her younger brother, even more than she had done. This helped Thuy concentrate on work and not worry about what needed doing at home. Hien and her brother would prepare the food, ready for her return from work. They continued to eat together as a family and there was still a lot of love to share. It was their time to share their day with everyone.

During dinner, Hien tentatively asked her mother.

"Mum, can I work part-time?"

"What are you going to do? Where? What about your studies? I don't want you to neglect them and you definitely can't drop out." Her mother said nervously.

"I won't drop out of school. Some of my classmates are applying for jobs at a coffee shop outside the centre. It'll just be part-time work." Hien said, smiling and comforting her mother.

"I know you want to help, but don't neglect your studies just because you want to earn money. As an older sister, you have to set a good example to your younger brother. I'm not going to say anymore, but you understand what I mean?"

"Don't worry mum, I won't let you down. A friend found this job for me and if you agree, I'll say I can only work on the weekends and only a couple of hours in the morning. Then I still have time to spend with you and Bac Hai. I promise I will still be able to help with the chores in the home too." Hien said, pleadingly.

"OK, I agree, but on the condition, you come home straight after you finish work. You can't go out with your friends and forget about us. Maybe you can work more hours during the summer holidays."

"Thank you, Mum!"

After the meal, Bac Hai volunteered to wash the dishes and promised that he would do them from now on to help more. It was a simple life for Thuy and her children. Time passed by like a peaceful river.

Hien took her A level exams to prepare for university and Bac Hai studied at a high school for boys. The two of them concentrated on their homework on the weekends and helped whenever they could during the school holidays. Thuy was proud of her children. She knew of families, where their children dropped out of school, or fell pregnant at a young age, or who were even addicted to drugs or caught stealing from their work place. This time she was the lucky one.

-----

In Vietnamese culture, when your parents pass away, you have to pay your respects at their graves. Thuy wasn't able to do this and her guilt was always there for not being able to fulfil her duty as a daughter.

With her retirement, Ms Hill was able to spend more time taking care of her elderly mother. Thuy and the children still visited them both when they could. Everytime they did visit, it made Thuy think about her family in Vietnam and she secretly wished that she could take her children to see her father and family there. This wish was never fulfilled, as one day there was a phone call from her younger brother informing her that their father was seriously ill and unlikely to survive.

She couldn't fly to Vietnam and say her goodbyes. She was devastated when he passed away. When her mother passed, she was studying far away and wasn't able to get back in time either.

**Six years later.**

On the day Bac Hai graduates with a first in his Bachelor's degree, his mother can hardly contain her pride. Her eyes shine as she watches him in his gown, a moment she's dreamed of for years. Thuy turns to Hien once again, gently reminding her about the camera, she doesn't want a single second of this day to go unrecorded.

"Don't worry, mum, I've got the camera. Wish dad was still alive..." Hien said, half to herself. Hien looked at her mother and didn't say any more. She didn't realise Thuy was thinking the same thing.

Thuy looked at her two children and was filled with pride. She thought to herself, how proud her husband would be if he was here too and they could celebrate this happy event together.

Bac Hai looked at his mother and sister and changed the focus of their thoughts.

"The University has a professional photographer, the photos are good but expensive, how many pictures do you want to get?" Bac Hai asked.

"I think two is enough? I know you two think I can't take nice photos, but I'll show you I can today!" Thuy smiled.

The three of them laughed happily as they got into the car and drove towards the graduation ceremony, hoping they wouldn't be late.

-----

Thuy was just over forty years old when she became a widow. It was meant to be the most beautiful age of a woman's life. For Thuy though, it was a heart-breaking time. In the middle of what should have been a long marriage together, she was left behind to raise two children on her own. She was in a country that was foreign to her and with no relatives to recognise her. When Binh died, their two children were still young. It was her responsibility to stay strong and show them a better future. All her sacrifices and hard work were for them.

God does not take everything away nor does he give everything to just one person.

Thuy's two children grew up with all their mother's love and nurturing. Hien and Bac Hai graduated from university, found good jobs, got married and lived happily with their families.

When Thuy retired, she didn't want to depend on her children for anything and continued to be truly independent.

Thuy joined the Elderly Association's Health Club. She practiced Tai Chi and attended line dance classes three days a week. She occasionally travelled with friends of the same age and took care of herself. She didn't want her children to worry about her, so made sure she was fit and healthy.

This life was unlike the traditional way of living in Vietnam. There, the children and even the grandchildren would be responsible for raising and taking care of elderly parents. Nowadays, life is different. Two generations of old and young living together are incompatible.

One morning, a message comes in for Thuy from her daughter. "Mum, are you going to Tai Chi today? Come over to our house when you're finished."

"What time?"

"Is 2 pm ok, Mum?"

"OK, I'll be there."

Thuy thought something must have happened, but hoped it wasn't anything serious. After practicing tai chi for almost two hours, she went home, took a shower, then made her way to Hien's house.

Hearing the knock on the door, the children rushed to open it. As soon as she stepped in, they rushed to her arms.

The house was bustling with laughter, there were a lot of delicious smells wafting from the kitchen. The big round table in the middle of the dining room was filled with many colourful dishes. Bac Hai's family had arrived just before Thuy. She looked around and saw that all the children were there. She knew it was difficult to get everyone together, as they were all so busy, so today was a special day.

Suddenly she remembered, today was her birthday! The children had organised a surprise birthday party for their mother. There was another knock at the door.

"We've got guests! We've got guests, Mum and Dad!" Lan Anh cried out, her voice ringing with delight as she came running in, Hien's five-year-old daughter practically bursting with excitement.

Bac Hai went to open the door.

"Hello! Am I on time?" Ms Hill greeted Bac Hai.

"Hi, Ms Hill, please! Come in, come in."

Everyone stopped and looked out, their faces beaming. Hien took Thuy to the door to welcome Ms Hill. Like two sisters who had not seen each other for a long time, Ms Hill opened her arms to hug and kiss her.

"Happy birthday Thuy, my dear friend!"

She handed over the gift bag, smiling happily. Thuy was surprised and moved to see Ms Hill.

"Thank you, thank you very much."

Yesterday Thuy had received her birthday card through the post, so she didn't expect to see her anytime soon. Miss Hill was still able to drive so drove to Hien's house and despite her age, she looked healthy and was still active.

Adults greeted each other with handshakes, while the children played with one another. There was laughter and lots of chatter, it was a joyous moment for Thuy and she was so pleased that Miss Hill was able to be there too. With all the decades they had known each other, and all the events they shared, Ms Hill was always a constant presence, a huge part of their lives to be cherished forever.

The meal was warm and full of love. The children and grandchildren were grateful to Thuy for everything they had.

The living room lights were off, Hien came out from the kitchen carrying a cake. The small candle in the middle flickered with Hien's footsteps. Everyone sang.

*"Happy birthday to you!*
*Happy birthday to you!*
*Happy birthday dear mum...."*

The room was loud with singing and chapping. Thuy looked at the cake clearly showing the number 70. The seventy years of a person's life, with so many events. Sadness and joy mixed together. It had been a bumpy and often uncertain life, but now things had finally settled down for her.

Thuy sat next to Ms Hill, surrounded by her daughter, son, daughter-in-law and son-in-law and her four grandchildren. She was touched and speechless. Tears of joy and happiness rolled down her cheeks. She smiled contently, knowing she had fulfilled her responsibilities as a mother as well as a father to her children./.

## Also published by Chu Minh Hạnh

1-**Hoàng Hôn (Sunset)** – Poetry by Chu Minh Hạnh & Lâm Hoàng Mạnh.
*A contemplative collection capturing the quiet beauty and fleeting emotions of life's endings.*
Nhân Ảnh, 2023

2-**Bình Minh (Sunrise)** – Poetry by Chu Minh Hạnh &Lâm Hoàng Mạnh
*Poems celebrating renewal, hope and the promise each new day brings.*
Nhân Ảnh, 2024

3-**Thùy** – Long story by Chu Minh Hạnh & Lâm Hoàng Mạnh
*An evocative story exploring love, resilience and the intricate tapestry of human experience.*
Nhân Ảnh, 2025

## Also published by Lâm Hoàng Mạnh

1-**Buồn Vui đời Thuyền Nhân** – A memoir
by Lâm Hoàng Mạnh
*A personal account of the joys and sorrows of Vietnamese boat people.*
Tiếng Quê Hương, 2011

2- **Idioms and Proverbs Handbook**
English to Vietnamese/ Vietnamese to English
by Lâm Hoàng Mạnh
*A practical reference for navigating Vietnamese and English expressions.*

3- **The Life of Chairman Mao** by Li Zhisui
Translated by Lâm Hoàng Mạnh & Nguyễn Học
*An intimate biography of China's controversial leader, from his personal physician's perspective.*
Nhân Ảnh, 2013

4- **Ho Chi Minh - A life** by William J. Duiker
Translated by Lâm Hoàng Mạnh & Nguyễn Học
*A comprehensive biography of Vietnam's revolutionary leader.*
Nhân Ảnh, 2014

5- **Hard Choice** by Hillary Rodham Clinton
Translated by Lâm Hoàng Mạnh
*Memoirs of political decisions and personal reflections from a former U.S. Secretary of State.*
Nhân Ảnh, 2016

6- **Còi Không Hụ Du Ký (Adventures Without Sirens)** – A travel diary by Lâm Hoàng Mạnh

*A lively account of travels filled with unexpected discoveries and adventures.*

Nhân Ảnh, 2018

7- **The Sorrow and Happiness of the Boat People** by Lâm Hoàng Mạnh

*Stories exploring the struggles and resilience of Vietnamese refugees.*

Nhân Ảnh, 2022

8- **Hoàng Hôn (Sunset)** – Poetry by Chu Minh Hạnh & Lâm Hoàng Mạnh

*A poetic reflection on endings, memories and fleeting moments.*

Nhân Ảnh, 2023

9- **Bình Minh (Sunrise)** – Poetry by Chu Minh Hạnh & Lâm Hoàng Mạnh

*Celebrating new beginnings and the hope that comes with each day.*

Nhân Ảnh, 2024

10- **Thùy** – Long story by Chu Minh Hạnh & Lâm Hoàng Mạnh

*A compelling long-form story exploring love, life and human resilience.*

Nhân Ảnh, 2025

Contact the author:
**Lâm Hoàng Mạnh**
m-v-lam@hotmail.com

ꕥ

Contact the publisher:
**Nhân Ảnh**
han.le3359@gmail.com

www.ingramcontent.com/pod-product-compliance
Lightning Source LLC
LaVergne TN
LVHW090255210926
848480LV00001B/23